THE PSYCHOLOGY
OF SECRETS

THE PLENUM SERIES IN SOCIAL/CLINICAL PSYCHOLOGY

Series Editor: C. R. Snyder

University of Kansas
Lawrence, Kansas

A Continuation Order Plan is available for this series. A continuation order will bring delivery of each new volume immediately upon publication. Volumes are billed only upon actual shipment. For further information please contact the publisher.

THE PSYCHOLOGY OF SECRETS

ANITA E. KELLY
University of Notre Dame
South Bend, Indiana

KLUWER ACADEMIC / PLENUM PUBLISHERS
New York   Boston   Dordrecht   London   Moscow

ISBN: 0-306-46657-0

©2002 Kluwer Academic / Plenum Publishers, New York
233 Spring Street, New York, N.Y. 10013

http://www.wkap.nl/

10 9 8 7 6 5 4 3 2 1

A C.I.P. record for this book is available from the Library of Congress

PREFACE

On an MTV special aired in 2000, young interviewees were asked to confess the worse thing they were ever told during a romantic breakup. One person tearfully responded "that I suck in bed." More recently, an acquaintance of mine admitted to his new girlfriend that he "has a mean streak." She decided not to date him after that. Another memorable and painful example of openness occurred years ago when I served as a member of a suicide intervention team. I was called to a very disturbing scene in an upscale neighborhood to console a woman who was threatening to take her life on the lawn in front of her children. Her husband had just confessed his long-term affair to her that morning and she felt that her world was coming apart. Fortunately, she did not take her life but was left with the humiliation of having her neighbors know about her private troubles. The question these examples bring to mind is, "Why do people so often reveal potentially stigmatizing personal information to others?"

The reader probably has an intuitive answer to this question already. It can seem like such a burden—even torture—to keep secrets from other people. Hiding such things as feelings of discontent from a boyfriend or girlfriend, violations of the law from close friends, and indiscretions from employers can be alienating. People want others to know them; therefore they often end up disclosing self-incriminating information. At the same time, however, people do not want to be reminded of the things that make them feel bad or ashamed. What can be done to alleviate this burden of secrecy? Will this anguish pass in time? What are the factors that should enter into making a wise decision to reveal a secret? These are three of the central questions addressed in this volume.

Psychotherapists dating back to Freud (1958) have promoted the revelation of therapy patients' secrets in treatment, no matter how humiliating or excruciating their secrets might be. In fact, such openness was the essence of Freud's Fundamental Rule of Psychoanalysis. Leaders of the encounter group movement in the United States in the 1960s, too, advocated getting one's secrets—as well as angry and painful feelings—out in the open when confronting interpersonal difficulties (see Bok, 1983). Such developments were precursors to the present-day emphasis that therapists, talk show hosts, and televangelists place on the cathartic benefits of revealing secrets. Talk show hosts like Jenny Jones and Jerry Springer almost daily elicit detailed accounts of sexual molestations, marital infidelities, and other painful private events on television. Revealing what were once considered extremely private matters to the media is becoming a new social norm (Krestan & Bepko, 1993). It is estimated that over 21 million viewers follow television talk shows that regularly encourage participants to reveal their deepest family indiscretions (Mitchell, 1993). One of the purposes of this volume is to question whether this movement toward openness has gone too far and to examine the negative consequences of revealing personal secrets. Another purpose is to look at when and why revealing secrets can be extremely helpful, leading to health benefits such as improved immunological functioning (e.g., Petrie, Booth, Pennebaker, Davison, & Thomas, 1995).

My interest in secrets began informally about 14 years ago when I observed the lack of discretion that some of my acquaintances and fellow psychology trainees seemed to have. They revealed others' secrets—even their therapy clients' secrets—at a rate that made me question whether I should reveal any private information to them myself. I knew several people who participated in mental health groups such as Al-Anon and Recovery. They would describe the details of meetings to me, including the names of fellow members, even though they acknowledged that the groups were supposed to be anonymous and had taken an oath of confidentiality as part of their membership. Moreover, as part of my doctoral training in psychology, I participated in a practicum support group that was supposed to be confidential. I happily unburdened my secrets to my trusted fellow group members only to discover later at least one of the other group members had revealed my secrets to people outside the group!

A little later in my training, I took great interest in social psychological research and was especially influenced by the work of Barry Schlenker, Roy Baumeister, and Dianne Tice on how a person's public self-portrayals can influence his or her private self-conceptions. Along these lines, it disturbed me that I had allowed others to know personal things that I did not want to keep in mind about myself. After all, once people have formed certain opinions of their peers—as my friends may have formed of me—

they tend to give the peers feedback that constrains them to being consistent with those impressions (e.g., Swann, 1996). It follows that people should not reveal to close others what they do not want to remember about themselves.

Another key, more formal observation occurred when I was conducting a study on secret keeping in outpatient therapy (Kelly, 1998). I asked 42 clients (who had received an average of 11 therapy sessions) to indicate what, if any, relevant secrets they were keeping from their therapists. As it turned out, just over 40% of them said that they were keeping such a secret. What was surprising was that when I asked them to indicate (on a 9-point Likert-type scale) how stressful it was to keep those secrets, many of them indicated that it was not at all stressful to keep the secrets from their therapists. This observation contradicted much of the published theoretical work on the stressful nature of secret keeping and made me wonder whether secrets may be burdensome at first but may become less so after people have kept them for some time. This idea is developed further in the last few chapters of this volume.

My perspective as a theorist and researcher is that informal observations such as those I have just described can serve as an informative starting point for theory development and subsequent research. Then, as the theory is formally tested using the research methods available to psychologists and as new data support or fail to support the theory, it must be revised accordingly. In essence, what began as my informal observations about the lack of discretion of my peers has led to my making more formal observations and theorizing about when people should and should not reveal their secrets. My theoretical model hinges on the features of the confidant, which are described in the last two chapters of this volume.

In contrast to this philosophical approach to conducting research, prominent psychology researchers have argued that because psychology in general (see Kagan, 1994) and counseling psychology in particular (see Hill, 1982) are so young, researchers should avoid overtheorizing and should attend only to the emerging facts from formal research. Kagan (1994) wrote, "Although I respect theory, I share Percy Bridgman's suspicion of a priori ideas, especially in young sciences like psychology. Too many investigators persuade themselves of the correctness of an idea through thought alone" (p. 117). However, my view is that researchers virtually always have preconceived ideas about how their studies will turn out, and I think it is better to articulate what these ideas are and then scrupulously revise these ideas based on the new evidence that emerges (see Strong, 1991, for a similar argument). Even though psychology is a young science and the formal study of secrecy is especially recent, there are many facts already available to help people predict, understand, and control the outcomes of their decisions to reveal their secrets. My purpose in this volume is to provide these facts in a manner that is held coherently together by theory. At the same time, however, I have been careful throughout this volume to point out the holes in the available data (partly the result of researchers' having paid more attention to studying self-disclosure than to studying secrecy).

I aim to identify the processes that may underlie the benefits or drawbacks to revealing personal secrets across many settings involving many different kinds of people. As such, I often rely on experiments conducted in the laboratory, even though they may be criticized for their artificial nature. Because experiments allow cause-and-effect inferences to be drawn, they lend more confidence to identifying the processes underlying the phenomena being studied; in this case, the effects of revealing secrets. Experiments are emphasized in this volume because as Mook (1983) so aptly put it, "experiments give us an understanding of real world phenomena ... because the processes we dissect in the laboratory also operate in the real world" (p. 156).

This is the first authored volume to provide a comprehensive description of the psychological benefits and drawbacks to revealing personal and potentially stigmatizing secrets. There also is an edited volume available, *The Secrets of Private Disclosures* (edited by Sandra Petronio) published in 2000, that has valuable chapters on the implications of disclosing HIV status and on gender and cultural differences in disclosure presented from a communications perspective. My volume differs greatly from that one in the sense that I have offered an integration of ideas from one consistent theoretical perspective of this growing literature on secrets, starting with redefining the nature of secrecy. I draw from clinical and social psychological research, including findings from my own research program, to explain why people keep secrets, what it is about revealing secrets that leads to health benefits, and when revealing secrets can backfire, even in psychotherapy sessions. I also present a theoretical model for making a wise decision to reveal a secret: This decision hinges on whether one's confidant is likely to react positively to the revelation.

The interest in empirically studying secret keeping is a very recent phenomenon. In fact, many of the studies on secrecy that I cite in this volume have been conducted only in the last few years. This interest has taken off with James Pennebaker's (e.g., 1989) work on the theoretical dangers associated with inhibiting the expression of traumatic events or emotional upheavals and with Daniel Wegner's (e.g., 1992) work on the paradoxical effects of the thought suppression that goes into keeping information secret. Also, the development of the Self-Concealment Scale to measure one's tendency to keep negative or distressing information from others (Larson & Chastain, 1990) has spawned a series of studies assessing how high self-concealers differ from low self-concealers on various measures of well-being. Because the interest in studying secret keeping is so recent, there is a growing (but still not huge) literature on the effects of secret keeper per se. Thus, there are times when I draw from research on related constructs, such as research on the inhibition of emotional expression, repressive coping styles, and inhibited temperal types, to fill in the gaps concerning how secrecy might affect our interpersonal relationships and physical and mental health. I also discuss the research on the benefits of writing about traumas, as opposed to writing about secrets per se, because often traumas are kept secret from at least some other people.

In Chapter 1 I define secrecy and its related constructs and describe the types of secrets people keep and why they keep them. In Chapter 2 I examine the evidence that people who do keep secrets—as compared with those who do not—tend to be less physically and psychologically healthy. In Chapter 3 I explain why secrecy has been linked to such problems and suggest that secret keeping per se may not be problematic. In Chapter 4 I look at the very compelling evidence that revealing secrets in anonymous and confidential settings leads to health benefits. In Chapter 5 I offer an explanation for why revealing secrets leads to such health benefits. In Chapters 6–7 I discuss the effects of revealing secrets to one's therapist in particular and offer a new self-presentational theory of psychotherapy to explain why high levels of clients' revelation in therapy are not associated with positive outcomes. In Chapter 8 I describe the dilemmas to revealing secrets to other people and illustrate how introducing different types of confidant feedback into the revealing process can dramatically alter the outcomes of revealing. In Chapter 9, the final chapter, I offer recommendations for when one should and should not reveal secrets. It is my hope that this final chapter will help secret keepers sort out the important factors in making a wise decision to reveal their secrets. Perhaps they can live better with decisions that are made consciously and deliberately, as opposed to unconsciously or passively.

ACKNOWLEDGMENTS

I thank the National Institutes of Health and the Graduate School of the Univeristy of Notre Dame for supporting my research between 1997 and 1999. I also thank Mercedes Kelly and Pascal Lavallee for their insights, my graduate and undergraduate research assistants for their hard work, and C. R. Snyder for encouraging me to write this volume.

CONTENTS

THE NATURE OF SECRECY

"I once killed for love." It was this late-night confession in August 1996, to two of her college roommates at the Naval Academy, that led Diane Zamora to a sentence of life in prison with no possibility for parole for at least 40 years. Zamora and her ex-fiancé, David Graham, were convicted of bludgeoning and shooting Adrianne Jones to death in 1995 (when all three were in high school together). The two had lured Jones to a remote area in Texas to kill her after Graham told Zamora he had slept with Jones. Zamora later confessed to the police that when Graham admitted to having had sex with Jones, Zamora had flown into hysterics, screaming, "Kill her, kill her!" (*People Magazine*, March 4, 1998, p. 67).

Stories such as this one are both disturbing and perplexing. In addition to the horror of wondering why someone would calculatingly "kill for love," they leave one wondering, Why did Graham tell his emotionally unstable fiancée that he had had sex with an extremely attractive rival? Perhaps more perplexing, why did Zamora tell her roommates and at least two other people, including her best friend, that she was involved in a murder? Later, at her trial, she tried to put a defensive spin on her previous confession to the police, saying that it was the domineering Graham who forced her to unwillingly partake in the murder. But it was too late to take back her confessions to so many people, including her own recorded words to the police.

The first question of why Graham confessed his affair to Zamora is perhaps a little easier to address. Marriage and family therapists have long believed that it is essential for a marital partner who has had an affair to confess to the other spouse (e.g., Brown, 1991; Pittman, 1989; Shlien, 1984) and their rationale also could apply to unmarried couples. Presumably, it is not the extrarelational sex that causes problems, but rather the secrecy surrounding the sex (Pittman, 1989). Keeping such a secret requires omitting truths or telling lies, and this deception may undermine a person's sense of self-worth (Shlien, 1984). The guilt and shame of the secret affair may become unbearable for the person who is having the affair (Shlien, 1984). Some marital therapists have even asserted the secret extrarelational affairs should be revealed even if they were brief and happened a long time ago because "hiding it means holding back a piece of oneself" (Brown, 1991, p. 138). This explanation could capture what Graham might have been experiencing: To continue to feel close to Zamora, he may have felt compelled to confess and clear his guilty conscience.

Zamora's motivations for confessing the murder to her roommates seem a bit more puzzling, because she had so much to lose by confessing and seemingly so little to gain. When the police had found Jones's body 9 months earlier, they declared the murder unsolved. Zamora must have known that her roommates were bound by both criminal and military laws to reveal such a confession to the authorities. If Zamora had just kept her secret, she would likely have been on her way to achieving her dream of becoming an astronaut by now, instead of being imprisoned for life.

Was her motivation based on feeling guilty about the murder? The answer to that question seems to be "no." One of the roommates, Jennifer McKearney, testified in Zamora's trial that when McKearney asked Zamora if she had any regrets about the murder, Zamora had said, "No, it had to be done" (*People Magazine*, March 2, 1998, p. 68). McKearney said that Zamora had claimed that anyone who got between herself and Graham would have to die, and that Jones was "a tramp and a slut" who deserved what she got. Perhaps Zamora felt that it was too much pressure to keep a secret that big to herself. Or perhaps as a midshipwoman, she took pride in her fierceness and daring in having taken the life of another. She may have been boasting and enjoying the attention that she received from such a bold, unique confession. It also is possible that even though she did not feel guilty about the murder, she did feel guilty about not letting her closest friends know such an important secret. People will probably never fully grasp the answers to these questions in this case, but researchers have begun to address the question of whether people have some sort of primitive or compelling need to confess emotional experiences to others (e.g., Rime, Mesquita, Philippot, & Boca, 1991a). In this chapter, I describe this research and explain why people sometimes reveal even very damaging personal secrets. But first, I define secrecy and describe the types of secrets people keep and why they keep them.

DEFINING SECRECY

Keeping secrets means to hide deliberately information from other people (Margolis, 1974). Secrecy also has been called "active inhibition of disclosure" (e.g., Pennebaker, 1989) and one's predisposition to engage in secrecy has been labeled "self-concealment" (Larson & Chastain, 1990). Secrecy can be experienced as burdensome and stressful (see Pennebaker, 1989, 1990), and as such it is not merely the opposite of self-disclosure (i.e., revealing personal information to others) (see Collins & Miller, 1994). Keeping secrets requires expending cognitive and emotional resources (see Lane & Wegner, 1995; Wegner, 1989, 1992, 1994; Wegner, Lane, & Dimitri, 1994), whereas simply not self-disclosing information does not involve such efforts. Factor analyses of measures of both self-concealment and self-disclosure have shown that self-concealment is empirically distinct from self-disclosure (Larson & Chastain, 1990).

As implied by the definition above, secrecy always involves at least two people. Secret relationships can involve only one person's knowledge of the relationship, such as in the case when someone has a secret sexual desire for a married friend or coworker (Wegner et al., 1994). But even in such cases, the very existence of the secret depends on the secret keeper's awareness of another person. People work to hide their secrets only if other people who are not supposed to know the secrets are around. For example, imagine a teenager who would feel comfortable telling his closest male friends about his exotic pornography collection but would be horrified if his mother found out about it. He would expend energy keeping the pornography hidden when she is present but not when the friends are present (unless he thinks they might tell her about the pornography). Hence, when discussing the essence of secrets, it only makes sense to think of them in terms of "keeping secrets *from whom?*"

It might seem obvious to many readers that the most crucial defining characteristic of secrecy—and the biggest determinant of its effects—should be the type of secret that a person is keeping. For example, keeping secrets about having committed a murder presumably would be more effortful and stressful, and thus more harmful, than keeping secrets about having smoked marijuana. However, it is the process of expending energy to keep information from other people that defines secrecy, not the type of secret. This book is written with this definition in mind and is about any personal information that people work to keep from others. For example, some people might view their admitting to having tried cocaine as actually enhancing their group's opinions of them (i.e., the group might see such experimentation as a sign of daring). Of course, other people, such as

George W. Bush, might see such an admission as an extremely risky act that could have cost a presidential election. In this example, the type of personal information is the same—trying cocaine—but in the latter case, it is a secret; and in the former case, it is not.

In understanding the nature of secrecy, it is important not only to keep in mind that secrets always have a social context but also to distinguish secrecy from privacy. Whereas privacy connotes the expectation of being free from unsanctioned intrusion, secrecy does not. Secrecy involves active attempts to prevent such intrusion or leaks, and the secret keeper exerts this energy in part because he or she perceives that other people may have some claim to the hidden information. For example, the hygiene rituals that people engage in on a daily basis are considered to be private in American society, because people agree that these practices are not for public display. However, having a hidden dangerous contagious disease would be considered a secret because society has a right or obligation to intervene in such cases. Also, the hidden rituals that members of various cults or religious sects engage in may be considered secret rather than private, because members of those sects are aware that the broader society does not necessarily expect such rituals to be confidential.

The distinction between secrecy and privacy is not a trivial one. It helps to explain why there has been so much controversy surrounding whether people who work in hospitals and other medical facilities or people who are about to marry should be tested routinely for HIV infection. In both cases, the public or another person's safety may be threatened by keeping such information secret, and thus people may feel that they are entitled to have access to that information. At the same time, the individual who is being tested for HIV may feel that he has a right to keep his medical records private, especially if he plans to use prophylactic devices at all times when treating patients or having sex (see Cline & McKenzie, 2000; Yep, 2000, for further discussion of the dilemmas to disclosing HIV-positive status).

What may be private information in one relationship may be secret information in another. For example, in some new romantic relationships, both partners may explicitly or implicitly agree that each may have sex with other partners as long as they use condoms. They may have an understanding that those other sexual encounters are private matters that do not need to be discussed. However, in relationships that are intended to be monogamous, such as the one between Graham and Zamora, both partners may expect full disclosure about any extrarelational activity. They also might expect disclosure about any previous sexual relationships, and any deliberate omission of such information would be considered a secret.

Even if one of the partners viewed such information as private before the relationship started, the fact that he is aware that she expects revelation might cause him to exert energy in hiding that information from her. This expenditure of energy occurs because in deciding that this information should be kept a secret, he must constantly monitor information that is consistent with the state of mind that he wishes to maintain as well as monitor the information that he wishes to hide from others (Wegner et al., 1994). It is not easy for people to engage in these dual processes: "The secret must be remembered, or it might be told. And the secret cannot be thought about, or it might be leaked" (Wegner et al., 1994, p. 288). In a nutshell, whether information is merely private or is secret depends on the expectations that the people in a particular relationship have about what should be disclosed. This distinction between secrecy and privacy is central to understanding the essence of secrecy and its contextual nature.

SECRECY VERSUS REPRESSION

As indicated earlier, by definition secrecy is a social phenomenon. But what about times when people are keeping secrets from themselves? Is that a form of secrecy? The concept of keeping secrets from oneself and not even realizing that one is engaging in such censorship has been called repression. Whereas self-concealment is defined as the "predisposition to actively conceal from others personal information that one perceives as distressing or negative" (Larson & Chastain, 1990, p. 440), the term "repression" has been used to mean keeping painful thoughts and impulses out of conscious awareness (Schwartz, 1990). People who deny symptoms and anxiety and who score high on measures of social desirability (i.e., they try to look like good people) have been referred to as having a repressive coping style (Weinberger, Schwartz, & Davidson, 1979). Although both self-concealment and repression are seen as types of defensive coping strategies or ways of avoiding dealing with unpleasant material (Spielberger et al., 1991), the main distinction between self-concealers and repressors is that the former engage in conscious secret keeping, whereas the latter engage in unconscious censorship of undesirable material.

Whereas the empirical study of self-concealment is relatively new (e.g., Larson & Chastain, 1990), repression and the broader concept of inhibition have received a good deal of attention since Freud's early theorizing about these concepts (see, for example, King, Emmons, & Woodley, 1992; Polivy, 1998). It is interesting that repression has received more research attention than self-concealment, given that repression is more difficult to study because researchers cannot directly assess unconscious processes. This greater emphasis on repression is perhaps a testament to the contribution of Freud's work on the unconscious aspects of personality in general and on repression in particular, which he depicted as the cornerstone of all defensive mechanisms.

Repression is conceptually but not necessarily empirically related to self-concealment. Spielberger et al. (1991) investigated the relationship between these two defensive coping strategies by asking German college students to complete the Self-Concealment Scale (SCS) (Larson & Chastain, 1990), the Marlowe-Crowne Social Desirability Scale (SDS-CM), and the Taylor Manifest Anxiety Scale (MAS) (Luck & Timaeus, 1969). (The combination of the latter two scales is a measure of the repressive coping style.) The scores on the SCS were positively correlated with scores on the MAS for both men and women, demonstrating that self-concealers report being high in anxiety. However, the repressors reported being low in anxiety. Based on the results from these self-report measures, Spielberger et al. (1991) suggested that self-concealment and repression tap different aspects of defensive coping. Likewise, other researchers have demonstrated that self-concealment is related to self-reported depression (e.g., Kelly & Achter, 1995; Larson & Chastain, 1990), whereas repression is not (e.g., Zung & Gianturco, 1971). For example, Zung and Gianturco (1971) observed a strong negative correlation between self-reported depression and repression among 159 patients seen in an outpatient clinic, and thus they concluded that the depressed patients did not repress or deny their illnesses and that they were sensitive to their symptoms.

However, it does not really make sense to use self-report measures to compare repressors with self-concealers, because by definition repressors deny being anxious or distressed, even though they might actually be distressed. Detecting differences between patients and controls with respect to inhibition of expression must be done instead with overt behavior and physiological assessments (Traue & Michael, 1993). For instance, when Anderson (1981) exposed patients with psychosomatic disorders to physical and mental stress, the patients who had the strongest physiological responses actually reported that they had experienced less stress than those who had weaker physiological responses. Researchers have shown that repressors, as compared with high-anxious or low-anxious participants, report fewer negative emotions in diary ratings (Shapiro, Jamner, & Goldstein, 1993) and fewer negative childhood memories (Davis & Schwartz, 1987). Repressors also report being older during their early negative memories (Davis & Schwartz, 1987; Myers & Brewin, 1994). Even though repressors seem to have trouble remembering early negative events, this trouble does not generalize to their recall of positive events (Myers & Brewin, 1994).

In sum, repression and self-concealment are conceptually related—both are seen as forms of avoiding threatening material—but they are not necessarily empirically related. Repression historically has received more empirical attention than self-concealment, even though it is more difficult to study. A way around the problem of trying to assess repression directly has been to consider people to be high in repressiveness (or high in repressive-defensive coping) when they score high on social desirability measures and report having low levels of anger or anxiety (Weinberger, 1990). These people may believe and act as though they have few problems, but they may actually be engaging in some kind of unconscious self-deception or denial (Weinberger, 1990). Thus, the major distinction between self-concealment and repression seems to be that the former involves suppression, which is conscious, and latter involves an unconscious avoidance of threatening information (King et al., 1992).

SECRECY VERSUS LYING

As implied earlier, secrecy typically carries the negative connotation of being a form of deception (e.g., Lane & Wegner, 1995). Whereas lying is deception by commission, secrecy has been described as deception by omission (e.g., Wegner et al., 1994). For instance, imagine a 40-year-old woman who cheated on her taxes when she was earning a lot of money at the age of 17 waitressing at an upscale restaurant. If she tells her husband, "I have never cheated on my income taxes," then she is simply lying. However, if she says, "I have never in all my adult life cheated on my income taxes," then she is keeping the adolescent cheating a secret from him. Either way, her intent is to mislead him about her record of integrity. But if she chooses to omit the truth rather than directly lie and if he ever happens to find out about the cheating, then she always can claim that she was merely protecting her privacy by not telling him about it.

An interesting note about secrecy is that concealing information from others may seem less reprehensible than actively lying to them because it is a passive process (Ekman, 1991). Gesell (1999) found that a sample of undergraduates did indeed rate secrets as less immoral than lies. Perhaps people feel that secrecy is not as bad as lying because when they have been deceived solely by omission, they can still feel that if they put a direct question to the deceptive person, the person could be relied on to give a truthful answer (or to decline to answer, and then the truth can be inferred from the silence). In contrast, once people recognize that someone has lied to them, they may feel that they can no longer believe anything that the person says. Even admitting to one friend about having lied to another friend can make the first friend wonder about the discloser's integrity.

However, there are likely to be cases when a person actually may feel more angered by concealment than by lying (see Sweetser, 1987). This anger stems from the fact that the target cannot complain about being lied to and may feel as though the deceiver got by on a technicality (Sweetser, 1987). A now-familiar example of this type of reaction to concealment was the Independent Counsel Ken Starr's outrage when former president Bill Clinton refused to answer questions about the precise nature of his intimate contacts with Monica Lewinsky. Clinton denied in the Paula Jones's deposition that he and Ms. Lewinsky had had a "sexual relationship." Clinton maintained that none of his sexual contacts with Ms. Lewinsky constituted "sexual relations" within a specific definition used in the Jones's deposition. Under that definition, a person engages in "sexual relations" when the person knowingly engages in or causes (1) contact with the genitalia, anus, groin, breast, inner thigh, or buttocks of any person with an intent to arouse or gratify the sexual desire of any person. "Contact" means intentional touching, either directly or through clothing. According to what the President testified was his understanding, this definition "covers contact by the person being deposed with the enumerated areas, if the contact is done with an intent to arouse or gratify," but it does not cover oral sex performed on the person being deposed. He testified: "[I]f the deponent is the person who has oral sex performed on him, then the contact is with—not with anything on that list, but with the lips of another person. It seems to be self-evident that that's what it is.... Let me remind you, sir, I read this carefully" (*Starr Report*, 1998).

The reason Clinton's testimony was so enraging to many Americans was that it was obvious his intention was to mislead them into believing that he had no sexual relationship with Monica Lewinsky when in fact he did have one. Perhaps a testament to the notion that secrecy is less reprehensible than lying is that fact that Clinton's job approval ratings stayed high throughout the impeachment hearings. Also, the US Senate did not find Clinton guilty of perjury, and thus did not force him to step down from the presidency. Later, during his final days in office, in a plea bargain to avoid further prosecution, Clinton finally admitted that his intent indeed was to mislead those putting him on trial as well as to mislead the American public. Right after this confession, his approval ratings plummeted and he received a resurgence of scrutiny of his actions as president. In particular, he fell under attack by prosecutors over his final-hour presidential pardons, especially the pardoning of billionaire Marc Rich. According to Crystal Champion (2001), there may be a trade-off associated with concealment and lying, such that concealment may make the recipient angrier about the deception but lying may do more damage to the deceiver's overall reputation as a moral, decent person. Clinton's decision finally to confess about the Lewinsky affair may have made people less angry about his sneaky omissions at trial, but it may have hurt him in terms of his overall reputation.

HOW COMMON IS SECRECY?

Even though researchers have not yet charted the frequency of secrecy in people's everyday experiences, undergraduates participating in a recent survey study perceived secrecy and lying to be equally common (Gesell, 1999), and lying has been found to be a very common occurrence (DePaulo, Kashy, Kirkendol, Wyer, & Epstein, 1996). In two separate diary studies, 77 college students and 70 demographically diverse members of the community kept track of how many times per day they told lies (DePaulo et al., 1996). The students reported that they lied about two times per day on the average and the community members reported telling one lie per day (DePaulo et al., 1996). The participants in those studies tended to tell relatively more other-oriented lies to women, such as "your hips don't look big in that skirt" in an effort to spare the women's feelings. In contrast, the participants tended to tell men more self-centered lies, such as "I am not attracted to your old girlfriend" in an effort to protect the liar's interests.

I contend that secrecy defined as deliberately keeping information from others—but not necessarily *all* others—is even more common than lying. It is such a common phenomenon that virtually all adults of normal intellectual and psychological functioning do keep personal secrets at one time or another. Anecdotal evidence for this suggestion comes from my own laboratory research on secrecy. Nine years ago, when I first started this line of research, I prescreened undergraduate participants for those who reported that they were keeping a personal secret, thinking that I would only ask those who had one to take part in my studies. However, I soon learned that such prescreening was not necessary. Virtually all the students who came into the laboratory without such prescreening could generate a personal and private secret that they had told no one or very few people. Likewise, in studies where large groups of people were asked to recall an emotional experience that they have never shared the majority said that they readily could recall such an experience (Rime, Philippot, Boca, & Mesquita, 1992). Also, Vangelisti (1994) found that 99% of her sample of undergraduates reported that they were keeping a secret from at least one of their family members.

Theorists have argued that secrecy may be considered a critical element in the development of one's ego boundaries or sense of identity (see Hoyt, 1978; Margolis, 1966; Taush, 1933). Learning about society's taboos (e.g., not to blurt out embarrassing observations, such as "Mommy, that man is missing a leg!") and learning to keep such information to oneself are thought to be central aspects of healthy development (Szajnberg, 1988). Developmental psychologists have noted that as children mature, they learn to conceal information from others and to use such information to influence or manipulate them (Peskin, 1992). In one study, 3-year-olds were not yet capable of strategically concealing information from others in order to obtain a desired object (a preferred sticker), whereas 5-year-olds were able to conceal information to obtain the object (Peskin, 1992). In sum, secrecy is a nearly universal phenomenon, and being able to keep personal secrets may even be seen as a sign of maturation.

TYPES OF SECRETS PEOPLE KEEP

People tend to keep their most embarrassing, disturbing, or traumatic personal experiences concealed. Secrets are likely to involve negative or stigmatizing information that pertains to the secret keepers themselves (Norton, Feldman, & Tafoya, 1974). These kinds of secrets are stigmatizing *personal secrets* (Kelly & McKillop, 1996) and they are the focus of this volume. There is a wide range of the types of personal secrets people keep, which includes secrets about being gay (Cole, Kemeny, Taylor, & Visscher, 1996) or lesbian, being raped (Binder, 1981; Burgess & Holmstrom, 1974), cheating on a test (Kelly, Klusas, van Weiss, & Kenny, 2001), and having medical conditions, such as AIDS (Larson & Chastain, 1990). Across a number of studies, one category of personal secrets emerges the most commonly occurring: sexual secrets (e.g., Hill, Thompson, Cogar, & Denman, 1993; Kelly, 1998; Kelly et al., 2001; Norton et al., 1974). In the following paragraphs, I provide more details on the kinds of secrets that people in both nonclinical and clinical samples have reported keeping and the kinds of topics couples and families consider taboo (i.e., off limits for discussion).

Undergraduates' Secrets

Norton et al. (1974) examined the frequency of themes for secrets written anonymously by 359 undergraduates in an encounter group exercise. Sex-related secrets occurred most often, followed by failure-related secrets. The researchers then drew a random sample of 49 secrets from the original 359 secrets and asked 190 other undergraduates to rate the levels of risk associated with the potential discovery of those secrets. Secrets ranged from the risky, "I have had incestuous relations with a member of my family" to the nonrisky, "I smoke dope." The secrets that were perceived as the most risky were those relating to sex, mental health, and violence or destruction.

In another study of secrets among undergraduates, my students and I invited 85 undergraduates to our laboratory where, after completing a stream-of-consciousness writing task, the undergraduates were asked to write confidentially and anonymously about the most personal and private secrets of their lives (Kelly et al., 2001). Specifically, they were asked to think of a secret that they had told no one or very few people. Among the 85 participants, 28 listed sexual secrets (e.g., about having been raped, experimenting with novel sexual acts, having had sex for money); 17 described secretly desiring or having a romantic relationship; 12 had family secrets (e.g., having been neglected as a child, having an unemployed father); 10 described interpersonal alienation; 7 listed secrets about death or suicide (e.g., their own suicide attempts); 4 listed delinquencies (e.g., cheating on a test); 3 listed an addiction/bulimia; 3 indicated abortion/pregnancy; and 1 described a health problem. Thus, once again it was sexual secrets that were most frequently mentioned.

Instead of asking participants to generate their own secrets, Lane and Wegner (1995) gave undergraduates a list of 50 topics and asked them to rate to what extent they kept those topics secret. The researchers then subjected the ratings to factor analysis and found that four distinct factors emerged. They labeled these "offenses," "worries," "sorrows," and "sins." Offenses included stealing things and masturbation; worries included getting mugged and failing a test; sorrows included being lonely; and sins included using marijuana and thoughts of the devil. The last two categories could be distinguished from the other categories in that sins referred to personal moral weaknesses, whereas offenses were socially disapproved of acts and often punished by society. The extent to which participants reported keeping the various events secret was found to be greatest for sorrows, next for offenses, next for sins, and least for worries.

Finkenauer and Rime (1998a) tried to capture the defining characteristics of secrecy by exploring the differences between secrets and nonsecrets in two studies. In the first study, undergraduates recalled the most recent important emotional event that they had shared with another person and the most recent important emotional event that they had not shared. The researchers focused their comparisons of the ratings of shared and non-shared events only on the negatively valenced events (i.e., they dropped the responses of participants who reported positive secrets). The second study was almost identical to the first, except that the participants in the second study were asked to recall either a shared or a nonshared event, not both. Also, participants in the second study were college students and their acquaintances who ranged in age from 15 to 75 years. For both studies, the researchers hypothesized that the emotional intensity, type of emotion (i.e., shame and guilt), and holding back from expressing emotions during the events would all discriminate between the secret and nonsecret events. Also, they predicted that keeping an emotional event a secret would make the participants ruminate over (i.e., mentally hold onto) the event more than if they had shared the event. The researchers based their predictions in part on the findings from a pair of surveys in which Wegner et al. (1994) showed that (1) past relationships that participants presently thought about were more likely to have been kept secret than ones that they did not think about and (2) participants who reported that a past relationship had been kept secret indicated that they were still preoccupied with thoughts of the relationship.

Contrary to Finkenauer and Rime's (1998a) predictions, in both studies the participants' ratings of the overall intensity of their emotional experiences failed to differentiate between shared and nonshared events. In Study 1, the participants indicated that the nonshared events were actually less negative than shared ones. Moreover, participants did not report that they ruminated more over nonshared events than over shared ones. Likewise, there were no differences in participants' ratings of how traumatic the events were and no differences in the extent to which they felt recovered from the event and its consequences. However, the type of emotion surrounding the events did distinguish nonshared events from shared ones. For nonshared events, participants reported greater shame, disgust (in Study 2 only), and guilt; increased appraisal of personal responsibility; and more holding back from emotional display during the event. They also reported that they had engaged in a greater search for meaning and efforts to understand what happened in the cases of nonshared events (Finkenauer & Rime, 1998a). Thus, the studies uncovered some expected differences in participants' past attempts to understand the two types of events but failed to uncover differences in how much participants currently ruminated over or were bothered by the events.

CLIENTS' SECRETS

Hill et al. (1993) asked 26 psychotherapy clients who had received an average of 86 therapy sessions to indicate what if any secrets they had not told their therapists. Secrets were defined as major life experiences, facts, or feelings that clients do not share with their therapists that occur over a relatively long time frame and do not necessarily stem from events within the therapy (Hill et al., 1993). Surprisingly, even though the clients were selected by their therapists for participation in the study, and even though the clients had paid a good deal of money for the therapy, nearly half of them (46%) reported keeping secrets from their therapists (Hill et al., 1993). The themes of the clients' secrets encompassed sex, failure, and mental health issues (Hill et al., 1993). For example, one of the clients reported that he was keeping his gay attraction toward the therapist a secret.

The themes to clients' secrets discovered by Hill et al. (1993) were similar to the themes described by encounter group and group therapy members in previous research (Norton et al., 1974; Yalom, 1985). Yalom (1985) reported that the three most common themes of secrets for group therapy members were: (1) a deep conviction of personal inadequacy, (2) a sense that they do not or cannot truly care for another person, and (3) some type of sexual secret.

Whereas both Hill et al. (1993) and Yalom (1985) asked clients about their secrets in general, I (Kelly, 1998) asked 42 short-term psychotherapy outpatients to indicate whether they were keeping secrets from their therapists that they believed were relevant to their treatment. The outpatients in this sample had received an average of 11 therapy sessions (ranging from 3 to 30) at a community mental health hospital. They completed confidential surveys that would never be seen by their therapists. Just over 40% of the outpatients said that they were keeping relevant secrets from their therapists. Consistent with Hill and colleagues' (1993) findings on keeping general secrets from the therapists, whether they were keeping relevant secrets was not related to how many sessions they had received. The types of relevant secrets that the 17 clients reported were as follows (they each listed only one secret, as it turned out): 7 said that they secretly were desiring the wrong person/had secret relationship difficulties; 4 indicated sexual secrets; 2 listed a health problem; 2 listed drugs/alcohol; 1 indicated lying/delinquency; and 1 said that he would take his secret to the grave. Hence, the relevant secrets from this sample of clients were similar to the secrets from other clinical and nonclinical samples: they most frequently were about sex and sexual desires.

TABOO TOPICS IN CLOSE RELATIONSHIPS

Related to the concept of secrecy are taboo topics—topics that are considered off limits for discussion—in relationships. Baxter and Wilmot (1985) interviewed 40 male and 50 female undergraduates and asked them to comment on taboo topics in their cross-sex relationships. Twelve of the relationships were platonic, 25 were romantic potential (i.e., they were not yet romantic but could become so), and 53 were romantic. The most frequently mentioned taboo topic, representing 34.4% of the total number of taboo topics mentioned, was the state of the relationship. The state of the relationship referred to how serious the romantic relationship was or to whether the platonic relationship would become romantic. Next was ex-trarelationship activity (15.7%), followed by relationship norms (12.8%), prior relationships (12.8%), conflict-inducing topics (11.0%), and negative self-disclosures (4.7%), such as having been arrested for shoplifting in the past.

FAMILY SECRETS

Secrets have been of particular interest to family systems researchers, largely because when families come in for therapy, secrecy is thought to be the source of the symptoms displayed by one or more family members (e.g., Saffer, Sansone, & Gentry, 1979). Vangelisti and Caughlin (1997) asked two large samples of undergraduates to recall and describe a secret that their family, as a group, kept from nonfamily members. The results showed that the types of family secrets they described could be cate-gorized as *taboo topics*, activities that are stigmatized or condemned by the family and the larger society; *rule violations*, which break rules common to many families; and *conventional topics*, which represent information that is not necessarily wrong but often is considered inappropriate for discus-sion (Vangelisti & Caughlin, 1997). Examples of taboo secrets were the lack of a previous marriage (when there was supposed to be one), substance abuse, finances, sexual preferences, mental health of family members, and physical abuse. Examples of rule violations were premarital pregnancy and cohabitation. Finally, examples of conventional secrets were physical health problems of family members, circumstances surrounding a family member's death, and personality conflicts among family members. Taboo secrets were the most common, with 75.4% and 74.1% of the participants in the two samples mentioning those; rule violations were mentioned by 14.7% and 9.5% of the participants; and conventional secrets were men-tioned by 9.9% and 16.4% of the two samples, respectively.

Even though it is interesting to read what kinds of secrets family members keep, predicting whether a member will keep a secret does not seem to be enhanced by knowing what type of secret it is (Vangelisti & Caughlin, 1997). Rather, such predictions are enhanced by looking at the functions of the secrets and at the relationships between the secret keepers and the people to whom the secrets pertain (Vangelisti & Caughlin, 1997). In particular, Vangelisti and Caughlin (1997) found that neither the valence of the secrets nor the extent to which family members identified with the secrets predicted whether they were likely to reveal it to outsiders. However, if the secrets served evaluation, maintenance, privacy, or defense functions, family members were unlikely to reveal them (Vangelisti & Caughlin, 1997).

SUMMARY

A number of typologies of secrets have emerged from research on undergraduates, psychotherapy clients, and families. Cutting across the different typologies, one can see that people most frequently report having sexual secrets and keeping secret their desires for (or involvement in) a romantic relationship. People also report keeping secrets that could make them look maladjusted: the mental health category from the Hill et al. (1993) study, the deep conviction of personal inadequacy sentiment expressed by group therapy members (Yalom, 1985), the sorrows category from the Lane and Wegner (1995) study, and the failure-related events category presented by Norton and colleagues (1974) all suggest that type of secret. As far as what seems to distinguish secrets from nonsecrets, Finkenauer and Rime (1998a) found support for the idea that people are inclined to keep secret events that they feel guilty about or ashamed of or that they feel are disgusting. However, they also found that people do not necessarily ruminate more over secrets as compared with nonsecret events.

WHY PEOPLE KEEP SECRETS

Having just identified the types of secrets people keep, I now pinpoint the reasons people give for keeping secrets. The 17 clients who reported keeping a relevant secret in psychotherapy were asked, "What has prevented you from sharing your relevant secret(s) with the therapist?" (Kelly, 1998). Five clients said that they were afraid to express feelings, three stated that they were too ashamed or embarrassed, three were concerned that revealing the secrets would show the therapist how little progress had been made, three stated that there was no time, two said that they would not tell anyone, two said that they were not motivated to address the secret, one indicated loyalty to another, and one said "nothing." In Hill and colleagues' (1993) study of the long-term therapy sample of clients, the most frequently listed reason for keeping secrets was that the clients felt too ashamed or embarrassed to share their secrets with their therapists. Regarding taboo topics, the primary reason respondents gave for not wanting to discuss the most frequently mentioned topic—the nature of the relationship—was "relationship destruction" (Baxter &

Wilmot, 1985). Specifically, both the more- and the less-committed partners feared that articulation of the unequal commitment levels would force the partners to recognize the inequity, and thus break up.

Consistent with these findings, a number of scholars have argued that people keep secrets because of their concerns about receiving disapproval from others (e.g., Bok, 1982; Larson & Chastain, 1990; Simmel, 1950; Stiles, 1987; Wegner & Erber, 1992). A potential outgrowth of such disapproval is being abandoned by confidants who have a negative reaction to a given revelation (see Kelly & McKillop, 1996). It would seem that underlying any decision to keep (or to reveal) a secret may be what Baumeister and Leary (1995) identified as a fundamental human motivation to belong to a community or group. Baumeister and Leary (1995) hypothesized that people need to form and maintain strong, stable interpersonal relationships and postulated that this need is for frequent, nonaversive interactions within an ongoing relational bond. They offered substantial support for their hypothesis by showing that people form social attachments readily under most conditions and resist the dissolution of existing bonds. Moreover, once people do adjust to the loss of a partner, they typically do quite well with a substitute romantic partner who fulfills their belonging needs. Baumeister and Leary (1995) also showed that a lack of attachments is linked to a variety of ill effects on health, adjustment, and well-being. They concluded that existing evidence supports the hypothesis that the need to belong is a powerful, fundamental, and extremely pervasive motivation that appears to have multiple and strong effects on emotional patterns and cognitive processes. It follows from their conclusions that people would go to great lengths to avoid revealing secrets that might leave them ostracized from their support network. Consistent with this idea are Norton and colleagues' (1974) findings that secrets relating to sex, mental health, and violence or destruction were perceived by a group of undergraduates as the most risky statements—those secrets might cost them precious relationships.

RULES OF REVEALING SECRETS

Now I address the flip side of concealing and describe the rules of revealing secrets, along with people's motives for revealing them. Based on their qualitative analysis of 24 secret revelations, Rodriguez and Ryave (1992) concluded that the revealing of secrets follows an organized sequence of events. The first step is the secret frame, wherein the revealer indicates that a secret is coming and indicates who should not be told. The second step involves the confidant's accepting the secret nature of the revelation and indicating that he or she can be trusted not to reveal it. The third step is the disclosure of the contents of the secret. The fourth and final step is the confidant's acknowledgment of having received and understood the secret. The first step in this sequence is similar to what Bellman (1981) termed the *preface*, which is the set of instructions a revealer gives to the confidant just prior to revealing the secret. Such instructions serve to inform the confidant that the secret must not be repeated. They also assure the confidant that the circumstances are appropriate for the revealing, and they unite the revealer and confidant. Last, they assure the confidant that the revealer can be trusted even though he or she is sharing a secret. Bellman (1981) notes that a contradiction arises when the secret that is being revealed pertains to someone else. Specifically, the confidant is being asked to keep a secret when the revealer himself or herself did not.

This seeming contradiction can be resolved by considering another rule to the transmission of secrets. People may expect to be told secrets that their closest friends know about individuals who are outside their immediate social circle. At the very least, they are likely to view less negatively revelations about acquaintances than about close friends. Yovetich and Drigotas (1999) found that college students were more likely to communicate private information gathered from a lower-level intimate to a higher-level intimate (upward transmission) rather than from a higher-level intimate to a lower-level intimate (downward transmission) in both imagined (Study 1) and actual (Study 2) instances of secret transmission. In addition, observers (Study 3) evaluated the revelation of a secret more negatively when an individual passed the secret from a higher-level intimate to a lower-level intimate. As these findings imply, people may excuse their closest friends for telling them other people's secrets.

WHY PEOPLE REVEAL SECRETS

Given that revealing personal secrets may make people look bad, as described earlier, why do people so often end up revealing their secrets to others? Derlega and Grzelak (1979) described five motives for revealing secrets and suggested that some combination usually accompanies the revealing. These are self-clarification, social validation, relationship development, social control, and expression. Self-clarification refers to the revealer's desire to acknowledge his or her position. For example, a woman might say, "Even though I am Republican, I am clearly pro-choice and had to have an abortion myself when I was 19." Revealing secrets based on wanting social validation is an effort to confirm one's sense of self-esteem. Relationship development motives often are spawned by hearing someone else's revelations and wanting to reciprocate to enhance an equitable, intimate bond. People who reveal secrets to establish social control are attempting or hoping to control the behavior of another by expressing disapproval of their actions. For instance, a man might tell his girlfriend who is considering a breast augmentation procedure that he left his previous girlfriend after she had that operation. Finally, the motive for expression is experienced as a compelling desire to talk about feelings or thoughts.

The motive for expression recently has received a good deal of attention in the clinical and social psychological literatures, with some researchers arguing that disclosing personal emotional experiences to others is a compelling need (e.g., Tait & Silver, 1989). In a number of studies involving both positive and negative emotional experiences, people have reported sharing the experiences with others, most of the time sharing the experiences repetitively and a short time after the experience (for reviews, see Rime et al., 1992; Rime, 1995a,b). Rime et al. (1992) found that for about 90 to 96% of the emotional experiences people had, they reported having disclosed the experiences to others. Rime and colleagues (Rime et al., 1991a; Rime, Noel, & Philippot, 1991b) also found that participants shared their emotionally intense experiences, as compared with less emotionally intense experiences, with others more frequently and over an extended period of time, a pattern that was replicated in diary studies in which participants kept track of their most emotional events of each day (Rime et al., 1995). The findings also were replicated in situations where people were contacted after some important emotional experience, such as the birth of a child or a car accident, and then again weeks later (Rime et al., 1995). In addition, when participants were induced to feel emotions in the laboratory, they shared the emotional experiences with others when they were given the opportunity to do so (Luminet, Bouts, Delie, Manstead, & Rime, 2000). These findings on expression of emotion pertain directly to expression of personal secrets to the extent that the secrets are charged emotionally.

Beyond describing the different motives for revealing, researchers have offered deeper explanations concerning why people reveal their emotional experiences to others. One explanation stems from the cognitive–motor view of expression (Rime & Schiaratura, 1991). According to this view, critical parts of one's experiences are encoded or retained at a nonverbal level in the form of mental images, bodily movements, and affect-related visceral changes (such as a churning stomach or racing heart). These nonverbal forms remain the focus of attention until they can be assimilated and put into words, particularly when the experiences are more emotionally intense. Another idea is that people experience emotion when their anticipations of how the world should operate are disrupted.

If the disruption is intense enough, it may challenge a person's basic assumptions about the self and the world (Janoff-Bulman, 1992). Such a person should be motivated to interact with others as a means of helping to confirm or disconfirm beliefs about the self and reconstructing assumptions about the world.

In both of these theoretical explanations, revealing is depicted as a way of making meaning out of emotional events, which is consistent with the commonly recognized *Zeigarnik effect*. Zeigarnik (1927) showed that people continue to think about and remember interrupted tasks more than finished ones, suggesting that they may have a need for completion or resolution of the events. Thus, people may reveal their secrets to others in order to try to get a sense of resolution on the secret.

These explanations for revealing make sense regarding emotional secrets, but they cannot account for the times when people choose to reveal a secret that is likely to cost them a relationship even though they do not necessarily need resolution on that secret. For example, imagine the following situation. A woman says to a potential dating partner, "I would not date a man who has ever had sex with a prostitute ... but other than that I don't care how many sexual partners he has had." Imagine, too, that he once did have sex with a prostitute but had never considered that information to be relevant to any new relationship. Paradoxically, now, just when the revelation might be most damaging to him, he may feel the most compelled to confess it. Thus, on his third date with the woman, he blurts out, "Actually, I have had sex with a prostitute, but it happened when I was just a teen." This perplexing confession stems from the fact that, as discussed earlier, private information can become secret information in the context of particular relationships. Just knowing that the woman would reject him for a revelation about his experience with a prostitute might make him focus on that information and cause him to suppress it. Ironically, at least initially, suppression makes information actually come to awareness more readily, particularly when the person is under stress (Wegner & Erber, 1992). If the woman said that she did not care about what he did before, then probably none of his specific sexual acts would have come to mind to be suppressed, and therefore he would not have become preoccupied with those thoughts and then blurted out the damaging confession (see Wegner, 1994; Lane & Wegner, 1995).

Certainly, he could have kept his experience with the prostitute a secret and dismissed his date's comments as too intrusive to be addressed. However, since the humanistic, encounter group movement of the 1960s, many Americans have come to expect openness about things such as previous sexual and assault histories when building new relationships (see Bok, 1982). Because of the cultural context, he may have felt that he should "come clean" with her to start things off and may have felt obligated to tell her about the prostitution. Otherwise, the belief is that what closeness he develops with her will be limited if she cannot completely accept him and what he has done.

In addition to the expectations for disclosure of one's relational partner, I contend that two other important elements go into whether one feels the need to disclose secret information. The first of these issues is the extent to which the secret keeper feels that the secret is central to his or her identity. If the man who had sex with a prostitute felt that this particular behavior is part of who he really is (i.e., it is part of his self-concept), then he might feel that it is important to reveal such information in an effort to be truthful with his new girlfriend. However, if he feels that the behavior was a rare exception for him, say, for example, that he was pressured to do it at a birthday party that happened a long time ago, then he may actually feel pleased to get away with keeping that information a secret. The interesting paradox here is that people may feel that their self-descriptions better represent who they really are when they lie about some things as opposed to when they are completely disclosing about their shortcomings. People generally view more desirable self-portrayals as compared with less desirable self-portrayals as more truthful or representative of themselves (Schlenker, 1980, 1986). For example, my colleagues and I (Kelly, Kahn, & Coulter, 1996) observed that in both samples of undergraduate and client participants, those who had rated themselves as being depressed as compared with those who had rated themselves as nondepressed viewed their self-descriptions as less representative of themselves. Perhaps this notion can explain why Bill Clinton said in his infamous quote about marijuana use, "I tried it, didn't like it, and didn't inhale." That statement seems absurd on its face, because people would agree that one has either tried pot or not; there is no half-trying! But if Bill Clinton felt that being a pot smoker was foreign to his self-concept, then he might have felt that it would be a more accurate reflection of himself to say that he did not really try it. (Of course, it is always possible that he wanted to make sure that he would win the election and that the veracity or representativeness of his statement was irrelevant.)

The second issue is that a secret keeper may fear that the secret will be discovered later and that then the relationship will be destroyed. This fear should be debilitating, given that, as described earlier, there is a good deal of empirical support for the notion that a fundamental human motivation is the need to belong. Fearing that the relational partner may ultimately abandon him or her because of a revelation is indeed a great threat, and it may help explain why people so often reveal their damaging secrets.

Getting back to the Graham–Zamora example of secrecy, I suggest that Diane Zamora may have revealed her secret to her friends because she may have feared that any relationships that she could develop with them would be impaired by her own knowledge of the secret and awareness of the possibility that they could later discover it. Now, anyone who gets to know and like Zamora does so with the knowledge of the murder. Even though it should be harder to get people to like her, at least when they do, she can trust that such liking will not be destroyed by a future revelation. Of course, I am merely speculating here; she just may have been bragging and not thinking about the grave consequences of her confessions.

CONCLUSION

Secrecy is an extremely common phenomenon and the ability to conceal information from others even may be seen as a sign of maturity or normal adult functioning. Secrets are those things that people hide from at least one other person; thus, it only makes sense to think of secrets in the context of relationships. The most frequently reported types of personal secrets that people keep are sexual secrets and secrets that make them look maladjusted, either like a failure or as though they are mentally ill. These themes refer to information that might make the people look like they are abnormal or are not living up to others' expectations and that might cause them to be rejected or ostracized from their groups. Being rejected by one's social group is no small event. A lack of attachments has been linked to a variety of ill effects on health, adjustment, and well-being (see Baumeister & Leary, 1995). This fundamental motivation to belong may explain both why people sometimes choose to reveal and sometimes choose to keep their secrets. They may choose to reveal some secrets in an effort to forge relational bonds with particular individuals and may choose to conceal those same secrets from other people in an effort to avoid being rejected by them. Another intriguing possibility for why people sometimes reveal damaging secrets to others is that people have a compelling need to disclose their emotional experiences with others (e.g., Rime, 1995a). However, it is not yet clear that such a need does exist, given that the primary evidence to support this notion is simply that people very frequently do share their emotional experiences, especially those more emotionally intense experiences, with others. It may be that because people feel an expectation from others to disclose their emotional experiences, they do disclose. It is possible that if these cultural norms changed, people would not disclose as often. Another intriguing explanation for why people reveal certain secrets but not others is that they are willing to reveal secrets that they feel depict who they really are. For example, if they felt that they did something that was unrepresentative of who they normally are, even if they were responsible for their actions, they would be less likely to reveal those events than if they felt that those secrets did capture who they really are. Given that people generally see more favorable events and descriptions of themselves as representative of who they really are, those secrets that they reveal are likely to be ones that still allow them to see themselves in a favorable light.

CHAPTER 2

INDIVIDUAL DIFFERENCES IN SECRET KEEPING

"I don't even know if I have the capacity for normal emotions or not because I haven't cried for a long time. You just stifle them for so long that maybe you lose them, partially at least. I don't know." (Jeffrey Dahmer on his confessions. http://serial-killers.virtualave.net/dahmer5.htm. Retrieved 5/10/00.)

Over the years, I have worked closely with a number of students in my laboratory. Some of them have told me a great deal about themselves and their families, others have been so secretive that I did not even know that they were seriously dating or engaged to another student in the psychology department. Most people probably have had similar experiences, in which they were shocked to discover hidden information about people whom they presumably knew well. Let me be clear right from the start of this chapter: these people who keep secrets and are hard to get to know are sicker, both psychologically and physically, than people who do not keep secrets.

An extreme example of this secretive kind of person was the late serial killer, Jeffrey Dahmer. His father, Lionel, told television reporters how just prior to his son's arrest in 1991, he had engaged in very mundane conversations with Jeffrey about Jeffrey's weight and job, as though nothing were wrong. He was pleased to see that Jeffrey seemed to be living a relatively normal existence, only to be stunned to discover later that Jeffrey was capable of keeping tremendous secrets from him. These secrets surrounded Jeffrey's gruesome killing of more than a dozen people. The aspect of this case that is most relevant to this chapter is throughout much of his life, the highly secretive Jeffrey experienced depression, anxiety, loneliness, and extreme shyness, just as people who conceal negative personal information in general are shy and vulnerable to depression, anxiety, cancers, infectious diseases, and other physical and psychological problems (e.g., Larson & Chastain, 1990).

In this chapter, I review the evidence that people who keep stigmatizing, negative, or distressing personal secrets tend to be sicker than those who do not, and I address the question, "Who are these secret keepers?" Part of understanding them involves contrasting self-concealment (i.e., the predisposition to keep secrets) with another, more frequently studied form of psychological inhibition: repression. Although as indicated in the previous chapter, secrecy necessarily involves at least two people, repression might be thought of loosely as keeping secrets from oneself. I explore how repression and self-concealment each relate to physical and psychological problems and then conclude by providing a profile of the secret keeper. Because of the difficulty in using self-report measures to assess the correlates of repression (i.e., repressors do not know when they are repressing unpleasant material) (Wegner, 1989), in my review of this research, I focus on studies that assessed physiological differences between repressors and nonrepressors. In contrast, in my review of the research on the correlates of self-concealment, I have included studies that used participants' self-reports, because self-concealment is a conscious process and self-concealers do not seem to deny their symptoms (see Kahn & Hessling, 2001; King et al., 1992).

CORRELATES OF UNCONSCIOUS INHIBITION AND THE REPRESSIVE COPING STYLE

At the age of 64, Jacqueline Bouvier Kennedy Onassis succumbed to non-Hodgkin's lymphoma. Her death saddened millions of people around the world, who remembered her as someone who was very modest about her achievements and who remained extremely composed during very trying times. She faced the emotional torment of the birth of a stillborn child in 1956 and the assassination of her husband, President John F. Kennedy in 1963 with quiet courage. Images still haunt Americans of her brave and contained behavior at her husband's widely publicized funeral. Because of her outward composure in such trying times, she frequently has been held up as an example of a life lived with courage, respect, and dignity. Yet one wonders whether such composure may have taken a toll on her health.

The inhibition of emotional expression has been seen as having mixed consequences. On the one hand, the inhibition of such expression helps avoid the escalation of angry feelings and potentially deadly aggressive acts (Suls & Fletcher, 1985). Avoidant strategies, as compared with non-avoidant ones, generally are associated with more positive adaptation in the short run (Suls & Fletcher, 1985). Moreover, the flip side of repression—being overly vigilant and disclosing of problems—has been linked to cardiovascular disease (Taylor, 1990). On the other hand, inhibited expressiveness has been identified as a risk factor for psychosomatic problems, such as back pain and headaches (Traue & Kraus, 1988), and a repressive coping style has been linked to problems as severe as cancer (e.g., Cox & McCay, 1982; Dattore, Shontz, & Coyne, 1980; Jensen, 1987; Kissen, 1966; Temoshok, 1987). For example, Garron and Leavitt (1979) found a small negative relation between self-reports of hostility and low-back pain levels among a large sample of medical patients. Garron and Leavitt (1979) interpreted this finding as supporting theories relating low-back pain to the inhibition of anger. Cochrane and Neilson (1977) found that psychiatric patients who were classified as being chronically or endogenously depressed tended to inhibit expression of aggression more than did patients who were not depressed. Moreover, engaging in inhibition is associated with the increased muscular activity that accompanies stress (Traue, 1995). It has been demonstrated in a number of studies that there is an inverse relation between emotional expression and autonomic reactivity (Buck, 1984; Hokanson & Burgess, 1962; Hokanson & Shetler, 1961). Finally, inhibited expressiveness may be a sign to other people that the person has deficits in emotions and communication (Traue, 1995). In the following paragraphs, I describe in more detail the findings on the harmful correlates of unconscious inhibition and the repressive coping style.

CANCER

Cox and McCay (1982) concluded that among a set of psychosocial variables, such as perceived social support, the strongest predictor of developing cancer is an antiemotional attitude, especially an inability to express negative emotions. Likewise, in a review of the research on the psychological antecedents of cancer, Greer (1983) found evidence that the development of cancer may be related to the predisposition to engage in emotional inhibition.

Further supporting the notion that unconscious inhibition is linked to cancer are the findings from a study of 52 women with a history of breast cancer and 34 healthy women (Jensen, 1987). The women were studied over the course of an average of 624 days to see what personality characteristics of the women predicted the recurrence of their cancer (Jensen, 1987). The spread and recurrence of cancer was greater on average in the women who had a repressive personality style and who tended to avoid expressing negative emotions. Jensen (1987) was able to show that these relations existed even when he statistically controlled for the stage of the disease at the time the women were diagnosed, age, total length of disease course, hematologic factors, and blood chemistries at the time of onset.

Even more compelling evidence that the repressive coping style may be linked to cancer comes from a prospective study of 400 women presenting with an abnormal lump and/or an abnormal mammogram (Flowers et al., 1995). The majority of the 36 women who were ultimately diagnosed with a malignant tumor were repressive copers, whereas repressive copers were not overrepresented among the woman who did not require a biopsy or who had a negative one.

Kneier and Temoshok (1984) found that repressive styles of coping with stressful emotions were associated with high cancer incidence and poor prognosis. They compared the repressive coping reactions of three matched groups of people ranging in age from 40 to 65 years: 20 malignant melanoma patients, 20 cardiovascular disease patients, and 20 disease-free controls. Repressive coping reactions were defined as reactions in which there was a discrepancy between self-reported anxiety and physiological response to anxiety-provoking statements. (The validity of this procedure was established through demonstrating correlations with other indices of repressive tendencies such as the Taylor Manifest Anxiety Scale.) The researchers found the melanoma group was significantly more repressed, whereas the cardiovascular disease participants were the least repressed or most sensitized. These differences in defensive posture were independent of disease severity; in other words, the differences were not merely the result of differences in disease-related anxiety. The researchers suggested that coronary-prone and cancer-prone individuals may be at opposite poles on the distributions of several coping and personality variables, with cancer-prone individuals being more likely to engage in repressive coping (Kneier & Temoshok, 1984).

Patients in another study who had malignant melanoma (i.e., a virulent form of skin cancer) and who reported little distress in the early phases of their cancer, despite their facing the same difficult situation as the other patients, tended to experience greater recurrences and had higher death rates than those who reported more distress (Fawzy et al., 1993). The researchers noted that this relationship was likely due to the fact that those who minimized their illness tended to cope less effectively with the cancer, such as not seeking medical treatment or complying with treatment.

In yet another study, Goldstein and Antoni (1989) investigated the relationship of three repressive coping styles to breast carcinoma incidence and metastasis. These three discrete repressive coping styles were labeled as Introversive, Cooperative, and Respectful, as measured by the Millon Behavioral Health Inventory (MBHI). Upon admission to a cancer treatment unit, 44 female patients recently diagnosed with nonmetastatic or metastatic breast carcinoma completed the MBHI. All patients received mastectomy, chemotherapy, radiation, and/or endocrine therapy. These patients were compared with 34 controls on measures of coping style and psychological distress. The cancer patients, as compared with the non-cancer patients, were more likely to employ a repressive coping style. Moreover, the only group to attain a clinically significant mean score on the Respectful scale was the group of cancer patients with metastasis. Goldstein and Antoni (1989) concluded that the incidence of repressive coping styles may be disproportionately high among breast cancer patients.

To obtain a better understanding of the inhibited emotional expression evident in breast cancer patients, Servaes, Vingerhoets, Vreugdenhil, Keuning, and Broekhuijsen (1999) compared 48 breast cancer patients and 49 healthy women on measures of disturbed emotional processes (i.e., alexithymia, or having a limited capacity to put feelings into words), emotional disclosure, emotional expression, assertiveness, repression, and distress. The patient group showed significantly more ambivalence over emotional expression, more restraint, and more anxiety than the healthy controls. No differences were found between the two groups in alexithymia, expressing emotions in general, or willingness to talk with others about emotions. The image of the breast cancer patient that emerged in the study was that of a person who has conflicting feelings with regard to expressing emotions, is reserved and anxious, is self-effacing, and represses aggression and impulsiveness. The researchers interpreted their findings to mean that cancer patients' inhibited behavior is a reaction to the disease rather than a reflection of a personality characteristic predisposing an individual to (breast) cancer.

In sum, the researchers who have examined the link between having a repressive coping style and cancer typically have looked at people who already have cancer and then measured their recovery/death rates. Although Servaes et al. (1999) suggested that repressive coping is actually a response, not a precursor, to the disease, what does seem clear is that once a person has cancer, this repressive coping response is linked to poorer prognosis and reduced recovery from the disease.

PHYSIOLOGICAL AROUSAL

Weinberger et al. (1979) studied the autonomic nervous system correlates of repression. They asked repressors (i.e., who were high in social desirability and low in self-reported anxiety) and nonrepressors to complete sentences that were aggressive, sexual, or neutral in nature. The repressors obtained significantly higher galvanic skin response, electromyogram, and heart rate scores, which suggests that they experienced more arousal and stress in response to the sentence completion tasks than did the nonrepressors.

Weinberger and co-workers' (1979) findings intensified researchers' interest in investigating the physiological consequences of repression, particularly concerning heart rate and arousal. For example, Siegman, Anderson, and Boyle (1991) subsequently replicated the link between the repressive coping style and elevated heart rate. However, they did not find a significant relationship between the repressive coping style and heightened blood pressure. The findings from other studies suggest that repression may be linked to heightened skin conductance levels, but not with heightened cardiovascular reactivity (Barger, Kircher, & Croyle, 1997; Pennebaker, Hughes, & O'Heeron, 1987).

Heart Disease

Denollet (1993) postulated that distressed individuals (characterized by elevated levels of type A behavior, anger, hostility, and life stress) and inhibited individuals (characterized by the nonexpression of anger) may be particularly coronary prone. Supporting this idea was an examination of 60 42- to 64-year-old males at high risk for coronary heart disease who were evaluated in terms of their expressive style, specific nonverbal cues, personality, and health (Friedman, Hall, & Harris, 1985). Judges watched videotapes of the participants and rated their appearance, the actual audio and video nonverbal cues that the participants emitted, and what they said (words in the transcript). As it turned out, the men who were rated as more repressed and tense, as opposed to more talkative and charismatic, tended to be more illness prone, thus supporting the notion that repression may be linked to heart disease (Friedman et al., 1985).

However, another study with male cardiac patients did not support this link (Denollet, 1991). Denollet (1991) investigated the potential influence of negative affectivity (NA) and repressive coping on cardiovascular fitness among 178 male cardiac patients (aged 31–76 years) who were undergoing rehabilitation. The patients were categorized as high in NA, low in NA, or as repressive copers. No association was found between coping style and cardiovascular fitness as measured by exercise stress testing.

Because both the inhibition of emotions, such as hostility, and the expression of such emotions have been linked to heart disease, Siegman (1993, 1994) focused his research efforts on clarifying the connection between hostility or anger and various negative physical side effects. He (1993, 1994a,b) challenged the widely held belief that the expression of anger is beneficial to mental and physical health. In particular, he reviewed experimental and correlational studies from several different laboratories, including his own, that demonstrated that the full expression of anger, with its vocal manifestations (loud and fast-paced), actually was associated with significant cardiovascular hyperactivity (e.g., Engebretson, Matthews, & Scheier, 1989; Siegman, Anderson, Herbst, Boyle, & Wilkinson, 1992; Suarez & Williams, 1990). Furthermore, epidemiological studies indicate that such expressions of anger also are related to coronary heart disease and to some physiological and hormonal changes that have been implicated in the pathophysiology of coronary heart disease. Siegman (1994b) concluded that neither the mere experience of anger nor its repression has any of the above negative cardiovascular consequences and that the expression of anger is most clearly related and consistently to coronary heart disease and its risk factors. Siegman (1994b) suggested that when dealing with negative emotions such as anger, people may benefit from speaking about these emotions in a calm, slow voice, as opposed to either repressing or venting the anger.

Cortisol Secretion

Roger and Najarian (1998) investigated the relationship between emotional inhibition and cortisol secretion (i.e., the release of a hormone involved in maintaining blood pressure) during stress among 51 student nurses (aged 18–42 years) undergoing a written examination as part of their training. The participants completed the Emotion Control Questionnaire, a measure of their tendencies to engage in mental rumination (i.e., the tendency to mull over mental events) and emotional inhibition, one month before the written exam. Cortisol secretion was selected as a measure of experiencing stress because it previously was demonstrated that parents who were less able to cope with the loss of fatally ill children tended to secrete more cortisol than parents who coped better (Wolff, Friedman, Hofer, & Mason, 1964) and that phobic participants tended to secrete more cortisol in response to provocation as opposed to neutral slides (Frederikson & Engel, 1985). The written examination was considered by the nurses to be a stressful event, given that the nurses' scores would have a direct bearing on their continued training. Urinary-free cortisol was assayed from samples taken immediately after the examination and again 3 weeks later (i.e., 2 days after their scores on the written examination were announced) as the control period. As it turned out, differences in cortisol secretions between the stressful event and control period were significantly positively associated with emotional inhibition and the tendency to engage in mental rumination. These findings are yet more evidence that repression is linked to harmful physiological consequences in the face of stress.

IMMUNOLOGIC FUNCTIONING

The link between repression and immunologic functioning recently has received much attention. For example, in one study, undergraduates were asked to complete self-report measures of repression and to write a letter to a friend about a highly stressful event that they had not widely discussed with others (Esterling, Antoni, Kumar, & Schneiderman, 1990). Blood was collected between 45 minutes to 4 hours after the writing and later tested for antibody titers to the latent viral pathogen that is very prevalent in the general population, the Epstein–Barr virus (EBV). This immunologic test was used because, among 20 immunologic variables studied, antibody titers against EBV have been found to be the most consistent and significant correlate of psychosocial stressors (Van Rood, Bogaards, Goulmy, & van Houwelingen, 1993). Increases in EBV are interpreted as a sign of experiencing stress. Judges coded the degree to which participants used emotional words out of total words in their writing. The participants who tended to use fewer emotional words actually had greater levels of EBV antibody titers after the writing than did participants who used more emotion words. Also, the participants who scored higher on the self-report measure of a repressive interpersonal style had greater levels of EBV antibody titers than did those who scored lower. The researchers interpreted their findings to mean that both having a personality that is inclined to avoid expressing negative emotions and engaging in such inhibition are associated with poorer cellular immune control over the latent virus. However, it is important to note it was not clear whether participants who used fewer emotional words were engaging in greater inhibition or simply were being less expressive. (As mentioned in Chapter 1, self-concealment and self-disclosure are empirically distinct and are not mere opposites.)

In another study, the link between having a repressive coping style and immunologic functioning was examined once again (Esterling, Antoni, Kumar, & Schneiderman, 1993). Specifically, Esterling et al. (1993) measured the production of antibody titers in response to an EBV viral capsid antigen in a normal, healthy college population made up of people previously exposed to EBV. These undergraduates completed a battery of physical status questions and items pertaining to potential behavioral immunomodulatory confounds, along with the Taylor Manifest Anxiety Scale and the Marlowe–Crowne Social Desirability Scale (i.e., low scores on the former and high scores on the latter indicate a repressive coping style). Participants reporting high and middle levels of anxiety had higher antibody titers to EBV, suggesting poorer immune control over the latent virus, as compared with the low-anxious group. Similarly, participants with a repressive coping style had higher antibody titers than their low-defensive counterparts. Thus, being too anxious or too repressed was associated with poorer immune response.

Researchers have suggested that the associations between repressive/defensive coping styles, enhanced stress responsivity, and reduced immunocompetence may be mediated by the hyperactivity of endogenous opioid systems (Jammer & Leigh, 1999). In other words, it is through this neurohormonal mechanism—the release of excess endogenous opioids—that a person could simultaneously experience reduced sensitivity to pain and distress and increased sympathetic nervous system and endocrine activity. Jammer and Leigh (1999) conducted a series of experiments and indeed did find some support for their hypothesis that endorphinergic dysregulation is associated with repressive/defensive coping styles. However, more research is needed to establish this underlying mechanism more definitively.

SUMMARY

Overall, research on the repressive coping style has supported the idea that repression is associated with increased cancer rates. Some studies also have shown that repression is linked to poorer immunologic functioning, increased skin conductance, and increased cortisol secretion in response to stress. However, the findings are less clear regarding the link between repression and elevated blood pressure (Siegman et al., 1991) or heart disease (Taylor, 1990). In fact, people who are overly vigilant and disclosing of problems have a greater likelihood of developing cardiovascular disease (Bonnano & Singer, 1990; Taylor, 1990). For example, with anger it is actually the expression, not the repression, of this negative emotion that seems to be linked to heart problems (see Siegman, 1994b). Apparently, either extreme of expressiveness or inhibition is problematic. Sigman's (1994b) solution is that when dealing with negative emotions such as anger, people should speak about these emotions in a calm, slow voice, as opposed to either repressing or venting the anger.

CORRELATES OF CONSCIOUS INHIBITION

In this section, I first identify the correlates of self-concealment, or the predisposition to keep secrets, and then identify the correlates of keeping a particular secret. I keep these reviews separate because the two have been studied separately; however, as the reader will see, both are related to a variety of problems.

SELF-CONCEALMENT

Since the introduction of the 10-item Self-Concealment Scale (SCS) (Larson & Chastain, 1990), this personality variable has received increasing attention among psychology researchers (e.g., Cepeda-Benito & Short, 1998; Kelly, 1998; Kelly & Achter, 1995; Larson, 1993a,b). Cramer and Barry (1999) evaluated the psychometric properties of the SCS and found that in a large sample of university students, it had both good internal consistency and reliability over time.

Researchers have shown that high scorers on the SCS—high self-concealers—have more physical and psychological problems than do low self-concealers (Cepeda-Benito & Short, 1998; Larson & Chastain, 1990; Ichiyama et al., 1993; Kelly, 1998; King et al., 1992). For example, among a sample of human service workers, self-concealment was found to be positively related to anxiety, depression, and bodily symptoms, such as back pain and headaches (Larson & Chastain, 1990). These relations held up after the researchers statistically controlled for participants' traumatic experiences, trauma distress, disclosure of the trauma, social support, social network, and self-disclosure (Larson & Chastain, 1990).

Similar relations between self-concealment and measures of psychological distress have been found in studies using samples of college students (Cepeda-Benito & Short, 1998; Ichiyama et al., 1993; Kahn & Hessling, 2001; King et al., 1992) and outpatient therapy clients (Kelly, 1998). For example, I found that the correlation between symptom (as measured by the Brief Symptom Inventory; Derogatis, 1993) and self-concealment scores was moderately strong ($r = .37$) among a sample of 42 psychotherapy clients (Kelly, 1998). In a separate study, John Achter and I found that the correlation between depression and self-concealment was quite high ($r = .50$) among a sample of 375 undergraduates (Kelly & Achter, 1995, Study 1). Interestingly enough, even though the women in our study had higher depression scores than the men, the women and men did not differ in their mean self-concealment scores.

In that same study, we asked the participants to imagine that they were experiencing a series of problems that college students commonly present to counselors and to report how likely they would be to seek counseling for these problems (Kelly & Achter, 1995, Study 1). We also asked them to indicate their general attitudes toward seeking counseling, as well as to rate how strong their social support networks were. As it turned out, high self-concealers, as compared with low self-concealers, reported a higher likelihood of seeking counseling, despite their more negative attitudes toward counseling. Moreover, although perceived social support was strongly negatively correlated with self-concealment ($r = -.45$), it was not a significant predictor of likelihood to seek counseling. In Study 2, we found that more high self-concealers (57%) reported having seen a counselor than did low self-concealers (37%). Thus, we concluded that high self-concealers are an enigmatic group in that they simultaneously have negative attitudes toward counseling and a high likelihood of seeking counseling.

Cepeda-Benito and Short (1998) attempted to replicate our findings by asking a large sample of undergraduates to complete questionnaires about their perceived likelihood of seeking professional psychological help, attitudes toward psychotherapy, fears of psychotherapy, psychological distress, social support, and self-concealment. In their study, as in ours, self-concealment was positively associated with self-reported distress ($r = .44$) and negatively related to perceived social support ($r = -.28$). However, unlike our results, they found that self-concealment was not significantly associated with reported likelihood of seeking counseling ($r = .06$). Also, in their sample, 21% of the high self-concealers versus 19% of the low self-concealers reported having seen a professional counselor, which was not a statistically significant difference. Thus, our earlier finding that high self-concealers, as compared with low self-concealers, are more likely to seek counseling may be the case only in groups of people who overall have a high rate of seeking counseling.

Recently, Macdonald and Morley (2001) asked 34 people referred to psychotherapy to keep a diary for one week of disclosed and nondisclosed emotions. They found that 68% of their emotions were not disclosed, as compared with much lower rates of nondisclosure observed in studies with nonclinical samples (e.g., Rime et al., 1991a). They suggested that the people in this clinical sample were habitual nondisclosers of emotional and personal experiences, which is consistent with our earlier observation that high self-concealers may be more likely to end up in therapy (Kelly & Achter, 1995).

In addition to being related to depression and anxiety, self-concealment has been linked strongly to social anxiety (Gesell, 1999), which refers to feeling tense when interacting with people at parties or other social settings, and to shyness and low self-esteem among college students (Ichiyama et al., 1993). Given their tendency to feel anxious in social settings, it is not surprising that high self-concealers report having a relatively strong need to be alone (Cramer & Lake, 1998). In two investigations using large samples of college students, the link between scores on the Preference for Solitude Scale (PSS) and Self-Concealment Scale was explored (Cramer &

Lake, 1998). The three subscales of the Preference for Solitude Scale identified by Cramer and Lake are: Need for Solitude (i.e., the desire to be alone), Enjoyment of Solitude, and Productivity during Solitude. Interestingly enough, of those three factors, only the Need for Solitude factor ($r = .38$) was correlated significantly with self-concealment, and that factor may be seen as the most negative of the three factors because it involves trying to get away from people as opposed to taking pleasure in being alone. Also, as in previous research, self-concealment was found to be significantly correlated with loneliness ($r = .54$), low self-esteem ($r = .54$), and social anxiety ($r = .29$) (Cramer & Lake, 1998).

King et al. (1992) explored the relations between self-concealment (as measured by the Self-Concealment Scale) and a variety of measures of constructs pertaining to the broader concept of inhibition. One such construct—conflict over emotional expression—involves wanting to express emotions and not being able to, as well as expressing emotions and wishing one had not (King & Emmons, 1990). In two previous studies, King and Emmons (1990, 1991) demonstrated that such conflict was associated with depression. In their study of 155 adults from the community and undergraduates, King et al. (1992) found that self-concealment scores were positively correlated with scores on measures of ambivalence over emotional expression ($r = .67$), emotional inhibition ($r = .39$), alexithymia (i.e., lack of access to one's emotions) ($r = .19$), emotional control rehearsal (i.e., a measure of rumination) ($r = .30$), and obsessional thinking ($rs = .39$ and .50, with scores on two separate measures of obsessional thinking). Obsessional thinking refers to the tendency to ruminate over details of events. Note that the correlations were particularly high for ambivalence over emotional expression and obsessional thinking. In contrast, self-concealment scores were negatively related to scores on measures of emotional expressiveness ($r = -.44$), self-control ($rs = -.27$ and $-.34$, with scores on two separate measures of the ability to delay gratification and control one's impulses), restraint (i.e., impulse control, consideration of others, suppression of aggression, and responsibility) ($r = -.29$), and self-deception ($r = -.33$). Self-concealment scores were not statistically significantly correlated with social desirability scores ($r = -.14$).

King and co-workers' (1992) next step in this study was to try to assess underlying factors to inhibition. They conceptualized the broader construct of inhibition as composed of the following three factors: rumination, behavioral control, and emotional constriction. Factor analyses of these three elements showed that rumination and emotional constriction were positively correlated with each other, whereas rumination correlated negatively with behavioral control. In factor analyses of scores on all their measures of inhibition, self-concealment loaded most highly on rumination. It also loaded on emotional constriction and loaded negatively on behavioral control. Thus, the picture of the self-concealer that emerges from the King et al. (1992) study is of a person who ruminates over problems, is ambivalent about emotional expression, does not engage in self-deception, inhibits expression of emotions, but does not necessarily inhibit behaviors.

Supporting the idea that self-concealers do not engage in self-deception were the findings from Kahn and Hessling's (2001) study of 279 undergraduates. Specifically, the undergraduates' self-concealment scores were significantly negatively correlated with their social desirability scores ($r = -.39$). Kahn and Hessling (2001) also found that self-concealment was negatively related to both extraversion ($r = -.24$) and social support ($r = -.33$), which is consistent with the earlier findings that self-concealers reported being shy (Ichiyama et al., 1993) and having relatively weak social support networks (e.g., Kelly & Achter, 1995).

KEEPING A PARTICULAR SECRET

Instead of using the Self-Concealment Scale to sort people into high and low secret keepers, some researchers have opted to compare people who have a particular secret with those who do not. For example, Finkenauer and Rime (1998b) asked 377 undergraduates and their relatives and acquaintances to complete questionnaires in which they were asked if they could recall an important emotional life event that they had kept secret. Approximately 42% reported having such a secret memory, whereas approximately 56% indicated that they had no such memory. Finkenauer and Rime compared these two groups on illness and life satisfaction self-reports. As it turned out, the respondents with a secret memory had greater total illness scores and were less satisfied with their lives than respondents without such a memory. The researchers showed that having a secret memory predicted illness scores, even when they statistically controlled for participants' levels of negative affect (i.e., the tendency to experience negative emotions and dissatisfaction). Moreover, based on their findings from path analyses on the links among having a secret memory, illness scores, and life satisfaction scores, Finkenauer and Rime (1998b) concluded that it is through making people ill that having a secret memory indirectly affects life satisfaction.

In a similar vein, researchers also have shown that gay men who tend to conceal their sexual orientation from others, as compared with those who do not, are at a greater risk for developing ailments such as cancer (Cole, Kemeny, Taylor, & Visscher, 1996a; Cole, Kemeny, Taylor, Visscher, & Fahey, 1996b). Specifically, one study involved 80 gay men who were HIV-seropositive but otherwise healthy at the beginning of the study (Cole et al., 1996b). These men were assessed a 6-month intervals for 9 years for signs of HIV progression. The measures included how long it took for the men to develop a critically low T-lymphocyte level, to receive an AIDS diagnosis, and to die from AIDS. As it turned out, the men who tended to conceal their homosexual identity experienced a more rapid progression to all these negative outcomes than did the men who were more "out of the closet." The researchers attributed these differences to the idea that it is stressful to inhibit the expression of one's sexual identity and that such stress can lead to negative health effects. They were able to rule out competing explanations for these remarkable findings by statistically controlling for various demographic characteristics, health practices, sexual behaviors, antiretroviral therapy, depression levels, anxiety levels, and degree of social support among the men in the sample.

In another study, these same researchers examined the incidence of cancer and infectious diseases among 222 HIV-seronegative gay men (Cole et al., 1996a). Those men who concealed the expression of their homosexual identity, as compared with those who did not, experienced a significantly higher incidence of cancer and several infectious diseases (i.e., pneumonia, bronchitis, sinusitis, and tuberculosis) over a 5-year follow-up period. These effects could not be attributed to differences in age, ethnicity, socioeconomic status, health-relevant behavioral patterns (e.g., drug use, exercise), anxiety, depression, or reporting biases (e.g., negative affectivity, social desirability) between the men who were "in the closet" and those who were "out of the closet." The researchers speculated once again that the findings support the notion that inhibiting expression of something as important as one's sexual orientation is stressful and can take a toll on one's health.

Likewise, Pennebaker and Susman (1988) discovered that survivors of childhood traumas who did not discuss the traumas with others, as compared with those who did discuss them, tended to develop more problems such as hypertension, cancer, and influenza. In addition, Pennebaker and Harber (1993) observed that among victims of the 1989 Loma Prieta Earthquake, the greatest amount of physical and psychological distress occurred during the time period 2 to 6 weeks after the earthquake that coincided with when the victims continued to think about the earthquake but squelched their desire to talk about it with others.

In yet another very important study, patients diagnosed with breast cancer who less openly shared with others their angry and depressed feelings about their cancer, as compared with those who were more open in their expression of these feelings, actually died sooner (Derogatis, Abeloff, & Melisaratos, 1979). Also, recent widows and widowers who talked less (e.g., with friends and family) about their spouse's death tended to have more health problems and tended to ruminate more about the death in the year following the tragedy (Pennebaker & O'Heeron, 1984). These correlations remained even when the researchers statistically adjusted for number of friends these individuals had before and after the loss of the spouse.

SUMMARY

There is mounting evidence that self-concealment is moderately strongly to very strongly linked to a variety of problems, ranging from depression and anxiety, to rumination, back pain, and headaches. Moreover, keeping a particular secret, such as being gay, has been linked to increased vulnerability to cancer, infectious diseases, and acceleration to AIDS symptoms.

At this point, one might ask the question, "Could this link between self-concealment and problems be explained by the possibility that secret keepers simply have had more negative life events than nonsecret keepers, and therefore they have both more things to hide and more problems?" Larson and Chastain (1990) addressed this possibility by statistically controlling for participants' reports of traumatic life experiences (e.g., having been raped or molested) before the age of 17, and they still found a moderately strong link between self-concealment and problems. However, one could argue that such a control was inadequate because although self-concealers may have been willing to admit to having the tendency to keep secrets, they did not want to admit to the specific traumatic experiences they had in their youth. Another problem is that Larson and Chastain's (1990) sample was composed of people substantially older than 17. The high self-concealers within the sample may have experienced more traumas since the age of 17 than the low self-concealers.

Another possible explanation for the link between secret keeping and problems is that it is really neuroticism or negative affectivity (i.e., the tendency to experience negative emotions and dissatisfaction) that underlies the link. Put another way, it could be that people who tend to complain and to admit to negative things are simply endorsing both high symptomatology and the negative quality of keeping secrets. However, as mentioned earlier, Finkenauer and Rime (1998b) showed that having a secret memory predicted illness scores, even when they statistically controlled for participants' levels of negative affect.

Although these two alternative explanations already have been addressed to some extent by researchers, they draw attention to the fact that the findings on the link between self-concealment and problems are correlational. As such, it is not possible to say that secrecy *causes* these problems. It is possible, however, at this point to describe what the secret keeper is like.

PROFILE OF A SECRET KEEPER

Even though the findings from the literature on conscious forms of inhibition have more direct bearing on profiling the secret keeper, who is defined as someone who keep secrets from others, the findings on both repression and self-concealment shed light on who these secret keepers are. People who keep secrets from themselves—repressors—do not report experiencing distress and problems, but they do show signs of physical weakness. Repressors have weaker immune responses to stress and tend to get more physiologically aroused by stress than do nonrepressors, which may make them vulnerable to cancers in the long run. There is some evidence that repression may have short-term benefits, such as avoiding the escalation of aggressive outbursts. Also, repressors are less likely to complain about problems, so they may be easier to be around in the face of an immediate problem or crisis.

People who tend to keep personal secrets from others— self-concealers—tend to be lonely, shy, and somewhat introverted. They are conflicted over the expression of emotion, and they tend not to be emotionally expressive. They also are socially anxious and have low self-esteem. To a lesser extent, self-concealers have an impoverished emotional life in the sense that they have a relatively low access to their emotions. They also report having a relatively strong need to be alone, perhaps because of their shyness and anxiety around others. They mull over their troubling thoughts and problems and are depressed and anxious generally. A troubling finding that has emerged from King and co-workers' (1992) study is that self-concealers report being somewhat impulsive and unable to inhibit or control their behaviors. Thus, they are in the unpleasant position of not being emotionally expressive, while behaving impulsively, which may explain their high levels of rumination and obsessional thinking. Specifically, these individuals are vulnerable to engaging in acts that they later will ruminate over and regret. Self-concealers report having more physical problems, too, like stomach pains and nausea. These people tend to have low levels of social support. Compared with low self-concealers, they are probably less well-liked and less able to form strong interpersonal bonds with others, given that the exchange of secrets is typically a part of forging relational bonds (see Derlega, Metts, Peronio, & Margulis, 1993), although this idea remains to be tested. Overall, high self-concealers are more likely to be unhappy, troubled individuals than are low self-concealers. Without much doubt, being a keeper of personal secrets seems to be negative. To date, there is no evidence that self-concealment is linked to any positive qualities or signs of healthy psychological functioning, with the exception that these individuals do not tend to engage in self-deception. But even with that quality, there is evidence that some self-deception is a positive or healthy quality that is associated with both well-being and the ability to care about others (Taylor & Brown, 1988, 1994).

Thus, self-concealers are enigmatic on three fronts: First, they are lonely, yet they report having a high need to be alone. Second, they report that they lack behavioral control (i.e., they are relatively impulsive in terms of their actions), but they also report that they inhibit their expression of emotions. Along these same lines, they tend to ruminate over negative events or question their behaviors after they have performed them. Third, they have negative attitudes toward counseling, yet they have more problems, and thus are more likely to seek counseling than are low self-concealers (Kelly & Achter, 1995).

I conclude by returning to the example of Jeffrey Dahmer, because he so epitomizes the extreme levels of self-concealment and the negative characteristics associated with being a high self-concealer. Until his arrest in 1991, he had concealed his problems from virtually everyone, including committing murders in his grandmother's basement and then in his own apartment without detection. Even in the face of a crisis when one of his victims almost escaped and the police entered his apartment, Dahmer calmly was able to conceal his murders from the police. Like other self-concealers, Dahmer was lonely and shy. Even as a young boy, his father recalls Jeffrey's having spent extensive periods of time alone in the woods. At the same time, the reason Dahmer gave police for why he killed his victims was that he was lonely and did not want them to leave him. Like other self-concealers, he had at one point sought professional psychological services. He had checked himself into an alcoholism rehabilitation center, but his treatment did not work. Finally, Dahmer was both impulsive in his actions—at one point he decided that he would no longer try to control his impulses to kill—and emotionally inexpressive. His behavior at his trial was characterized as emotionless. However, like other self-concealers, he did not deny his troubles or try to present himself in a favorable light. When his crimes were finally discovered by the police, he admitted to feeling "thoroughly evil."

CHAPTER 3

WHY SECRECY IS LINKED TO PROBLEMS

Just as Jeffrey Dahmer represents an extreme version of the high self-concealer (not to mention a sociopath), Katherine Power seems to epitomize the problems associated with keeping an important, troubling secret (see Burger, 1997; Polivy, 1998). She was a Brandeis University student who drove the getaway car in 1970 for a revolutionary group who performed a bank robbery in Boston that went terribly wrong. A police officer was killed. After the robbery, Power went underground, eventually settling near Corvallis, Oregon. She married and bore a son and was teaching and working as a chef under the alias Alice Metzinger. However, in September 1993, Power finally turned herself in to Massachusetts police, pleaded guilty to manslaughter, and was sentenced to 8 to 12 years in prison. What is intriguing about this case is that her name was removed from the FBI's most wanted list after 14 years, and it seemed as though she had gotten away with the crime. Yet in 1992, she had become anxious and depressed and sought therapy, telling her psychotherapist about the crime in the second session (Burger, 1997). "Power was so desperate to talk about her crime that she had become seriously depressed" (Polivy, 1998, p. 188).

As described in the previous chapter, there is evidence that people who keep secrets have poorer mental and physical health than those who do not. But does secret keeping actually cause problems as it seems in Katherine Power's case? More broadly, why do secret keepers have such problems? Answering these questions is the focus of this chapter.

As I alluded to in the previous chapter, researchers have attempted to explain the link between secrecy and symptoms by arguing that keeping secrets or actively inhibiting self-disclosure is stressful and that such stress makes one sick (e.g., Pennebaker, 1985, 1989, 1990). Although this inhibition idea has received the most attention from psychologists, other researchers from both clinical and social psychology (e.g., Derlega, 1993; Temoshok, 1983) have proposed their own explanations for the link between secret keeping and health problems. In this chapter, I describe these explanations and the evidence that has been offered to support them. I conclude this chapter by proposing a new explanation for the link between secrecy and problems that is based on the possibility that people who are born with the predisposition to inhibit social expression also may be born with the predisposition for various kinds of illnesses.

INHIBITION MODEL

Because the notion that the inhibition of feelings can lead to illness (Pennebaker, 1985) has received the most attention, I begin by evaluating the inhibition model as a means of explaining the link between secrecy and problems. Roughly 15 years ago, Pennebaker and Chew (1985) noted that the act of inhibiting ongoing behavior requires physiological work, and they demonstrated that undergraduates who were induced to inhibit their expression of the truth (i.e., to lie) to experimenters experienced elevated skin conductance levels relative to their baseline skin conductance levels. Shortly thereafter, Pennebaker (1985, 1989, 1992) proposed a model of the relationship between traumatic experience and psychosomatic disease that included the following three propositions: (1) To inhibit actively one's behavior is stressful and disease-related; (2) when individuals do not or cannot express thoughts and feelings concerning a traumatic event (i.e., when they engage in behavioral inhibition), there is an increased probability of having obsessive thoughts about the event and of having illnesses in the long run; and (3) conversely, the act of confiding or otherwise translating the event into language reduces autonomic activity (in the short run) and leads to long-term reductions in disease rates. According to Pennebaker (1997a,b), how the event is discussed, the possibility of ever coming to terms with the event, and the ultimate consequences of discussing the experience are all variables that may influence the outcomes of confiding, inhibition, and, down the road, health. Temoshok (1983) earlier had expressed a similar idea in her multidimensional model of illness, in which she depicted a coping style that involves an insufficient expression of thoughts or emotion as a part of the development of psychosomatic disturbances.

Pennebaker (e.g., see 1997a,b) cited a good deal of experimental research from his own laboratory to support his inhibition model. However, for obvious ethical reasons, these experiments were not designed to test the idea that secret keeping causes negative health effects. What Pennebaker's experiments were designed to show—and did show—is that revealing previously undisclosed traumatic experiences in a confidential, anonymous setting leads to health benefits. As such, these experiments will be described in the next chapter. Because of the ethical constraints involved in inducing people to keep secrets to see whether they become sick, as yet no published experiments have tested directly the long-term health effects of secret keeping. In several experiments, however, investigators have assessed the effects of inhibiting the behavioral expression of emotions, and the results of these are described next.

Cioffi and Holloway (1993) asked undergraduates to endure a cold pressor pain induction to their hands. The participants were randomly assigned to conditions in which they were instructed either to (1) concentrate on their room at home (distraction), (2) pay close attention to their hand sensations (monitoring), or (3) remove awareness of those sensations from mind (suppression). During the 2 minutes immediately following the withdrawal of the painful cold induction, the participants in the monitoring condition reported the most rapid recovery from the pain. Participants in the suppression condition reported the slowest recovery. What is most interesting about Cioffi and Holloway's findings is that later during the experimental hour, the participants in the suppression condition as compared with the other participants interpreted an innocuous vibration against their necks as more unpleasant. The researchers suggested that the suppression task had drained participants' capacities to cope with pain, and that, therefore, the suppression of pain is not an effective coping strategy.

However, Colby, Lanzetta, Kleck (1977) found that inhibiting expressions of pain reduced the distress associated with the pain. Ten male undergraduates were asked to pose three levels of pain expression while they were receiving electrical shocks, which they terminated at their tolerance level. It was found that even though pain tolerance levels were not related to their level of expression, participants' skin conductance levels were. Specifically, when participants inhibited their expressive behavior, they experienced decreased skin conductance responses to the shock, suggesting that they were less distressed by the shock.

Lanzetta, Cartwright-Smith, and Kleck (1976) uncovered a similar pattern in three experiments in which they asked participants either to conceal, freely express, or exaggerate their facial displays associated with the anticipation and reception of painful shocks. Participants in the conceal conditions, as compared to those in the free-expression or exaggeration conditions, experienced lower skin conductance levels and reported feeling less pain.

In another experiment, women were instructed to imagine three positive and three negative emotional scenes (McCanne & Anderson, 1987). During the initial imagination of each scene, the participants were told simply to imagine the situation. They next were instructed to imagine the situation again and enhance the muscle tension in the respective muscle groups in their faces that corresponded with the emotions in the positive and negative scenes. The participants then were instructed to imagine the scene a third time and suppress the muscle tension in the same muscle groups. They were successful in altering their muscle tension in accord with the experimental instructions, with no overt signs of changes in their faces during imagination of the scenes. The participants reported that they experienced less enjoyment and more distress during positive affective trials in which they suppressed the muscle activity in their faces. Thus, inhibiting the expression of positive emotion reduced the subjective experience of it.

To investigate further the effects of inhibiting emotions, researchers have conducted a series of experiments using the following paradigm: Participants are presented emotional films and asked to inhibit or express their emotions while watching the films, and then their physiological and self-reported changes in emotion are assessed. In one such experiment, undergraduates were exposed to six negative videotaped scenes and were randomly assigned to conditions in which they produced facial expressions of suppression, spontaneous behavior, or exaggeration while watching the scenes (Zuckerman, Klorman, Larrance, & Spiegel, 1981). As it turned out, higher levels of facial expressiveness were accompanied by higher levels of autonomic activity and higher levels of self-reported emotion. These relationships were obtained in comparisons across experimental conditions as well as in correlational analyses within conditions, once again supporting the idea that inhibition of the behavioral expression of negative emotions decreases the experience of those emotions.

In a similar experiment, Bush, Barr, McHugo, and Lanzetta (1989) examined the impact of facial control on undergraduates' self-reported responses to dubbed and undubbed comedy video clips. The dubbing involved inserts of smiling people. The participants were randomly assigned to conditions in which they either freely expressed their emotional responses to the video clips (spontaneous condition) or controlled their facial reactions (inhibition condition). The presence of dubs increased electromyogram (EMG) activity over cheek and eye muscle regions for the participants in the spontaneous condition but not for participants in the inhibition condition. Participants in the spontaneous condition increased smiling at dub points and reported significantly greater amusement to dubbed compared with undubbed routines. Most important for the present discussion, those participants in the spontaneous condition, as compared with participants in the inhibition condition, reported significantly more amusement to dubbed routines. Thus, inhibition led to less enjoyment of the amusing films.

Likewise, Labott, Ahleman, Wolever, and Martin (1990) found that inducing the inhibition of expression of negative emotions can offset negative changes in both immunologic functioning and mood. Labott and coworkers recruited a sample of undergraduate women who considered themselves to be emotionally expressive in response to movies, and they showed these women both sad and humorous movies. Before watching the movies, the women were randomly assigned to conditions in which they were told either to inhibit totally their expression of emotions or to express overtly their emotions as much as possible. Unfortunately, the instructions to inhibit or express emotions did not necessarily correspond with actual behavior of the women. Seven women were dropped from each experimental group because they either did not inhibit their laughter or did not express sadness through crying, leaving eight women in each group. As it turned out, regardless of the overt laughter that the women expressed, the humorous stimulus resulted in improved immunity. Moreover, the expression of sadness through overt crying was associated with a reduction in immunologic functioning, whereas the inhibition of crying in the context of the same sad stimulus was not. Also, following the sad stimulus, participants who were in the expression condition as compared with those in the inhibition condition had more negative moods. Although these results seem to support the idea that inhibition of negative moods has positive effects, one must keep in mind that roughly half the women were dropped from the study. The women who were retained because they were able to cry in the expression condition may have been more vulnerable to experiencing negative shifts in their immunologic functioning that the women who were dropped from the analyses.

In another experiment that involved the suppression of negative emotions, 43 men and 42 women were asked to watch a short disgust-eliciting film while their behavioral, physiological, and subjective responses were being recorded (Gross & Levenson, 1993). The participants were randomly assigned to conditions in which they were either told simply to watch the film (no-suppression conditions) or to watch the film while behaving "in such a way that a person watching you would not know you were feeling anything" (suppression condition). Participants in the suppression condition did in fact reduce their expressive behaviors. At the same time, they experienced a mixed physiological state: On the one hand, they showed decreased somatic activity and decreased heart rate. On the other hand, they exhibited increased blinking and indications of increased electrodermal responding (i.e., elevated skin conductance levels)—both signs of stress. Despite these physiological differences between the participants in the suppression and no-suppression conditions, there were no differences between the two groups in their subjective experiences of emotion. Thus, it seems that the participants in the suppression condition were showing some physiological signs of experiencing stress from their suppression efforts but not other physiological signs of stress; and they were not feeling any more or less disgust than the other participants.

More recently, Gross and Levenson (1997) assessed the physiological effects of inhibiting negative and positive emotions in 180 female undergraduates who watched amusing, sad, and neutral films. Half these participants were randomly assigned to a condition in which they were instructed to inhibit the expression of their emotions while they were watching the films, and the other half were instructed simply to watch the films (i.e., control group). Participants in the inhibition condition, as compared with those in the control group, reported that they felt less amusement during the amusing film; but there were no differences between the groups in reported level of sadness during the sad film. The participants in the inhibition condition experienced a greater increase in sympathetic activation of the cardiovascular system than did the participants in the control group when they watched either the amusing or sad film. In contrast, when they watched neutral films, there was no difference in sympathetic activation between the two groups. Given that an increase in sympathetic activation is a sign of experiencing stress, Gross and Levenson (1997) suggested that their physiological findings support the notion that hiding negative emotions is unlikely to make one feel better. The researchers concluded that whereas the suppression of a neutral stimulus (i.e., one that does not produce the impulse to express emotions) seems to have little physiological impact, the "suppression of both positive and negative emotions exacts a palpable physiological cost" (Gross & Levenson, 1997, p. 101).

SUMMARY

Overall, the findings on the physiological effects of inhibiting the behavioral expression of emotions are quite complicated and they do not seem to show consistent patterns. In one study, suppressing pain led to reduced recovery from the pain (Cioffi & Holloway, 1993). However, in other studies, inhibiting the expression of pain led to reduced skin conductance levels (Colby et al., 1977; Lanzetta et al., 1976) and reports of feeling less pain (Lanzetta et al., 1976). Regarding the inhibition of emotions, suppressing amusement and sadness led to increased sympathetic activation of the cardiovascular system (Gross & Levenson, 1997). Yet in other research, inhibiting the expression of the emotions of pain, pride, and amusement was found to decrease one's self-reported experience of these emotions (Bush et al., 1989; McCanne & Anderson, 1987; Zuckerman et al., 1981). Also, inhibiting the expression of disgust did not lead to increases in self-reported experiences of that emotion (Gross & Levenson, 1993). Likewise, as mentioned in the previous chapter, discussing anger in a calm voice seems to be better at decreasing the experience of anger than expressing the anger with agitated behavior (see Siegman, 1994b). Despite other researchers' conclusions to the contrary (see Gross & Levenson, 1997; Polivy, 1998), thus far there seems to be more evidence that supports as opposed to contradicts the notion that inhibition of both positive and negative emotions reduces the experience of those emotions at both physiological and subjective levels. Moreover, none of these studies involved an investigation of the long-term consequences of inhibiting the behavioral expression of emotions. Therefore, it remains to be seen whether the foundation of the inhibition model—that is, the notion that actively inhibiting one's behaviors is stressful and disease-related—will receive clear or consistent empirical support.

PREOCCUPATION MODEL

Another popular explanation for the link between secrecy and problems is what Lane and Wegner (1995) called the preoccupation model of secrecy. They used this model to explain how attempts to keep information secret can cause intrapsychic problems, especially obsessive preoccupation with the secret. According to Lane and Wegner, obsessive preoccupation develops in the following way: First, to keep a thought secret, people engage in thought suppression, which is the conscious avoidance or active inhibition of a thought. Second, thought suppression causes intrusive thoughts. Third, intrusive thoughts cause individuals to renew their efforts at suppression in attempts to keep the thought secret. The second and third steps of thought suppression and intrusion cycle back and forth, causing the secret keeper to experience "continuing mental unrest" (Lane & Wegner, 1995, p. 239). According to Lane and Wegner, the secret keeper is unable to break the cycle and reach resolution of the secret without revealing it. They suggested that obsessive preoccupation develops, continues (and possibly even escalates) over time, and can develop into psychopathology such as having a full-blown obsession (see also Wegner, 1989, 1992, 1994; Wegner et al., 1994). Most relevant for this volume, they proposed that obsessive preoccupation does not cease unless the secret is revealed, and even after the secrecy has been lifted, preoccupations may persist. The bottom line to the preoccupation model is that there are cognitive and emotional consequences of secret keeping, making secrecy a threat to one's mental health.

The process through which thought suppression ironically may make the suppressed information more accessible to awareness, the second step of the model, has been termed the *hyperaccessibility* of suppressed information (Wegner & Erber, 1992). In keeping a secret, one must simultaneously monitor information consistent with the state of mind one wishes to maintain and keep track of the information one wishes to hide from others (Wegner, 1994; Wegner & Wenzlaff, 1996). For example, if an untenured professor has had a sexual affair with a student, she must continually watch against revealing that information when she is in the presence of other faculty members. These others may actually come to serve as negative cues or reminders of the suppressed information, and their mere presence may make it very difficult for her to keep the secret out of mind (see Wegner, 1989, 1992, 1994).

Prior to the publication of the preoccupation model, Wegner and colleagues gathered evidence to support the idea that suppressing information makes that information hyperaccessible (Wegner & Erber, 1992; Wegner, Schneider, Carter, & White, 1987; Wegner, Shortt, Blake, & Page, 1990; Wenzlaff, Wegner, & Klein, 1991). For example, Wegner and Erber (1992) asked undergraduates to complete Stroop (1935), or color-naming, tasks under time pressure. Those participants who were instructed to suppress particular words as compared with participants who were not told to suppress the words actually had those words come to mind more readily. Likewise, in another two experiments, undergraduates who were asked to suppress thoughts of a no-longer-desired past relationship experienced increased expressions of the thoughts after they suppressed them (Wegner & Gold, 1995).

Lane and Wegner (1995; Studies 1 and 2) also demonstrated that keeping a secret enhanced the cognitive accessibility of the secret and that secrecy and thought suppression were both associated with increased intrusiveness of the suppressed thoughts (Studies 3 and 4). Specifically, they tested the idea that induced secret keeping (of a word) would be associated with increased intrusiveness of that secret word (Study 3). They presented undergraduates with four target words (e.g., car, child, house, or mountain) one at a time and asked them to write about their stream of consciousness following different instructions pertaining to each word for a series of four 5-minute periods. The instructions were to (1) try to think about the target word, (2) try not to think of the target word, (3) try to keep the word a secret (from a group of experts who ostensibly would review the writing and try to guess what the word was), and (4) simply to write about their stream of consciousness with no special instructions regarding the word. As it turned out, during the secrecy condition, participants' ratings of their efforts to keep the word a secret were positively associated with both the extent to which they intentionally and unintentionally thought of the target word. Also, across all four conditions, attempts to keep the word a secret were associated with efforts to suppress the word. However, comparisons of the means across the conditions showed that the mean for participants' unintentional thinking of the target was significantly lower in the suppression and secrecy conditions than in the think condition. Moreover, the means for unintentional thinking in the suppression and secrecy conditions did not differ from the mean for the control condition. Despite these observations, Lane and Wegner (1995) concluded that overall their findings support the idea that when people are keeping a secret, their efforts to engage in thought suppression and their intrusive thinking become linked.

In the fourth study of that series, which was described in Chapter 1, Lane and Wegner gave undergraduates a list of 50 preselected topics that included such items as masturbation, lying, dying, mother, father, and being in love. They asked the participants to rate how intrusive their thoughts were about each topic, how often they tried to suppress thoughts of these topics, and how much they kept each of these topics secret from others. There was a significant positive correlation between thought suppression and secrecy ($r = .31$), between the intrusiveness of the thoughts and secrecy ($r = .32$), and between the intrusiveness of the thoughts and thought suppression ($r = .23$). Lane and Wegner (1995; Study 4) concluded that they demonstrated that secrecy and thought suppression were both associated with increased intrusiveness of the suppressed thoughts. One must keep in mind, however, that this study was limited by the possibility that participants may have rated as more secret and more intrusive the topics that were relevant to them, thus making it seem as though secrecy and intrusiveness are related. Also, as the researchers themselves noted, the causal direction of these factors could not be established in this fourth study, given its correlational design.

In addition to the limitations of those studies, there are limitations to other studies in which the researchers concluded that people become more preoccupied with their self-generated disturbing thoughts after suppressing them. In the Wegner and Gold (1995) studies, for example, participants who suppressed thoughts of a still-desired past relationship did not show subsequent increases in expressions of the thoughts (although their skin conductance levels, or indications of their emotional arousal, were elevated following suppression). In another study (Trinder & Salkovskis, 1994), undergraduates who were asked to suppress their negative, personally intrusive thoughts for 4 days, as compared with participants who were asked either to try to focus on the thoughts (i.e., the focus group) or simply to keep track of the thoughts (i.e., the control group), reported more intrusions of the thoughts. However, the control group and the focus group received added reassuring instructions (i.e., "It doesn't matter if the thought comes often or not; I'd like you to think about it for as long as possible without changing it, just stay with it") that were not provided to the suppression group. These added instructions may have led to the group differences by suggesting only to the participants in the control and focus groups that it was acceptable to have the intrusive thoughts. A similar laboratory experiment showed that suppressing a negative, personally intrusive thought for 5 minutes led to greater intrusions of the thought than did merely keeping track of the thought (Salkovskis & Campbell, 1994). But this study too included the reassuring instructions that were read only to the control group.

Despite these limitations, there have been recent attempts to apply the preoccupation model to real-world health issues that often are kept secret, such as abortion and eating disorders. Major and Gramzow (1999) noted that having an abortion often is kept secret for good reason, given that one in five adult women in the United States has had an abortion and yet roughly half the adult population views abortion as the (im)moral equivalent to murdering a child. They investigated the stigma of abortion and the psychological implications of concealing the abortion among 442 women followed for 2 years from the dates of their abortions. As expected, the women who felt stigmatized by abortion were more likely to report that they felt the need to keep it a secret from family and friends. Keeping the abortion a secret was associated with suppressing thoughts of the abortion and with disclosing abortion-related emotions to others less frequently. Increased thought suppression was associated with experiencing more intrusive thoughts of the abortion. Both suppression and intrusive thoughts surrounding the abortion, in turn, were positively related to increases in psychological distress over the 2-year period. Emotional disclosure moderated the association between intrusive thoughts and distress in the following way: Disclosure was associated with decreases in distress among women experiencing intrusive thoughts of their abortion, but it was unrelated to distress among women not experiencing intrusive thoughts. Major and Gramzow (1999) concluded that secret keeping put women at risk for experiencing increased intrusiveness of thoughts of the abortion. However, it is important to note that the secrecy, thought-suppression, and intrusive-thoughts measures were all administered at the same time (i.e., at 2-year follow up), leaving open the possibility that intrusive thoughts led to thought suppression. Moreover, contrary to Major and Gramzow's predictions, intrusive thoughts were positively associated with disclosing emotions surrounding the abortion. Also, after the researchers statistically controlled for the women's personal conflict over the abortion and their positive and negative affectivity in general, secrecy surrounding the abortion was not associated with greater distress.

Smart and Wegner (1999) examined the psychological effects of concealing the stigma of having an eating disorder during an interaction with another person. They recruited undergraduate female participants who either did or did not have eating-disordered characteristics. The participants were asked to play the role of someone who did or did not have an eating disorder in an interview in which they would be answering questions that were related to the eating disorder. In Study 1, participants with an eating disorder who role-played not having an eating disorder exhibited more secrecy, suppression, and intrusive thoughts of their eating disorder and more projection of eating disorder-related thoughts onto the interviewer than did those participants with an eating disorder who role-played someone with an eating disorder or those participants without an eating disorder who role-played someone without an eating disorder. In Study 2, the researchers found both increasing cognitive accessibility of eating disorder-related words during the interview and after the interview among those participants with concealed stigmas. The researchers concluded that the participants who concealed their stigmas became preoccupied with the control of stigma-relevant thoughts (Smart & Wegner, 1999).

Closer scrutiny of their data, however, shows that in Study 2 among the participants with eating disorders there was no difference in intrusions of the thoughts between those who played the role of someone without a stigma and those who played the role of someone with a stigma. Also, although scores on the cognitive accessibility measure increased more sharply during the interview for those with a concealed stigma, the scores were actually higher overall for the participants with an eating disorder who played the role of someone with an eating disorder. The only clear and consistent finding that supported the researchers' hypotheses surrounding the preoccupation model across Studies 1 and 2 was that secrecy was linked to greater thought suppression. In fact, in both Studies 1 and 2, judges rated the participants who played the role of someone without an eating disorder as less neurotic and more comfortable during the interview than those who played the role of someone with an eating disorder. The data in Study 2 on cognitive accessibility via a word completion task showed that at the end of the interview participants with eating disorders had high accessibility of eating disorder-related words relative to participants without eating disorders, whether they were in the no-stigma or stigma role playing conditions. Taken together, these findings do not provide support for the preoccupation model. More important for this volume, interpersonal impressions were enhanced by the concealment. Also, in Study 2 participants with an eating disorder who played the role of someone without an eating disorder did not show impairments in their cognitive functioning. The researchers suggested that a possible explanation for this finding that contradicted their model was "that the women with actual EDs [eating disorders] in this study were so practiced at secrecy that their cognitive functioning was not influenced by their high level of preoccupation with the stigma" (Smart & Wegner, 1999, p. 484).

Jeffrey Kahn and I earlier had made a similar claim that practice at suppression can actually reduce its negative cognitive effects (Kelly & Kahn, 1994). We demonstrated that undergraduate participants who suppressed their own intrusive thoughts experienced a reduction in intrusions of the thoughts relative to participants who expressed their own intrusive thoughts (Exp. 1). Thus, we challenged the idea that over time suppressing can lead to preoccupation with a secret. We suggested that perhaps with experience suppressing their private thoughts, people develop strategies and techniques that become virtually automatic and require little thought or effort (Kelly & Kahn, 1994). Such experience controlling their thoughts could make keeping secrets from others less difficult, so that people could avoid sharing secrets and the rejecting feedback that is associated with sharing altogether.

Additional findings that were contrary to Lane and Wegner's (1995) and Major and Gramzow's (1999) conclusions about the link between secrecy and thought intrusions (i.e., contrary to the preoccupational model) were the findings described in Chapter 1 from Finkenhauer and Rime's (1998a) studies, in which participants' ratings of events that they kept secret and events that they had shared were compared. As mentioned in Chapter 1, participants in both Studies 1 and 2 indicated that they did not ruminate more over an event that they kept secret as compared with one that they had shared with others. However, Finkenhauer and Rime's (1998a) studies were limited by the fact that participants were asked to generate only one emotional event in either the shared- or non-shared-event categories. The participants might have picked a shared (i.e., non-secret) emotional event that was not representative of their shared emotional events in general. The fact that it came to mind when they were asked to pick an event during the study suggests that they were thinking and maybe even ruminating about that event more than their other shared events.

Fish and Scott (1999) obtained findings that more clearly contradicted the preoccupation model. They investigated the relation between forgetting childhood abuse and the level of secrecy surrounding the abuse, and they discovered that self-reported forgetting and secrecy were positively related, not negatively related. Specifically, among a nonclinical sample of 423 adults (mean age 43.4 years) who completed a questionnaire regarding childhood abuse history, 32% reported childhood abuse. Of those reporting abuse, 52% noted periods of forgetting some or all of the abuse, and 76% indicated there had been a time when no one but themselves and their abuser knew about the abuse. Also, 47% of the respondents reporting abuse indicated that an abuser tried to get them to keep the abuse a secret. (That is, 47% said that there was a time when no one else but the abuser knew the secret.) Most important for the present discussion, the respondents who had periods of forgetting the abuse, as compared with those who had continuous memories of the abuse, were more likely to report that there was a time when the abuser tried to get them to keep the abuse secret.

These findings make sense in light of Koutstaal, Schacter, Johnson, Angell, and Gross's (1998) finding that mentally reviewing events actually increases memory of those events. These researchers examined the degree to which adults' memory for everyday events was improved by later seeing photographs or reading brief verbal descriptions of those events. Both older and younger adults watched everyday events on a videotape. When the participants reviewed the events with either verbal description or photographs, as compared with when they did not have any review, they recalled more events and in greater detail. Thus, the researchers demonstrated that recalling an event at one time often increases the likelihood that it will be remembered at a still later time. Verbal descriptions enhanced later recall to the same degree as reviewing photographs. Koutstaal et al. (1998) concluded that postevent review has clear potential practical benefits for improving memory.

SUMMARY

What can the reader make of these conflicting findings on the association between keeping an event a secret and ruminating over the secret event, and thus of the preoccupation model of secrecy? There is only mixed support for the idea that people tend to ruminate more over events that they keep secret. In several correlational studies, thought suppression has been associated with secrecy. Suppression also has been linked with increased intrusiveness of the suppressed thoughts (e.g., Lane & Wegner, 1995; Major & Gramzow, 1999). However, it may well be that people suppress thoughts that are intrusive, rather than the thoughts that they suppress become intrusive. Wegner addressed this possible concern by demonstrating in several experiments that suppressing a thought, such as the thought of a white bear, led to increased preoccupation of that thought (e.g., Wegner et al., 1987) and that suppressing thoughts made them hyper-accessible (e.g., Wegner & Erber, 1992). However, Jeff Kahn and I (Kelly & Kahn, 1994) found the opposite result with people's own unwanted intrusive thoughts. Moreover, to date, the long-term effects of thought suppression and secret keeping have not been assessed directly (i.e., experimentally), only correlational assessments of the long-term link between these two variables have been conducted. Major and Gramzow (1999) studied the relation between keeping a secret about abortion and distress and found no significant association when they controlled for key personality variables. Given the conflicting findings, it is far from clear that keeping an event secret is associated with becoming more troubled by that event.

SELF-PERCEPTION MODEL

In his influential self-perception theory, Bem (1967, 1972) postulated that because people's internal states often are ambiguous (e.g., anger and sexual arousal are quite similar emotions at a physiological level), people look to their behaviors to determine these internal states. For example, if a woman kisses a man whom she is not certain that she is attracted to, she may say to herself, "Well, I kissed him, therefore I must be attracted to him."

Some researchers have used self-perception theory to explain why secret keeping is linked to problems. Specifically, people, such as those who have been raped, feel shame about having experienced the stigmatizing traumatic event, and thus they choose to conceal the event from others (Derlega, 1993; Pennebaker, 1985, 1989; Silver, Boon, & Stones, 1983). Such individuals may then tell themselves that because of the fact that they have hidden the experience from others, the event must indeed be very negative or shameful (Derlega, 1993). It is through this self-perception process (Bem, 1967, 1972) that people might develop lowered self-esteem (Derlega, 1993). Ichiyama et al. (1993) used this idea to explain why lowered self-esteem was linked to self-concealment among a sample of college students.

There is correlational evidence that secrecy is linked to shame. For example, as mentioned in Chapter 1, Finkenhauer and Rime (1998a) found that participants indicated higher ratings of guilt and shame over non-shared events as compared to shared events. That finding is consistent with the findings from Frable, Platt, and Hoey's (1998) study in which 86 Harvard undergraduates were asked to describe the who, what, and where of their daily lives over 11 days and to rate their momentary self-esteem and affect. Those participants with concealable stigmas (students who indicated that they were gay, that they were bulimic, or that their family earned less than $20,000 each year) reported lower self-esteem and more negative affect than both those whose stigmas were visible and those without stigmatizing characteristics.

To try to demonstrate whether concealment causes a negative evaluation of the concealed information, Fishbein and Laird (1979) conducted a clever experiment in which they induced participants either to reveal or conceal an ambiguous piece of information (i.e., their score of +4.6 on an intelligence test) from a confederate. The participants in the concealment condition later rated that score as more negative than did participants in the disclosure condition. Fishbein and Laird discussed the implications of this finding in terms of self-perception theory (Bem, 1972). Specifically, the participants looked to their actions (i.e., their revealing or concealing information) to determine the meaning of the ambiguous information. The researchers extended these findings to say that people might run the risk of seeing themselves in unfavorable ways if they choose to hide information about themselves from others. They speculated that such concealment of information over time can lead to lowered self-perceptions of one's self-worth. The reader should note that one problem with that study was that the participants knew that the experimenter was aware of their scores when the experimenter advised them either to reveal or conceal them. As such, the participants in the concealment condition may have thought that the experimenters were trying to protect them from embarrassment in suggesting that they not mention their score to the "other participant" (i.e., confederate). Therefore, before feeling confident in the finding that secrecy actually caused a negative evaluation of the secret information, researchers will have to replicate these findings in a study without that confound. Regardless, the findings offer the most direct support for negative self-perception processes involved in concealment thus far.

Khersonskaya (2001) conducted a similar experiment that assessed what happened when participants were asked either to reveal or to conceal ambiguous information. Like Fishbein and Laird (1979), she found that participants in the conceal condition were less willing to have their scores be made public. However, she also found no differences in their satisfaction with their scores for the participants in the reveal versus conceal conditions. Khersonskaya suggested that participants were less willing to reveal simply to be consistent with their earlier instruction, rather than because they viewed concealed material more negatively.

SUMMARY

Self-perception theory has been used to explain how people may come to view negatively the information that they keep secret (e.g., Fishbein & Laird, 1979; Ichiyama et al., 1993). Simply observing one's own secret keeping behavior may make one assume that the hidden information should be kept secret and may even lower one's self-esteem.

DIMINISHES SOCIAL SUPPORT

Larson (1993b) suggested that self-concealment is problematic on two fronts: It in itself causes distress and it prevents people who are in need of social support from receiving it. In fact, as mentioned in Chapter 2, self-concealment has been found to be both positively related to depression and negatively related to perceived social support (e.g., Kahn & Hessling, 2001). Larson (1993b) noted that people in stressful situations, such as patients and staff in an oncology clinic, are faced with the dilemma of whether to conceal or reveal the distress they are experiencing. According to Larson (1993b), self-concealment as a coping response increases stress and simultaneously diminishes the likelihood of helpful, empathic responses from others. Therefore, he concluded that oncology staff must find safe contexts and confidants for sharing their inevitable fears, self-doubts, and uncomfortable feelings and must help patients resolve the distress–disclosure dilemma that attends the cancer experience.

Although Larson (1993) was not suggesting that the lower levels of social support cause the distress surrounding secret keeping, he was suggesting that the lack of social support accompanying the concealment prevents one from recovering from distress. However, in a study that I conducted with John Achter (Kelly & Achter, 1995), we found that whether or not we statistically controlled for participants' social support levels, self-concealment was strongly positively associated with depression. Likewise, even when Larson and Chastain (1990) statistically adjusted for levels of social support, they still found that self-concealment was related to physical and mental symptoms. The same was true in Cole and co-workers' (1996b) study of HIV-positive gay men who were either in or out of the closet. Even statistically controlling for levels of social support, Cole et al. found that being in the closet predicted faster progression of HIV infection. These findings do not support the notion that it is through reduced social support that self-concealment leads to physical and psychological symptoms.

SUMMARY

Several explanations have been offered in the psychological literature for why secret keepers, as compared with nonsecret keepers, tend to have more mental and physical problems. These explanations are the inhibition, preoccupation, diminished social support, and the self-perception models of secrecy. Regarding the inhibition model, Pennebaker has conducted a series of experiments that have demonstrated that revealing secrets leads to health benefits (see Chapter 4, this volume), but it does not follow that concealing secrets necessarily leads to health problems. To date, there is no direct, experimental evidence that secrecy causes health problems. Researchers have explored the possibility that inhibiting behavioral expression of one's emotions is physiologically taxing, but the evidence is quite mixed. The preoccupation model of secrecy also does not offer a satisfactory explanation for the link between secrecy and problems. There is evidence that with new thoughts, such as the thought of a white bear, suppressing the thoughts leads to increased preoccupation with the thoughts (Wegner et al., 1987). However, people do not seem to become more preoccupied with their own intrusive thoughts as a result of suppressing them (Kelly & Kahn, 1994). The self-perception and diminished social support models have not yet received much testing. The little testing the social support model has received does not point to the notion that it is through lowered levels of social support that secret keeping is associated with problems.

A PREDISPOSITIONAL EXPLANATION

Thus far, none of the proposed models has offered a compelling explanation for the link between secrecy and problems, given the mixed or limited findings for each. An element that has been missing from this discussion is the notion that genetics may play a central role both in why people inhibit social expression and why those same people are likely to have more physical and psychological problems. Pennebaker (1993) noted that inhibition can reflect genetic proclivities to be hypersensitive to novel stimuli and that individuals predisposed to be hypersensitive tend to engage in processes of inhibition that can impede the normal cognitive changes that help them cope with upsetting experiences. He observed that inhibition processes can completely disrupt normal social interaction, resulting in further isolation by the traumatized individual. I speculate that a more simplified version of this explanation could fit the existing evidence on the correlates of self-concealment: It is possible that the kind of person who has the genetic predisposition to inhibit social expression also may be the type of person who is more vulnerable to developing the kinds of problems that have been linked with self-concealment. Along these lines, it may be the case that keeping a particular secret per se is not necessarily problematic; keeping a secret may not cause the symptoms that have been associated with self-concealment.

INHIBITED TEMPERAMENTAL TYPES

Indirect support for my suggestion comes from research by Kagan (1994) and others (e.g., Kagan, Reznick, & Gibbons, 1989; Suomi, 1991), who have provided evidence for a part genetic origin to what they call inhibited and uninhibited temperamental types. Kagan (1994) identified two behavioral profiles linked to these two temperamental types. Inhibited children tend to be reluctant to initiate spontaneous comments with unfamiliar people, show caution in situations requiring decisions, smile less, have unusual fears and phobias, show large heart rate accelerations to stress, and have atopic allergies. It is estimated that two out of every ten healthy Caucasians inherit a physiology that leaves them inclined to be aroused and disturbed by stimulation such as a colorful mobile early in the first year and initially avoidant of novelty in the second and third years (Kagan, 1994). This physiology in inhibited children is thought to be a more reactive circuit from the limbic area of the brain to the sympathetic nervous system. Specifically, this more reactive circuit involves a low threshold of excitability in the central and basolateral areas of the amygdala and in the projections from these areas to cortical, motor, and autonomic targets. This low threshold is believed to leave inhibited children especially vulnerable to the state of fear of the unfamiliar. In contrast, about four out of every ten children seem to inherit a physiology that biases them to be relaxed at 4 months and relatively fearless in early childhood (Kagan, 1994).

Kagan (1994) has demonstrated that infants who display a high-reactive behavioral profile at 4 months (i.e., those who arch their backs, pump their limbs, and fret or cry in response to novel stimuli) show higher levels of early childhood fears of things such as unfamiliar people, unfamiliar facial expressions, and intrusions into their personal space than do children who display a low-reactive profile. In turn, high fear at 9 months, which was observed in only 10% of the infants, was a good predictor of high fear at 14 and 21 months. The relation between early reactive profiles and later categorization of inhibited typologies is as follows: Half the low-reactive infants displayed uninhibited profiles at 3½ years, whereas 14% were inhibited; 40% of the high reactives were inhibited at 3½ years, whereas 25% displayed uninhibited profiles (Kagan, 1994).

Moreover, it has been demonstrated that there is predictive utility of the typologies from age 7 to adolescence (Kagan et al., 1989). Using a combination of observers' ratings of spontaneous conversation and smiling to create indexes of an inhibited or uninhibited style, Kagan et al. (1989) found that two thirds of the children who had remained in the inhibited category from the second to the seventh year were quiet and serious around age 13. Among the children who had remained uninhibited between the second and seventh year, 40% remained uninhibited from age 7 to age 13. He argues that such early demonstration of the existence of the two typologies and relatively high consistency for the typologies across one's childhood support the idea that the typologies may have stemmed in part from genetic structure. Specifically, he argues that one's genetic makeup affects whether one will have an overaroused limbic system. Some children—those who are inhibited—show very early signs of having an overresponsive amygdala. Kagan contends that this heightened sensitivity leads them to avoid conflict and the stimulation of novel inputs. Support for this argument can be found in studies of identical twins who show similarity in inhibited or uninhibited behavioral patterns and found in research that has demonstrated consistent associations between the two typologies and their sympathetic reactivity and asymmetry of cerebral activation. In particular, high-reactive infants showed increase sympathetic activity in the cardiovascular system even before 4 months. Reactivity to novel stimuli, as evidenced by limb thrashing, arching of the back, and so on, at 4 months was a good predictor of later childhood fears (see Kagan, 1994).

Given that there is evidence of a genetic component to the development of an inhibited personality and that central elements of this temperamental type are that the person inhibits social expression, has more fears, and tends to be less cheerful and more serious than the uninhibited type, it is reasonable to think that having symptoms such as anxiety, physical pain, and depression may be linked to a partly biologically based tendency to self-conceal.

Possessing a Secret Is Not Necessarily Related to Symptoms

Additional evidence for the predisposition argument comes from research that suggests that keeping a secret is not related to symptoms when researchers statistically account for other dimensions of concealment. In a series of studies, Jeff Kahn and I (Kahn & Kelly, 1998) found that the Self-Concealment Scale was composed of three separate factors, which we labeled the Possession of a Distressing Secret, Apprehension about Disclosure, and Self-Concealment Tendency. The first factor, the Possession of a Distressing Secret, seems to reflect the extent to which an individual holds some important, distressing secret. Within this factor, there is no discrimination between holding one secret or more than one; items that assess both load on this factor. An example is, "I have an important secret that I haven't shared with anyone." The second factor of the Self-Concealment Scale, Apprehension about Disclosure, seems to reflect a person's fears and concerns about the consequences of disclosing negative information. Apprehension about Disclosure pertains specifically to the fear a person reports experiencing when faced with revealing personal information. An example is, "I'm often afraid I'll reveal something I don't want to." Third, Self-Concealment Tendency reflects more of a chronic behavior of withholding personal information. This factor does not reflect the possession of a secret or fears about disclosing information; rather, Self-Concealment Tendency seems to describe a behavior of concealing potentially negative self-relevant information from others. An example is, "When something bad happens to me, I tend to keep it to myself."

Consistent with Finkenhauer and Rime's (1998b) findings that people who could recall a secret memory were sicker than those who could not, we (Kahn & Kelly, 1998) found that the Possession of a Distressing Secret was significantly correlated with symptomatology, as measured by the Brief Symptom Inventory ($r = .28$). Apprehension about Disclosure and Self-Concealment Tendency also were significantly correlated with symptomatology scores ($rs = .42$ and $.26$, respectively). However, after conducting a multiple regression analysis in which all three factors of the Self-Concealment Scale were entered into a model to predict symptomatology scores, we discovered that although Apprehension about Disclosure still was significantly positively related to symptomatology (standardized B = .38), Possession of a Distressing Secret and Self-Concealment Tendency were not (standardized βs = .04 and .07, respectively). This pattern of findings suggests that holding a particular secret does not relate to psychiatric symptoms when other dimensions of self-concealment are accounted for statistically. It seems that the link between self-concealment and symptomatology observed by many researchers may be driven by this Apprehension to Disclose factor, not by possessing a particular secret. Thus, the widely accepted idea that keeping particular secrets is stressful and may lead to symptoms (see Pennebaker, 1989, 1990) begins to be challenged by these data. However, the findings will need to be replicated before researchers can feel confident about this pattern. I am especially cautious because there were only two items in the Self-Concealment Tendency factor, making that subscale less than optimally reliable.

In another study, mentioned in Chapter 1, I (Kelly, 1998) assessed secret keeping and symptomatology levels in a sample of 42 therapy outpatients. As could be expected, the participants' self-concealment scores were positively related to their symptomatology scores ($r = .37$) and to their reports of whether they were keeping a relevant secret from the therapist (r = .42). However, when I statistically controlled for the clients' self-concealment scores, I found that keeping a particular relevant secret from the therapist was associated with a significantly greater reduction in symptoms across an average of 11 therapy sessions. This finding supports the idea that although the type of person who keeps secrets has greater symptomatology levels, keeping a secret per se is not necessarily problematic (see Kelly, 2000a).

Kahn, Achter, and Shambaugh (2001) measured 45 counseling center clients' predispositions to disclose (versus conceal) psychological distress at intake and then measured their self-reported stress and symptomatology at termination, which occurred on average after six or seven sessions. As it turned out, the clients who scored higher on distress disclosure and lower on concealment at intake experienced a greater reduction in self-reported stress and symptomatology over the course of counseling. Kahn et al. (2001) interpreted their findings to mean that "clients who come to their intake session with a tendency to share personally distressing information with others possess important interpersonal qualities that would likely facilitate the counseling process" (p. 200). However, I suggest that their findings may be explained in a more parsimonious fashion as a classic regression to the mean phenomenon. Specifically, the clients who were higher in distress disclosure and lower on self-concealment may have started out in a state of unusually high distress for them, and as might be expected just with the passing of time, they became less distressed than their high self-concealing counterparts. In essence, I am suggesting that they regressed to their mean state of being healthy, whereas the more chronically symptomatic high self-concealers stayed less healthy, independent of any process of concealment of distress during their treatment.

The reader may be skeptical about my separating the process of keeping a particular secret from general self-concealment in predicting the outcomes of concealment. This skepticism is reasonable given the findings described in the previous chapter that keeping a particular secret about being gay (Cole et al., 1996a,b) was predictive of illnesses years later and that people who could recall a secret memory were sicker than those who could not (Finkenhauer & Rime, 1998b). However, I suggest that these previous patterns could be explained by the fact that the researchers did not statistically control for what Kahn and I (Kahn & Kelly, 1998) labeled as the Apprehension to Disclose, which may be a similar construct to the general predisposition to be inhibited described by Kagan (1994). This predisposition to be inhibited is likely to be linked with both keeping a particular secret and symptomatology, and as such the relation between keeping a particular secret and symptoms may be a spurious one. If what I am suggesting—that the type of person who keeps secrets is vulnerable to illnesses and that secret keeping per se is not necessarily illness inducing—is true, then other researchers who control for this factor in the future will probably not find a link between keeping a particular secret and illness.

SOCIAL ANXIETY IS RELATED TO SYMPTOMS

In another correlational study, undergraduates were asked to report on how much they keep secrets and to complete the Self-Concealment Scale (Gesell, 1999). These scores were combined to create a composite secret keepers score. Then, a number of personality variables, including social anxiety, manipulativeness, need for control, and sociability, were entered into an analysis that was designed to predict secret-keeping tendency. Social anxiety was most strongly associated with secret keeping (standardized β = .66). In addition, a separate analysis entering social anxiety and secret keeping together to predict symptomatology showed that whereas secrecy in and of itself still predicted symptomatology scores, the personality dimension of social anxiety accounted for much of the predictive effect that secrecy has on symptomatology. Specifically, social anxiety could explain 80% of the variance in symptomatology. In other words, self-concealers tend to be socially anxious, and it is the social anxiety that is more strongly related to symptomatology than secret keeping. I see this finding as further (indirect) support for the notion that inhibited personality types are more susceptible to symptoms, and that it is not secret keeping per se that causes illness.

SHY OR INHIBITED PERSONALITY TYPES

In the previous chapter, I reviewed a number of findings on the correlates of self-concealment and repression. Given that Kagan addressed the inhibited temperament in his research, which involves shyness and the inhibition of behavioral expression, I now provide evidence that shy or inhibited personality types do tend to have greater illness rates than do uninhibited type.

In one study, women with rheumatoid arthritis rated themselves as definitely more shy and inhibited than their healthy sisters (Moos & Salomon, 1965). In another study, Biederman et al. (1990) examined psychopathological correlates of behavioral inhibition in 30 children (aged 4–7 years) who were high-risk offspring of parents with panic disorder and agoraphobia and 20 healthy controls (aged 4–20 years). The participants were evaluated with the Diagnostic Interview for Children and Adolescents—Parent Version. As it turned out, the inhibited participants, as compared with the healthy controls, had higher rates of multiple anxiety disorders, accounted for by high rates of overanxious disorders and phobic disorders. The researchers concluded that behavioral inhibition to the unfamiliar may be one of multiple risk factors contributing to the development of childhood anxiety disorders.

Schmidt and Fox (1995) also demonstrated the relation between extreme shyness and emotional and psychosomatic problems. They asked female undergraduates to rate themselves on measures of shyness, sociability, personality variables, and the prevalence of various disorders and then to interact with a female confederate. After the interaction, they were rated by independent observers for their level of shyness. Extreme shyness, as rated by the participants themselves and the observers, was found to be a significant predictor of emotional and psychosomatic problems, such as allergies and gastrointestinal functioning. It also was associated with self-reported depression, loneliness, fearfulness, social anxiety, neuroticism, inhibition, and low self-esteem. Thus, consistent with Kagan's (1994) findings with children, a picture of the shy, inhibited person with a number of physical and psychological ailments emerged from this study.

Finally, Windle (1994) too found that behavioral inhibition was linked to problems in a sample of 4462 male US military veterans. They measured inhibition using an index of behavioral inhibition on the Minnesota Multiphasic Personality Inventory (MMPI). Higher behavioral inhibition was associated with somewhat higher levels of cortisol, lower levels of social support, and a higher prevalence of lifetime generalized anxiety and major depressive disorders.

Summary

I have offered a part-genetic predispositional explanation for why secret keepers tend to have high levels of symptomatology. This explanation is based largely on Kagan's findings that there are very early, relatively stable signs of inhibited and uninhibited temperaments. Given that the types show up so early, it seems that there may be a genetic element to them. Kagan and other researchers have shown a link between shyness-inhibited personality and symptoms such as allergies and fears. Based on these findings and on preliminary findings that keeping a particular secret is not linked to symptoms when the general apprehension to disclose is accounted for statistically, I am suggesting that the kind of person who keeps secrets may be vulnerable to illness, rather than that secret keeping per se causes problems. This emphasis on a part-biological explanation to account for the covariance of self-concealment and symptoms fits rather neatly into a broader background of trait-based approaches to personality. After observing the findings from the many family, adoption, and twin studies conducted by different researchers across the globe (e.g., Jang, McCrae, Angleitner, Riemann, & Liveslez, 1988; Loehlin, 1992), Costa and McCrae (1998) concluded that genetic influences account for 40 to 50% of the variance in measured personality traits. However, McCrae and Costa (1995) acknowledged that even if personality traits have a biological basis, they still are psychological phenomena that must be understood in terms of how they interact with people's actions and experiences.

Whether or not this predisposition to be inhibited is part-genetically based as Kagan's findings suggest, my point is that the link between keeping a secret and becoming ill may be a spurious one that perhaps could be explained by the fact that each of these variables (i.e., keeping a secret and becoming ill) is linked to the predisposition to be inhibited. It is important to note, however, that the evidence to support this idea is correlational, and as such it is not possible to say with any certainty that such a predisposition causes people both to keep secrets and to become ill. This idea may best be viewed as another of a series of possible explanations for the link between secrecy and problems that requires much more empirical testing. Another limitation to my proposed idea is that I have used the terms "apprehension to disclose," "social anxiety," "shyness," and "inhibited temperament" loosely to refer to a common underlying personality construct, and future researchers will need to tighten the definition and assessment of this dispositional factor before further examining the predispositional idea.

CONCLUSION

In the chapter, I reviewed several competing theories for why secret keeping is linked to problems and presented the mixed evidence concerning each of these theories. I also offered another possible explanation based on the idea that secret keepers may have the biological predisposition to become sick. However, the reader may still be thinking, "Yes, but I know that secret keeping is stressful and likely to cause problems." Katherine Power's story of being on the lam for years seemed to illustrate this point so well. It is difficult to pinpoint cause-and-effect links in such cases, however, because it may have been her fear of getting caught rather than the secrecy per se that drove her to become anxious and depressed. Also, in her case, the secret involved something she owed to others: prison time. She probably felt guilty about her crime and as though she deserved to be punished for it. Her feelings of guilt alone could have made her depressed. Imagine if the situation had been identical except that everyone knew about her crime. Imagine too that prosecutors were spending years

deciding whether to seek to convict her. Under such circumstances—
awaiting the prospect of punishment without secrecy—she still may have
become depressed. For researchers to investigate the harmful effects of
secrecy, they will need to tease secrecy apart from feeling guilty or feeling
that something is owed. Also, it will be interesting to see how fears of
being caught play a role in the effects of secrecy. Perhaps if there had been
some statute of limitations on murder, such that she could not have been
prosecuted after her 23 years on the run, Katherine Powers might have
been able to keep her secret and not become depressed.

A very promising research direction is to see how one's level of self-
concealment interacts with a decision to reveal or conceal a secret in
influencing the outcomes of that decision. I predict that, on average, the
kind of person who normally conceals and then chooses to reveal a secret
will be worse off in terms of physical and mental health than a person who
normally reveals and then chooses to conceal a specific secret. I say this
partly because of the evidence that high self-concealers tend to ruminate
more than do low self-concealers; I suspect that they would worry about
the implications of their revelations long after the revealing. I also make
this prediction based on the evidence that high self-concealers would start
out sicker than low self-concealers before any decision to reveal or conceal
a secret would even be made.

HEALTH BENEFITS
OF REVEALING

Psychologists and laypersons alike believe that "confession is good for the soul," a theme that frequently has been depicted on talk shows and in popular movies. For example, in the popular 1996 British film. "Secrets and Lies," Hortense, a young black optometrist, sets out to find her birth mother after her adoptive mother dies. Hortense is disturbed to find out that her birth mother, Cynthia, is white. Cynthia is a factory worker who lives in a run-down house with her whiny, moody daughter Roxanne. Hortense calls Cynthia, who initially bursts into tears and refuses to see her. Cynthia has difficulty acknowledging (first to herself, then to others) that Hortense is her daughter. One of her first reactions to seeing Hortense is a sincere denial that she has ever "been with a black man." But before long, a suppressed memory jolts into her consciousness. Eventually, the two develop a warm friendship, and Cynthia invites Hortense to a party with her family and friends. One of the characters in the film notes that it is "Best to tell the truth, isn't' it? That way nobody gets hurt." At the party, Cynthia pretends that Hortense is her factory co-worker, which leads her to ever-more convoluted lies. The film climaxes with all the secrets and lies finally spilled out and all the people at the party hugging one another. Cynthia says near the end, "This is the life, innit?" The intention of the filmmakers seemed to be to demonstrate how difficult it can be to face up to ugly truths, even while the evasions and unspoken grievances slowly choke the secret keepers, but that in the end it is better to reveal these truths. Finally embracing her daughter and coming forward with the truth brings both mother and daughter new insights and joy.

In the December 1995 movie with a similar theme, "Dead Man Walking," the male protagonist Matthew Poncelet brutally kills a teenage couple but denies responsibility for his crimes. In the end, he finally does confess the truth to his spiritual advisor, Sister Helen Prejean, and the audience gets the sense that despite his execution, this confession has freed his soul.

Matthew Poncelet's character was largely based on the real-life Robert Lee Willie, who was executed in Louisiana in 1980 for the kidnapping and killing of a teenage girl. Sister Prejean had already learned many of the details of his crimes by reading police reports, which included a confession in which Willie provided a great deal of information to the deputy sheriff, Mike Varnado, who investigated these crimes. Like movie makers, police officers frequently appeal to people's beliefs in the benefits of open confession. This is especially evident when they coax confessions out of suspected criminals under the pretext that the criminals will feel better afterward. The following are excerpts from a transcript of a Public Broadcasting Service special on these crimes:

> MIKE VARNADO: According to Willie, he took this knife and he cut her throat, like this. And in his version he gave me in the confession, he said Joe was between her legs, taking the knife and jugging her as deep as it would go in her throat. I was outraged immediately that they would bring this girl up in here—this is her home—and do these—do these vile things to her. ... And the key to him confessing is—he asked me a question. He said, "I guess I'm a big man" or "I'm making the headlines down there a lot" and things like that. And I said, "Yeah." I said, "You are." I said, "You could be like Jesse James," you know? And he said, "Yeah, I'll tell you about it. Yeah, I killed her."
>
> ROBERT LEE WILLIE: [*police audiotape*] I asked her, I said, "Do you want a ride?" She said yes. So she got in the middle of the seat, between me and Joe, and we rode around and went up to Frickie's Cave and—
>
> MIKE VARNADO: Willie showed absolutely no remorse through the whole thing. None. He was proud of what he had done. He talked to me like this was a Sunday afternoon football game we were discussing.
>
> ROBERT LEE WILLIE: [*police audiotape*] He says, "You know where we can go fuck this whore?"
>
> MIKE VERNADO: He didn't have any—any problem telling me what they had done, the brutal details. The problem he had was actually owning up to being the one that actually cut the girl's throat. I guess he felt awkward about doing that.
>
> ROBERT LEE WILLIE: [*police audiotape*] Joe blindfolded her and we went down in the bottom of the hill and Joe made her lay on the ground and he had this big old knife and he just cut her throat and just started jugging her in the throat with it, man—just jugging her and jugging her and— (http://www.pbs. org/wggh/pages/frontline/angel/angelscript.html; retrieved May 14, 2000)

Whereas Willie's confession to the police may have been motivated by his desire to appear dangerous and powerful, his confession to Sister Prejean seemed to be motivated by a genuine desire to purify himself of his terrible deeds. Even though ironically Willie's confession to the police almost surely contributed to losing his life to execution, revealing secrets has been shown to be beneficial under certain circumstances.

As mentioned in the previous chapter, it is difficult from an ethical standpoint to try to demonstrate experimentally that keeping secrets makes people become ill. However, researchers have been able to study whether revealing secrets leads to health benefits. Investigators conducting experiments in confidential and anonymous settings have shown that talking or writing about private traumatic experiences leads to health benefits, such as fewer physician visits (Pennebaker & Beall, 1986; Pennebaker, Colder, & Sharp, 1990), improved immunological functioning (Pennebaker, Kiecolt-Glaser, & Glaser, 1988; Petrie, Booth, Pennebaker, Davison, & Thomas, 1995), and longer survival periods in advanced breast cancer patients (Spiegel, Bloom, Kraemer, & Gottheil, 1989). In this chapter, I review this remarkable evidence in detail, describing the many experiments that have established a cause-and-effect relationship between revealing and healing.

It is worth emphasizing that the experiments reviewed in the following paragraphs usually took place in confidential and anonymous settings, thus avoiding the confounding influence of confidant feedback on the health effects of revealing. It also is worth noting that many of the following experiments did not address the revealing of secrets per se. However, they are relevant in this volume on secrets because they did address the effects of revealing traumatic or distressing events, which often are kept secret.

REVEALING TRAUMATIC VERSUS TRIVIAL EVENTS

In a seminal experiment, Pennebaker and Beall (1986) studied the health effects of writing about private traumatic experiences as compared with writing about trivial events in a confidential and anonymous setting. The more specific aim of the experiment was to determine whether revealing the facts or revealing the emotions surrounding such traumas had a greater influence on the relief associated with revelation. Undergraduates were randomly assigned to groups in which they were asked to write for four consecutive days about either (1) a trivial event, (2) the facts surrounding a personal traumatic event, (3) the emotions surrounding a personal traumatic event, or (4) the facts and emotions surrounding a personal traumatic event. As it turned out, those participants who wrote about the facts and emotions surrounding the trauma actually made fewer health center visits during the 6 months after the writing experience than did participants in the other groups. Given that one of the three trauma-writing groups significantly differed from the group that wrote about trivial events, this experiment provided initial support for the idea that writing about traumas leads to health benefits. Pennebaker and Beall (1986) reported not only that writing about both the thoughts and emotions surrounding a trauma were important for health benefits but also that the health benefits depended, at least in part, on how deep the expressions of thoughts and emotions were.

Pennebaker and Beall's (1986) findings spawned efforts to explain why participants who wrote about the facts and emotions surrounding traumatic events had fewer physician visits. In one such effort, Pennebaker et al. (1988) sought to determine whether revealing traumas actually could lead to improved immune functioning. Undergraduates were asked to write for 4 consecutive days either about trivial events or about personal traumatic events (i.e., the facts and emotions surrounding the traumas) (Pennebaker et al., 1988). The participants' proliferative response of lymphocytes (white blood cells) to stimulation of two mitogens (substances foreign to the body) were assessed both before and after the writing period. Any increase in lymphocytes in response to these mitogens would be a sign of improved immune functioning. As it turned out, by the end of the writing intervention, participants who were in the trauma-writing group as compared with those in the trivial writing group did indeed have significantly higher proliferative responses to one of the mitogens (Pennebaker et al., 1988). Thus, these findings extended the findings of Pennebaker and Beall (1986) by demonstrating that writing about traumas can actually improve the functioning of the immune system.

In another experiment on immune functioning, medical students were randomly assigned to write about either private traumatic events or control topics for 4 consecutive days and then were vaccinated against hepatitis B (Petrie et al., 1995). As it turned out, the group who wrote about traumatic events as compared with the control group had significantly higher antibody levels against hepatitis B at the 4- and 6-month follow-up periods. These findings once again demonstrated that the emotional expression of traumatic experiences can lead to improved immune functioning.

Lutgendorf, Antoni, Kumar, and Schneiderman (1994) also studied the effects of revealing distressing events on immune functioning. In particular, they investigated how cognitive changes and experimental involvement during an emotional disclosure relate to changes in antibody titers to the Epstein–Barr virus (EBV) in healthy undergraduates. In this case, any significant *decrements* in the presence of these antibody titers would be a sign of improved immune functioning. Undergraduates were assigned randomly either to discuss a stressful topic that they had previously discussed only minimally or to undergo assessments (including blood tests and a mood checklist) only. As it turned out, the participants in the disclosure condition did not differ from the assessment-only control group in terms of EBV antibody titers. However, the participants who disclosed more about and avoided less of the stressful topic during the course of the 3-week period did experience antibody decrements. As such, Lutgendorf et al. provided correlational, although not experimental, support for the notion that revealing emotional events is associated with improved immune functioning.

Given that Lutgendorf and coworkers' (1994) experimental induction did not result in improved immune functioning, researchers assessed once again whether disclosure of emotions through writing about upsetting events would result in changes in blood-associated immune variables (Booth, Petrie, & Pennebaker, 1997). Using healthy adult volunteers in two different experiments, Booth et al. (1997) randomly assigned them to write about either emotional issues or trivial topics for 4 consecutive days. The participants' levels of what are called circulating lymphocytes and T-lymphocyte subsets (CD4 and CD8), as well as a variety of standard hematological markers, were measured both before and after the writing intervention. Immediately following the interventions in the two experiments, there were significant differences between the emotional disclosure and control groups in CD4, CD8, and total circulating lymphocyte numbers (but not in CD4/CD8 ratios or any other hematological variables), suggesting better immune functioning for the emotional disclosure group. More specifically, the circulating lymphocyte numbers in the emotional writing group remained relatively stable over the course of the experiments, suggesting that the difference between the groups was due to a fleeting elevation in postwriting blood lymphocyte levels (i.e., a sign of poorer immunological functioning) in the control group. Moreover, the participants in the emotional disclosure group as compared with those in the control group reported that the writing intervention was more stressful. In a nutshell, Booth et al. (1997) offered an important contribution to the literature by showing that although participants felt distressed by their writing about traumas, they did not experience increases in immunological markers of stress, and in fact they showed better immune functioning after their writing than did the control group.

Spera, Buhrfeind, and Pennebaker (1994) conducted an experiment that went beyond assessing the internal markers of the benefits of revealing private traumas to looking at how such writing could influence adjustment to job loss. Their specific objective in this experiment was to determine the influence of disclosive writing on subsequent reemployment activity and success. Sixty-three adults who had just lost their jobs were recruited for the study and 41 of them were assigned randomly to either experimental writing or control writing conditions. The remaining 22 participants who did not sign up for the writing phase of the study were included as nonwriting controls. As it turned out, the participants who were in the group that wrote about the trauma of losing their jobs as compared to those in the control groups were more likely to find reemployment in the months following the study. Interestingly enough, these effects did not seem to be caused by any heightened motivation or job-seeking efforts of those in the writing group. Specifically, the participants in the experimental group did not receive more phone calls, make more contacts, or mail out more job-related letters than did those in the control groups.

SUMMARY

Using the basic paradigm comparing the health effects of writing about traumatic events versus writing about trivial ones in an anonymous and confidential setting, researchers have discovered that writing about traumatic events leads to fewer physician visits, improved immunologic functioning, and even increased reemployment rates. Because these results were obtained using experimental designs, one can conclude that there is a cause-and-effect relationship between writing about traumas and receiving health benefits.

REVEALING TO A PSYCHOTHERAPIST VERSUS REVEALING PRIVATELY

Given that writing alone led to health benefits in the experiments just described, one may wonder to what extent psychotherapists are needed to help people with their problems. Murray, Lamnin, and Carver (1989) compared the effects of emotional expression in written essays versus in psychotherapy on changes in emotions surrounding distressing events. Undergraduates completed a measure of their current moods and then were assigned randomly to written expression, psychotherapy, or written trivial (control) conditions. Participants in the written expression condition wrote about a disturbing event and its accompanying emotional experiences, participants in the psychotherapy condition described (orally) a disturbing event and their emotional experiences to a therapist, and participants in the control group wrote descriptions of their room and clothes closet. The participants in the psychotherapy group met with psychotherapists who focused on reflecting feelings and content, using empathy, clarifying meanings, and encouraging the participants to explore the deep understandings of their specific distressing events. Participants in all three conditions engaged in their respective experimental tasks for 30 minutes. They all completed a mood inventory again, rested for 15 minutes, and completed the mood inventory a third time. They performed all these tasks again 2 days later. As it turned out, the participants in written expression condition temporarily experienced increased negative affect, and they ultimately did not change their feelings about the disturbing events. In contrast, the participants in the psychotherapist condition experienced less negative affect, and they showed more cognitive reappraisal (i.e., made more new meanings out of the disturbing events) and a dramatic shift to positive affect than did participants in either of the writing groups (Murray et al., 1989). Thus, talking to a psychotherapist had a more positive impact than writing about distressing events.

Donnelly and Murray (1991) obtained a slightly different pattern of results in their study in which they randomly assigned undergraduates to one of three conditions. These conditions involved writing about traumatic events, receiving psychotherapy about traumatic events, or writing about trivial events (control group) over 4 consecutive days. The researchers conducted content analyses of what was expressed during the intervention phase of the study and discovered the following pattern: Both the written expression and psychotherapy groups as compared with the control group expressed more positive and negative emotions, and they showed more cognitive, self-esteem, and behavior changes during the intervention. Moreover, the participants' positive emotions, cognitive changes, and self-esteem improvements increased over the 4 days, whereas the negative emotions decreased. Their degree of pain and upset about the traumatic events decreased over the days for both treatment groups. After the experiment, both treatment groups reported feeling more positive about their topics and themselves. Despite the positive changes on those measures, measures of mood taken before and after each session showed that participants in the written expression group reported an increase in negative mood immediately after each session, whereas the psychotherapy participants did not. Based on these findings, Donnelly and Murray (1991) suggested that the key role of the therapist may be to provide support in facing emotional traumas.

Segal and Murray (1994) followed up that study with a test of whether psychotherapy is more effective than an expression of thoughts and feelings into a tape recorder. They recruited 60 undergraduates with unresolved traumatic experiences and asked them either to participate in a brief course of cognitive therapy or to talk into a tape recorder. As it turned out, both procedures were similarly effective in reducing negative mood and negative thoughts, although the course of cognitive therapy was somewhat more effective on two outcome measures. Specifically, at 1-month follow-up, the participants in the cognitive therapy group as compared with those in the tape-recorder group felt significantly better about themselves and thought differently about their topic to an even greater extent.

In sum, Murray and colleagues conducted a series of studies with healthy participants who either underwent very brief therapy or revealed their distressing experiences privately. Under these conditions, therapy was found either to have a similarly favorable outcome as or to have a slight advantage over revealing privately. It seems that in particular one's immediate mood after a revelation may be more positive with than without a therapist. The reader must keep in mind, however, that although participants talked about events that they rated as equally personal, the participants in the writing group generated more negative emotion during their expression task than did participants in the psychotherapist condition (see Murray et al., 1989). It may be that participants disclosed more negative details during their expression period, and therefore their mood was lower than it was for participants in the psychotherapist condition. In essence, it may have been what they chose to reveal, rather than the support of the therapist, that led to the group differences.

WRITING VERSUS TALKING

In Murray and his colleagues' experiments, psychotherapy was superior in terms of improving affect to writing about distressing events (Donnelly & Murray, 1991; Murray et al., 1989), but it was not superior to talking alone (Segal & Murray, 1994). This pattern begs the question of whether talking is superior to writing about distressing events. Therefore, Murray and Segal (1994) conducted another experiment in which they compared these two processes. They randomly assigned undergraduates either to express vocally or to write down their feelings about either interpersonal traumatic events or trivial events in 20-minute sessions over 4 days. As it turned out, similar emotional processing was produced by vocal and written expression of feeling about traumatic events. Specifically, the painfulness of the topic decreased steadily over the 4 days, with both groups reporting positive cognitive changes and feeling better about their topics and themselves. The researchers conducted a content analysis of the sessions and discovered greater overt expression of emotion and related changes for participants in the vocal condition than for those in the writing condition. Moreover, there was an upsurge in negative emotion after each session of either vocal or written expression. Murray and Segal (1994) suggested that previous findings that psychotherapy ameliorated this negative mood upsurge cannot be attributed to the vocal character of psychotherapy.

Pennebaker (1997a) and Esterling, L'Abate, Murray, and Pennebaker (1999) conducted separate literature reviews on the health benefits of revealing private traumatic experience and concluded that expression in either written or vocal form is healthful. In one of the key experiments described in both reviews, healthy undergraduates who were seropositive for the EBV (which is extremely common) were randomly assigned to write or talk about stressful events or to write about trivial events (control group) during three weekly 20-minute sessions (Esterling, Antoni, Fletcher, Margulies, & Schneiderman, 1994). The participants completed a personality inventory and provided blood samples before their writing or talking period and then provided a blood sample after the final intervention period. After the final intervention, the participants in the talking/ stressful group as compared with those in the written/stressful group had significantly lower EBV antibody titers, which suggests better cellular immune control over the latent virus. In turn, the participants in the written/stressful group had significantly lower EBV antibody titers than did the participants in the control group. Thus, the investigators demonstrated that either talking or writing about distressing experiences leads to improved immunologic functioning. Moreover, content analysis of the written or oral expression indicated that the talking/stressful group achieved the greatest improvements in cognitive change, self-esteem, and adaptive coping strategies (Esterling et al., 1994).

REVEALING PREVIOUSLY DISCLOSED VERSUS UNDISCLOSED EVENTS

As explained in the previous chapter, at one point, Pennebaker (e.g., 1989) postulated that part of the benefit in revealing comes from no longer having to expend energy in inhibiting one's expression of the traumatic experience. Greenberg and Stone (1992) subsequently tested Pennebaker's (e.g., 1989) inhibition model directly. Following Pennebaker's (e.g., see 1989) writing paradigm, they asked healthy undergraduates to write for 20 minutes across 4 consecutive days about undisclosed traumas, previously disclosed traumas, or trivial events (Greenberg & Stone, 1992). As it turned out, the three groups did not significantly differ in their subsequent use of health care services and/or in their self-reports of physical symptoms. With the follow-up analyses, however, Greenberg and Stone were able to show that the participants who disclosed more severe traumas as compared with those who disclosed less severe traumas and control participants reported fewer physical symptoms in the months following the study. Greenberg and Stone suggested that health benefits occur when severe traumas are disclosed, regardless of whether previous disclosure has occurred. However, they noted that this conclusion was based on their correlational findings only, given that they found no between-groups differences to suggest that writing about traumas *causes* these health improvements. They also noted that their one of their main manipulation checks (i.e., that assessed the extent to which participants reported that they previously had held back from revealing their traumatic events) did not show the expected differences between the undisclosed trauma and the previously disclosed trauma groups. This result calls into question whether they really offered an adequate test of Pennebaker's inhibition theory.

REVEALING REAL VERSUS IMAGINED TRAUMAS

In another clever experiment, Greenberg, Wortman, and Stone (1996) questioned the basic assumption behind the writing studies: they challenged the idea that writing about real experiences is healthful. Specifically, they examined whether disclosing emotions generated by imaginative immersion in a novel traumatic event would enhance health and adjustment in a manner similar to that caused by disclosing real traumatic events. College women were recruited on the basis of their having experienced a traumatic event that was perceived as severe (e.g., rape, violent assault, abandonment by a parent, witnessing a gruesome event). The women then were assigned randomly to write about their own real traumas, imaginary traumas, or trivial events. Those in the imaginary trauma group were given real traumas to write about, so that the content of their writing would be equivalent to the writing of those in the real trauma group. As it turned out, at the end of the experiment, the imaginary trauma participants were significantly less depressed than real trauma participants, but they were similarly angry, fearful, and happy. Interestingly enough, at 1-month follow-up, both trauma groups made significantly fewer illness visits than did the control group participants. However, the real trauma participants reported more fatigue and more avoidance of certain ideas, feelings, or situations than did the other groups. Greenberg et al. (1996) speculated that the health benefits for the participants in the imaginary trauma group could have resulted from their gaining catharsis, engaging in emotional regulation, or constructing resilient possible selves (i.e., views of self as competent and successful; see Markus & Nurius, 1986). Most relevant for the present review, these findings point to the possibility that simply writing about traumatic events—not even necessarily one's own—is healthful.

HEALTHY UNDERGRADUATES VERSUS CLINICAL SAMPLES

Bootzin (1997) and Kevin McKillop and I (Kelly & McKillop, 1996) criticized Pennebaker's (e.g., see 1997a,b) work on the health benefits of revealing traumatic events by noting that the experiments have relied almost exclusively on relatively healthy individuals, begging the question, What happens when groups from clinical populations reveal their private traumas through writing? Do they experience health benefits?

One experiment provided evidence that sharing private, negative information in therapy may actually help diseased individuals live longer (Spiegel et al., 1989). Advanced-stage breast cancer patients were randomly assigned to psychosocial support groups or to routine oncological care groups. Those who had participated in the support groups survived significantly longer ($M = 36.6$ months) than did those who received the routine care ($M = 18.9$ months). The researchers argued that it was the group members' revealing of their private fears to other group members that helped them maximize the benefits from therapy and contributed to their living longer. However, there was no direct empirical evidence that it was the revealing of fears per se that led to the group differences. There were other differences between the two groups that also could have led to these findings. For instance, it may be that listening to others' problems and realizing that the support group members were not alone in the troubles led to the group differences.

Smyth, Stone, Hurewitz, and Kaell (1999) more recently addressed this issue of the reliance on samples of healthy undergraduate by conducting a trauma-writing experiment with outpatients suffering from mild to moderately severe asthma or rheumatoid arthritis. The outpatients were assigned randomly to conditions in which they either wrote for 3 consecutive days about "the most stressful life experience that they had ever undergone" (p. 1305) or about their plans for the day (control group). Amazingly, and much like the results from experiments with healthy undergraduates, at 4-month follow-up, 47.1% of the 70 outpatients in the experimental group as compared with only 24.3% of the 37 outpatients in the control group experienced clinically meaningful improvement in health outcomes. In particular, the asthma patients and arthritis patients in the experimental group experienced significantly more improvement in lung functioning and in overall disease activity, respectively, as compared with the asthma and arthritis patients in the control group.

META-ANALYSES

As alluded to earlier, several reviews have been conducted on the health effects of revealing private traumatic or distressing experiences. For example, Esterling et al. (1999) reviewed studies on the use of writing, alone or in conjunction with traditional psychotherapy, noting that an interest in such effects has increased substantially in recent years. They concluded that talking with friends, confiding to a therapist, praying, and even writing about thoughts and feelings can be physically and mentally beneficial.

Smyth (1998) conducted a more specific review of 13 well-controlled published and unpublished experiments on the health benefits of writing about emotional events. He concluded that the overall effect size of the writing on health was .42, which is considered to be between a medium and a large effect size. He also noted that Pennebaker was involved in 8 of the 13 experiments. Smyth compared the eight studies involving Pennebaker with the five studies that did not involve him and found that if anything the effects of writing were even greater in the studies not involving Pennebaker (although the difference was not statistically significant). Thus, it seems clear that revealing private traumatic experiences in confidential settings is healthful, and while Pennebaker has been the leading researcher in this area, he is not the only researcher to have observed these remarkable benefits of revealing secrets.

SUMMARY

Although to date there is no direct (i.e., experimental) evidence that keeping secrets causes health problems, there is direct evidence that through keeping a secret a person may miss out on the health benefits of revealing it. These documented health benefits have ranged from healthy undergraduates' improved immunologic functioning (e.g., Petrie et al., 1995) to advanced-stage breast cancer patients' living longer (Spiegel et al., 1989). It seems that whether talking or writing, revealing anonymously or to a therapist, or revealing previously disclosed or undisclosed traumatic events, revealing private and disturbing experiences is healthful. The one glitch that emerges from drawing clear implications from this research is that revealing either an imagined or real trauma has been found to be healthful (Greenberg et al., 1996). This finding does not undermine the conclusion that writing anonymously about disturbing events is healthful, but it does call into question what it is about revealing such events that is healthful. This issue is addressed in the next chapter.

CONCLUSION

The implications of the results from these experiments are clear: If one wants to feel better about a private traumatic experience as well as feel healthier overall, one should write or talk about it either anonymously or to a trusted person, such as a psychotherapist. There is evidence that such expression about both the facts and feelings surrounding the traumatic event actually can lead to improved immune functioning and fewer physician visits (e.g., Pennebaker & Beall, 1986). The findings have been obtained not only by Pennebaker and colleagues but also by other researchers who have observed even larger effect sizes for these health benefits (see Smyth, 1998). Such findings may make the reader wonder why everyone does not write about his or her traumatic experiences in either a diary or journal. Murray and colleagues (e.g., 1989) shed some light on this question by demonstrating that people feel negative in the short run as they are writing and that a therapist may be able to help offset that negativity. Greenberg et al. (1996) too showed that participants who wrote about their own traumatic experiences as opposed to those who wrote about imagined ones experienced more negativity and avoidance of certain thoughts and feelings surrounding the trauma. These findings help to explain why people do not always take advantage of such a seemingly simple route to improved health. However, if they can tolerate the negative feelings in the short run, the potential benefits seem worth the trouble.

WHAT IS IT ABOUT REVEALING SECRETS THAT IS BENEFICIAL?

Given the substantial evidence described in the previous chapter that revealing private traumatic or negative experiences is associated with psychological and physiological benefits, the question remains, Why is revealing secrets helpful? One commonly held view among scientists is that through gaining new insights into the secrets people feel better about them. Another idea is that through venting emotions or gaining catharsis people come to feel better about their secrets. In this chapter, I review the evidence on these two ideas and then describe in detail a pair of studies that my students and I conducted (Kelly et al., 2001) in which we teased apart the effects of gaining new insights versus catharsis.

NEW INSIGHTS

Searching for meaning in life has been described as one of the primary motivations for human beings (see Frankl, 1976/1959), and this search seems particularly acute after a traumatic experience. Making sense of such an experience is considered to be a necessary part of regaining mental and physical health (Antonovsky, 1990; Baumeister, 1991; Lifton, 1986). Baumeister (1991) stated that "when a major personal trauma or setback occurs, for example, the initial response may be the rejection of meaningful thought, as in denial. Then, gradually, the person copes with the crisis by finding a new way to interpret what went wrong and to put the world back together" (p. 75). If people do not talk or write about their traumatic experiences and choose instead to keep them secret, they may miss precious opportunities to get new perspectives on the secrets and develop a sense of closure on the events (Kelly & McKillop, 1996; Pennebaker, 1989, 1997b; Pennebaker & Hoover, 1985; Tait & Silver, 1989). People often find meaning in the experiences by getting a new perspective on them and then assimilating them into their worldviews (Horowitz, 1986; Meichenbaum, 1977; Pennebaker et al., 1988; Silver et al., 1983). In fact, many counseling approaches have grown out of the idea that reinterpreting or reframing experiences is critical in helping clients get better (e.g., see Dowd & Milne, 1986; Kelly, 1955). Across many types of brief therapy interventions, interpretations made by the therapist have been found to be associated with client improvement (see Hill, 1992), apparently because the interpretations provide clients with new perspectives on their problems.

When people are not able to incorporate their personal traumas into their lives, they may find ways to escape themselves through such self-destructive means as suicide, masochism, alcoholism, bulimia, or excessive religiosity (see Baumeister, 1990, 1991). A "tunnel vision" thought process seems to precede suicide, such that suicidal people become rigid in their thinking and will no longer try to make meaning out of the events in their lives or gain insight from experiences (Shneidman & Farberow, 1961, 1970). In one study, suicidal people as compared with nonsuicidal people were significantly less able to come up with solutions to interpersonal problems in their lives (Shneidman & Farberow, 1970). Moreover, in Silver and co-workers' (1983) study of survivors of father–daughter incest, the women who had not made meaning of their incest experiences as compared with the women who had done so reported more psychological distress, poorer social adjustment, and lower levels of self-esteem.

Foa, Molnar, and Cashman (1995) observed the importance of meaning making in women who had experienced sexual assault and then had undergone therapy that involved their repeatedly reliving and recounting their trauma in a treatment referred to as *exposure therapy*, which is used for treating anxiety disorders such as phobias and posttraumatic stress disorder (PTSD) (Foa & Kozak, 1986; Foa & Rothbaum, 1989). Following the treatment, the women had more thoughts in which they attempted to organize the trauma memories, and these organized thoughts were negatively correlated with depression.

Along these same lines, after reviewing the studies on the physical and mental health benefits of revealing private traumatic experience, Pennebaker (1997a) concluded that gaining new insights is an important part of recovery from distressing experiences. Pennebaker (1997a) observed that although a reduction in inhibition may contribute to the disclosure phenomenon, changes in basic cognitive and linguistic processes during writing predict better health. The key, he noted, was the level of insight people used during their writing. In particular, he found that a high use of positive emotion words and moderate levels of negative emotion words were associated with positive health outcomes.

Suedfeld and Pennebaker (1997) observed this pattern when they explored whether the recall of very unpleasant memories would occur at a different level of complexity in meanings from that of neutral memories and whether differences in such complexity would be related to health outcomes. Two groups of undergraduates wrote an essay each day for 4 days: one group wrote about a trivial topic and the other wrote about a negative (traumatic) life event for a previous study. The complexity scores of these two types of essays were compared and they were correlated with a composite measure of well-being (immunologic assays, visits to the Student Health Center, and self-reported distress and substance abuse). As it turned out, the essays about negative experiences were significantly higher in complexity, suggesting that the participants put more mental effort to their writing. Among these essays, there was a significant relationship between the complexity of meanings in the writing and improvement in the participants' health, such that moderate levels of complexity (i.e., scores closest to the median for the group) were associated with the most improvement. Apparently, very high levels of complexity represent feeling quite troubled and may be an indication of a continued lack of resolution surrounding the negative event, and low levels of complexity may mean that the person did not put in the mental energy needed to gain closure on the negative event (see Pennebaker, 1997a).

In a separate analysis of a series of writing about trauma studies, Pennebaker, Mayne, and Francis (1997, Study 1) observed a mixed pattern regarding the links between gaining new insights into the trauma and experiencing changes in physical versus mental health. When participants increased their use of words associated with insightful and causal thinking over the course of their writing, they experienced improved physical health. However, their increased use of insightful words was not associated with improved mental health (Pennebaker et al., 1997).

Nolen-Hoeksema, McBride, and Larson (1997) also observed mixed results regarding attempts to make sense of a trauma. They found that among recently bereaved men, those who analyzed the meaning of their loss as compared with those who engaged in less analysis reported greater positive morale 1 month after the loss. However, these men experienced more persistent depression and lack of positive states of mind over the 12 months after the loss (Nolen-Hoeksema et al., 1997). As the researchers themselves noted, because of the correlational nature of the study, it was not clear whether the analysis caused the depression, or whether the particularly troubled men simply tended to engage in more analysis.

Lepore (1997) acknowledged the importance of making meaning out of distressing experiences and tried to go one step further in understanding how it reduces stress surrounding the events. In particular, he explored whether expressive writing improves emotional adaptation to distressing events by reducing event-related intrusive thoughts—unwanted thoughts that pop into people's heads—or by desensitizing people to such thoughts. He asked undergraduates who were preparing for their graduate school entrance exams either to write their deepest thoughts and feelings about the exam (i.e., experimental group) or to write about trivial events (i.e., control group). Participants in the experimental group experienced a significant decline in depressive symptoms from 1 month (Time 1) to 3 days (Time 2) before the exam. In contrast, the participants in the control group maintained a relatively high level of depressive symptoms over the same period. Expressive writing did not affect the frequency of intrusive thoughts, but it did seem to affect the impact of intrusive thoughts on depressive symptoms. Specifically, intrusive thoughts at Time 1 were positively related to depressive symptoms at Time 2 in the control group and were unrelated to symptoms in the expressive writing group. Lepore speculated that one possible explanation for this finding was that "people who engage in thinking about and expressing their stress-related thoughts and feelings may gain some insight into the stressor, which in turn renders any reminders or memories of the stressor comprehensible and nonthreatening" (p. 1034). However, he acknowledged that it is not possible to know whether that explanation is better than the notion that the participants habituated to (i.e., got used to) the stressors when they wrote or talked about them (cf. Bootzin, 1997).

Bootzin (1997) criticized the research on the effects of writing about traumas in general by pointing out that efforts to explain these health benefits have been correlational in nature. As such, researchers have not been able to establish cause-and-effect relationships between the proposed mechanisms that underlie the benefits of writing and the health outcomes. For example, one cannot be certain from studies such as Silver and co-workers' (1983) study of survivors of incest whether meaning making caused the psychological benefits observed or whether a third variable, such as participants' intelligence levels, could explain these benefits (see Kelly et al., 2001). The participants with higher intelligence as compared to those with lower intelligence simply may have been better at developing new insights and coping with their problems.

In sum, it has been observed in a number of writing studies that there is a link between making meaning of traumatic events and improved health. However, given the correlational nature of these analyses, more research is needed to try to establish whether a cause-and-effect relation exists between meaning making and subsequent mental states (see Boot-zin, 1997; Kelly et al., 2001).

CATHARSIS

As mentioned earlier, another popular explanation for why revealing secrets leads to health benefits is that revealers have the opportunity to gain catharsis. Breuer and Freud (1975) were early proponents of catharsis and stated that "the patient only gets free from the hysterical symptoms by reproducing the pathogenic impressions that caused it and by giving utterances to them with an expression of affect, and thus the therapeutic task consists solely in inducing him to do so" (p. 283). Consistent with his interpretation of Freud's cathartic method, Pennebaker (1997b) defined catharsis as the linking of emotion and insight. However, researchers and therapists in general have come to use the term catharsis to mean a venting of pent-up emotions or an expression of emotions behaviorally (e.g., Bush-man, Baumeister, & Strack, 1999; Polivy, 1998; Tice & Ciarocco, 1998). In his catharsis theory, for example, Scheff (1979) contended that recalling the facts of an emotional experience is unnecessary, whereas discharging one's emotions is both necessary and sufficient for therapy. Catharsis will be used here to mean a venting of emotions.

Many psychotherapists today continue to believe that catharsis is beneficial, as illustrated by the fact that it has been an integral part of a number of the more recent approaches to psychotherapy, such as reevalua-tion therapy (Jackins, 1962), primal therapy (Janov, 1970), new identity therapy (Casriel, 1972), psychodrama (Moreno, 1958), and short-term dy-namic psychotherapy (Davanloo, 1980; Nichols & Efran, 1985; Sifneos, 1979). Laypersons, too, often consider catharsis to be helpful. For example, in a survey I (Kelly, 1997) conducted a few years ago, undergraduates rated gaining catharsis as a highly effective strategy for dealing with their own troubling secrets and perceived that other people would view gaining catharsis as significantly more beneficial than gaining new insights into troubling secrets.

In her review of the research on catharsis, Polivy (1998) concluded that even though some studies have raised the question of whether catharsis actually purges or provokes emotions, catharsis seems to reduce one's level of emotional arousal surrounding a troubling event more often than not. Two studies with Holocaust survivors provided indirect empirical support for the idea that catharsis is beneficial (Pennebaker, Barger, & Tiebout, 1989; Shortt & Pennebaker, 1992). As the survivors related their previously suppressed stories to the researchers, their skin conductance levels fell, indicating that they became more relaxed (Pennebaker et al., 1989; Shortt & Pennebaker, 1992). Similarly, informal studies of suspected criminals who were given lie detector tests demonstrated that when the suspects confessed, their skin conductance levels dropped, and they appeared more relaxed to observers (see Pennebaker, 1985, 1990). Moreover, student outpatients at a university clinic who received cathartic psychotherapy, as compared with those who received insight-oriented psychotherapy, reported more improvement on a measure of life satisfaction (Nichols, 1974). However, in that same experiment, the outpatients who received insight-oriented therapy reported a greater reduction in symptomatology.

Mendolia and Kleck (1993) conducted a pair of experiments that suggested that there may be delayed benefits to catharsis. They examined the effects of talking to another person about either the facts or emotions surrounding a stressful event on the physiological arousal of the discloser. In Experiment 1, undergraduates viewed an affect-neutral videotape followed by a stress-inducing videotape (i.e., of gruesome woodshop accidents). The participants then talked about either their emotional reactions to the stressful videotape (emotion condition), the sequence of events within it (fact condition), or the sequence of events within the neutral videotape (distraction condition). All the participants were then reexposed to the stressful accident episode. As it turned out, the participants in the emotion condition as compared with those in the fact condition were more autonomically aroused (i.e., distressed) during the second exposure to the accident episode, demonstrating that expressing negative emotions had an untoward immediate effect. In Experiment 2, 48 hours separated participants' talking about their first exposure to the stressful stimulus from their second exposure to it. This time, participants in the emotion condition as compared with those in the fact condition had lower levels of autonomic arousal while viewing the stimulus again and reported more positive affect after watching it. In essence, although gaining catharsis was not helpful over the short run, it was beneficial over the longer duration perhaps because it allowed participants to get used to their negative emotions surrounding the distressing videotape (Mendolia & Kleck, 1993).

However, other researchers have speculated that the scientific community has abandoned catharsis theory because of the research that has failed to support the benefits of venting one's emotions (Bushman, Baumeister, & Stack, 1999). For example, in one experiment, participants who expressed a fear of public speaking were asked to make speeches before an audience (Tesser, Leone, & Clary, 1978). They were randomly assigned to a condition that required them to focus on why they had those feelings, a catharsis-only condition, or a control group. It was found that participants

exhibited the highest levels of digital perspiration in the catharsis condition and reported feeling significantly worse than did the participants in
the condition that focused on why they had those feelings (Tesser et al.,
1978). In another experiment, participants were assigned to take part in
one of three conditions: (1) interpersonal, which involved a 20-minute
counseling session, (2) silence, which allowed for 20 minutes to take time
to review feelings in silence, and (3) catharsis, which provided a tape
recorder so the participant could "get things off (his/her) chest" (Bohart,
Allen, Jackson, & Freyer, 1976). Participants in the interpersonal group
reported the greatest improvement in affect, whereas participants in the
catharsis group showed the least improvement (Bohart et al., 1976). In yet
another study, men in a daily stress-coping skills group who were told
to use a cathartic release strategy reported increases in negative affect
relative to their original levels (Stone, Kennedy-Moore, & Neale, 1995).

In a study by Siegman and Snow (1997), each of 24 participants took
part in three conditions: (1) anger-out, in which previously experienced
anger-arousing events were described loudly and quickly, (2) anger-in, in
which anger-arousing events were relived inwardly, in the participant's
imagination, and (3) mood-incongruent speech, in which anger-arousing
events were described softly and slowly. As it turned out, only the anger-
out condition was associated with high cardiovascular reactivity levels,
and self-reported anger was highest in the anger-out condition, moderate
in the anger-in condition, and lowest in the mood-incongruent condition.
Based on these findings, Siegman and Snow concluded that the full-blown
expression of anger is problematic and that the mere inner experience of
anger is not.

Similarly, after comparing the effects of cognitive therapy with talking
into tape recorder (described in the previous chapter), Segal and Murray
(1994) concluded that even though the talking into a tape recorder was
almost as effective as cognitive therapy for dealing with traumatic experiences, the mechanisms through which the two groups benefitted seemed
to differ. Across both groups, the arousal of negative affect was inversely
related to positive outcome, whereas the reduction of negative affect and
negative thoughts was positively related to outcome. Participants in the
tape-recorder condition talked about negative emotional content persis-
tently over the 4-day period, whereas participants in the cognitive therapy
group were encouraged by their therapists to switch their focus to examining their negative thoughts and cognitive distortions. The researchers
concluded that "the sheer arousal of negative affect by itself does not seem
to be therapeutically valuable as might be expected from simple catharsis
theories" (p. 204).

In sum, whereas Polivy (1998) suggested that catharsis is associated with benefits more often than not, Bushman et al. (1999) argued that the scientific community has all but abandoned catharsis theory. In a number of experiments involving the venting of emotions, such venting has led to increased negative affect relative to earlier emotional states (e.g., Stone et al., 1995). However, Mendolia and Kleck (1993) found that the negative emotional states were only temporary and were followed by improved affect, suggesting that any future study of catharsis must include both short-term and long-term assessments of changes in affect.

NEW INSIGHTS VERSUS CATHARSIS

Although I have presented gaining new insights (i.e., meaning making) and catharsis as opposing explanations for the benefits of revealing secrets, they often have been depicted as processes that combine to lead to the physical and mental health benefits associated with the revealing of private traumatic experiences (e.g., Bohart, 1980; Greenberg et al., 1996; Murray et al., 1989; Pennebaker, 1989, 1990; Pennebaker, Colder, & Sharp, 1990). For instance, Berry and Pennebaker (1993) suggested that the effectiveness of many common expressive therapies (e.g., art, music, cathartic) would most likely be enhanced if clients were encouraged both to express their feelings nonverbally and to put their experiences into words.

Similarly, Pennebaker et al. (1990) proposed that emotions were a part of the experiences that must be recognized and that the expression of emotions would facilitate new insight or meaning into the experiences. They asked college freshmen to write about either coming to college or superficial events. Following the writing, only 10% of the participants mentioned the value of venting emotions or gaining catharsis, whereas 76% of them said that they felt the study was valuable because it helped them to understand better their own thoughts, behaviors, and moods. Moreover, as described in the previous chapter, Pennebaker and Beall (1986) found that participants who wrote about the facts and emotions as compared with participants who wrote about only the facts or emotions surrounding their traumatic experiences made fewer health center visits during the 6 months after the writing experience. The researchers reported that the health benefits depended at least in part on how deep the expressions of thoughts and emotions were.

One limitation of those studies is that they could not tease apart the effects of gaining new insights and catharsis because they did not involve a direct experimental manipulation of these variables. All of the published studies on the health benefits of revealing have utilized correlational analyses to establish a link between gaining new insights and benefits (see

Bootzin, 1997). Thus, my students and I (Kelly et al., 2001) conducted a pair of studies designed to disentangle the effects of gaining catharsis from the effects of gaining new insights on improving one's affect surrounding a secret. We predicted that participants' trying to gain new insights into their secrets would be more helpful than trying to gain catharsis alone, because purely venting their emotions surrounding their secrets could actually intensify the emotions. Furthermore, we expected that the more the participants developed new insights into their secrets, the more relief they would experience.

In Study 1, we assessed whether participants' having gained catharsis or new insights into their secrets from revealing them to confidants in the past was associated with recovery from the secrets. In Study 2, we followed up these correlational findings by attempting to establish a cause-and-effect relationship between participants' gaining new insights into their secrets and experiencing improved affect surrounding the secrets.

STUDY 1

One hundred thirty-seven undergraduates were asked to (1) select the most private, personal secret that they had ever shared with another person, (2) describe to what extent they experienced catharsis and gained new insights into the secret after revealing it, and (3) indicate how they felt when thinking about the secret now. We hypothesized that having gained new insights into the secret would be the better predictor of feeling positive about the secret at the time of the study.

PROCEDURE

The participants were given questionnaire during their regular class time and were asked not to write their names anywhere on the questionnaires. They read the following instructions:

> Virtually everyone keeps secrets, or hides personal information from others at some point in time. In other words, we hold private information that we would want very few other people (or no one) to know about. Please take a moment to reflect on a time in which you shared a very private and personal secret with someone else. Select a secret from the past or present that involves you directly and personally. Select the most private, personal secret that you have ever shared with another person, but do not write it down.

The participants then completed scales assessing the extent to which they had gained new insights and catharsis from having revealed their secret to the confidant. Specifically, a modified version of the Therapy Session

Report (TSR) (Orlinsky & Howard, 1966) was used to measure the extent to which participants felt that they had gained catharsis and new insights from having disclosed their secrets to their confidants in the past. We adjusted the questionnaire to correspond with our research goals by prefacing the items with, "What do you feel you got out of sharing your secret with this person?" (i.e., their confidant). The subscales were what Howard, Orlinsky, and Hill (1970) called catharsis (e.g., "a chance to let go and get things off my chest"; "relief from tensions or unpleasant feelings") and mastery/insight (e.g., "more understanding of the reasons behind my behavior and feelings"; "ideas for better ways of dealing with people and problems"). We also assessed participants' current positive and negative feelings about their secret. In particular, participants were asked to reflect on the secret they thought of earlier in the session, to feel the emotions associated with this secret, and to "indicate to what extent you feel this way whenever you think about your secret." The positive affect measure included items such as "interested," "alert," and "inspired"; and the negative affect measure included items such as "irritable," "distracted," and "ashamed" (see Watson, Clark, & Tellegen, 1988).

RESULTS AND DISCUSSION

Study 1 assessed whether gaining catharsis or new insights from revealing secrets to confidants in the past was associated with improved affect surrounding the secrets at the time of the study. As it turned out, gaining new insights (as measured by the mastery/insight subscale of the TSR) was correlated significantly with positive feelings surrounding the secrets, whereas gaining catharsis (as measured by the catharsis subscale of the TSR) actually was correlated with negative feelings surrounding the secrets.

The finding that gaining new insights was associated with positive affect surrounding the secret is consistent with previous research that showed that across therapeutic techniques interpretations provided by the therapist were associated with positive client outcomes (Hill, 1992). Such interpretations are likely to provide people with new perspectives on their problems or difficulties and help them make sense of their troubles.

In addition, the finding that catharsis was associated with negative feelings surrounding the secrets is consistent with results from a classic study by Ebbesen, Duncan, and Konecni (1975). These authors interviewed 100 technicians and engineers who had just been laid off from their jobs at an aerospace company and asked some of them anger-eliciting questions like, "What instances can you think of where the company has not been fair with you?" (p. 446). When these same individuals were later asked to rate their attitudes toward the company, they were more hostile toward the company than were those who had not been asked the anger-eliciting questions initially. Thus, getting one's feeling out in the open may intensify the negative emotions one feels.

A qualifier to this conclusion is that it is possible that participants told their confidants more negative secrets in cases when they needed (and got) catharsis as compared with when they needed new insights. Because these individuals may have started out with more negative secrets, they still may have had more negative feelings about the secrets at the time of the study, even if experiencing catharsis had been beneficial to them. In essence, an important drawback to interpreting these findings is that the data are correlational, thus making it impossible to determine whether gaining catharsis and new insights actually caused participants to feel worse or better about their secrets. Moreover, participants' reports of whether they gained catharsis or new insights from revealing their secrets to their confidants were retrospective, and it is unclear whether their recollections were accurate. As such, Study 2 was conducted to address both of these issues. In it, we utilized an experimental design to explore whether gaining catharsis or new insights into one's secrets would lead to differences in affect surrounding those secrets.

STUDY 2

Eighty-five undergraduates were brought into the laboratory and randomly assigned to one of three groups in which they were asked to write about either (1) their secrets while trying to gain new insights into them, (2) their secrets while trying to gain catharsis, or (3) their previous day (i.e., control group). They were asked to generate the secrets and rate their feelings about them before the manipulation was introduced. After two sessions of identical writing tasks spanning one week, participants were again asked to rate their feelings surrounding the secrets. Given the findings from Study 1, we predicted that the new-insights group would show significantly greater improvements in affect surrounding their secrets than would either the catharsis or control groups, and that those participants who reported making the most meaning out of their secrets would show the greatest improvements. Likewise, we predicted that participants who were most able to come to terms with their secrets during their writing would experience the greatest improvements in affect. This prediction was based on previous theoretical work suggesting that gaining closure is a central part of coping with private traumas (see Pennebaker, 1997b). We also expected that the catharsis group would fare no better than the control group in terms of changes in affect.

It is important to note that we were interested in studying the effects of the process of gaining insights, as opposed to what the new insights were. Our basis for this focus was that Silver et al. (1983) found

> no evidence to suggest that the specific type of answer our respondents generated from their search for meaning was important in terms of coping effectiveness. Rather ... what appeared to be critical was whether the women were able to make *any* sense of their incest experience at all. (p. 91, italics in original)

Moreover, we studied the effects of gaining new insights and catharsis both immediately and after 1 week to address the possibility that there could be some delayed benefits to catharsis (see Mendolia & Kleck, 1993).

PROCEDURE

Participants were brought into the laboratory in groups of one to three and seated in separate cubicles. The experimenter told them that their responses would be confidential and anonymous and that even the experimenter her- or himself would not have access to the locked box where they would leave their completed packets.

After the opening instructions, participants were asked to report on their stream of consciousness for a 3-minute writing period. The purpose of this task was to acclimate them to writing about their personal thoughts and feelings. Then they were asked to generate a very private and personal secret that they had told no one or very few people. They were asked to describe one secret only and not to go into any detail in their description. After they listed their secret and turned the page over, they were asked to complete several 9-point items. These items were: "How disturbing is this secret to you?" (from not at all = 1 to extremely = 9); "How private is this secret to you?" (from not at all = 1 to extremely = 9); "How often have you thought about this secret during the last week?" (from never = 1 to extremely often = 9); and "To what extent have you come to terms with this secret?" (from not at all = 1 to full = 9). They then completed for the first time the same measure of their positive and negative affect that was used in Study 1. As in Study 1, we asked the participants to reflect on the secret they thought of earlier in the session, to feel the emotions associated with this secret, and to "indicate to what extent you feel this way as you are thinking about your secret now."

Next, the manipulation was introduced. Participants were randomly assigned to spend 25 minutes writing according to one of the following sets of instructions: (1) The new-insights group was instructed to "focus on making sense out of the secret or gaining new insights into the secret. Develop this new perspective on your secret by changing your thoughts about it. Your sole purpose in writing is to make meaning out of your secret—to gain a new perspective or new understanding of the secret." (2) The catharsis group was instructed to "focus on what you are feeling about the secret and getting those feelings out in the open. Write about your feelings without rationalizing or explaining them. Your sole purpose in writing is to get your feelings about the secret off your chest—to really pour out your emotions and release them." (3) The control group was asked to describe "in detail what you did yesterday from the time you woke up till the time you went to bed. It is important that you describe things exactly as they occurred. Do not mention your own emotions, feelings, or opinions. Your description should be as objective as possible."

After they were done with the writing task, all three groups completed the measure of their positive and negative affect surrounding their secrets a second time and items that asked how many people they had told their secret before the study, along with some distracter items. They were thanked for completing the first portion of the study and reminded about their session scheduled for the next week. To bolster the manipulation, the new-insights group was told, "if you wish to discuss your secret and continue to make meaning out of it with other people whom you trust, please feel free to do so"; the catharsis group was told, "if you wish to discuss your secret and continue to get your feelings about it off your chest with other people whom you trust, please feel free to do so."

The participants returned exactly 1 week later. The experimenter reminded them of the anonymity and confidentiality of their responses and gave them the measure of the positive and negative affect surrounding their secrets a third time. After they completed this inventory, they were given the identical 25-minute writing instructions that they had received the previous week (i.e., the new-insights group received the instructions to try to gain new insights, the catharsis group received the instructions to vent their emotions, and the control group received the instructions to write about their previous day). After this writing period, they completed the measure of their positive and negative affect surrounding their secrets a fourth time and were asked the following items (along with some distracter items): "To what extent did you get your feelings off your chest in writing today"; and "To what extent did you make sense or meaning out of your secret in writing today?" They rated these items on 9-point scales from not at all (1) to to a great extent (9).

Results and Discussion

In Study 2, we sought to determine whether there was a cause-and effect relationship between being instructed to focus on gaining new insights into personal secrets and feeling more positive about those secrets. The participants wrote down very personal secrets, some of which were highly disturbing, including secrets about being raped, experimenting with sexual acts, having attempted suicide, and cheating on a test (see Chapter 1 for a complete list). There were no significant differences across the three groups for participants' ratings of how disturbing or private the secrets were, and none for how often they thought about the secrets and how much they had come to terms with the secrets. There also were no differences across the groups for how many people they had told their secrets before the study. Participants indicated that they had told an average of between two and three people their secrets and that they had actively held back from telling others to a fair extent.

Participants in the new-insights group experienced significantly greater improvements in positive affect surrounding their secrets than did participants in the catharsis and control groups. Moreover, the extent to which participants gained new insights into their secrets from their writing, as rated by judges, was significantly correlated with participants' reports of increased positive affect surrounding their secrets. When participants' own ratings of the extent to which they gained catharsis and made meaning of their secrets were entered in a multiple-regression analysis together with initial positive affect scores, meaning making was a significant predictor of increased positive affect, whereas catharsis was not. Regarding negative affect, there were no significant differences across the three groups. However, we found that participants' coming to terms with their secrets during their writing (as rated by judges) was associated with less negative affect. These findings provide strong support for the conclusion that, not only are people able to create new insights into their secrets on their own, but engaging in this process is an effective coping strategy that is superior to merely venting their emotions about the secrets.

To assess the *pattern* of improvement in the affect scores for the new-insights group as compared with the catharsis group, a repeated-measures analysis was performed on the four administrations of the affect measures (i.e., Time) for the new-insights and catharsis conditions using the negative affect scores subtracted from the positive affect scores at each of the four administrations. As shown in Table 1, the participants in the new-insights group had significantly greater improvement in affect across time than did those in the catharsis group. The difference in mean affect scores between the new-insights and catharsis groups was significantly greater at Time 4 than at Time 1 ($P = 0.4$) or at Time 3 ($P = .007$), but not significantly greater than at Time 2 ($P = .13$). This finding is important, because Pennebaker (e.g., 1997a) established that improvement in affect over the course of writing about emotional events was associated with health benefits. This

TABLE 1. Means and Standard Deviations of Negative
Affect Scores Subtracted from Positive Affect Scores
across the Four Administrations

Condition	Administration of affect scales			
	Time 1	Time 2	Time 3	Time 4
New insights (n = 35)				
M	−5.19	.59	1.76	4.52
SD	13.94	12.10	10.49	11.24
Catharsis (n = 33)				
M	−5.55	−2.42	−.58	−1.64
SD	11.95	13.24	8.99	9.22
Control (n = 17)				
M	−6.18	−2.65	−1.76	−1.35
SD	13.58	9.88	9.02	8.09

pattern also is important because it illustrates that there was no delayed benefit to catharsis relative to the other groups (see Mendolia & Kleck, 1993).

One might argue that the results were simply an artifact of the differential demand characteristics inherent in the writing tasks. Specifically, participants in the new-insights condition may have believed that this task was supposed to help them, whereas participants in the catharsis condition may have been skeptical about the effectiveness of catharsis. Therefore, participants in the new-insights group may have reported that they felt more positive about their secrets than did participants in the catharsis group. However, a recent survey showed that a sample of 99 undergraduates rated gaining catharsis and new insights into a secret as equally highly effective for helping them cope with troubling secrets (P > .05) (Kelly, 1997). The means for new insights and catharsis were 7.44 (SD = 1.20) and 7.19 (SD = 1.31), respectively, on 9-point scales from not at all helpful (1) to extremely helpful (9). When those same participants were asked to rate how effective other people thought the two coping strategies were, the participants reported that others would view catharsis as significantly more helpful than gaining new insights (Kelly, 1997). These results directly contradict the demand-characteristic explanation for the findings.

One reason why gaining new insights is likely to be curative may be that people are able to find closure on the secrets and avoid what has been termed the Zeigarnik effect (Zeigarnik, 1927), wherein people actively seek to attain a goal when they have failed to attain the goal or failed to disengage from it (Martin & Tesser, 1993; see also, Pennebaker, 1997a). As mentioned in Chapter 1, Zeigarnik (1927) showed that people continue to think about and remember interrupted tasks more than finished ones, suggesting that they may have a need for completion or resolution of the events. Thus, revealing a secret with the explicit intention of gaining a new perspective on it may help people feel a sense of resolution about the secret. Evidence for this idea comes from two separate analyses of the data from Study 2. In one analysis, as expected, judges' ratings of the extent to which participants gained new insights into their secrets during their writing significantly predicted their final positive affect scores, even after we statistically adjusted for participants' initial positive affect scores. In another analysis, we found that not coming to terms with their secrets was a strong predictor of feeling negative about the secrets, even after we statistically adjusted for initial negative affect scores.

DISCUSSION

We conducted these studies in an effort to disentangle the effects of gaining catharsis from the effects of gaining new insights, which have been blended in previous research that has examined the benefits of revealing emotions and facts surrounding private traumas (e.g., Pennebaker & Beall, 1986; Pennebaker et al., 1990). The experimental (and correlational) findings from Study 2 and the correlational findings from Study 1 converged to support the conclusion that focusing on gaining new insights into one's secrets is a useful strategy for increasing positive affect surrounding the secrets, whereas merely attempting to gain catharsis is not helpful. Study 1 even showed that gaining catharsis was associated with negative affect surrounding the secrets.

The implications of these results are that people should try to gain new insights into and come to terms with their troubling secrets, if their goal is to make themselves feel better about the secrets. However, one might argue that some secrets are difficult to construe in new ways and that it may take a long time to create new meaning for particularly excruciating or humiliating secrets. In his theory of personality, George Kelly (1955) proposed that people are not just capable of actively constructing their realities and seeing their problems from alternative perspectives, but they are naturally inclined to seek these meanings. Silver et al. (1983) showed that the great majority of their sample of survivors of long-term father–daughter incest sought to make meaning of the experiences, and a number of them were able to do so, despite the terrible nature of their experiences. Other researchers also have shown that many people do come to make meaning out of their negative life experiences (see Andreasen & Norris, 1972; Chodoff, Friedman, & Hamburg, 1964; Cornwell, Nurcombe, & Stevens, 1977; Doka & Schwartz, 1978; Helmrath & Steinitz, 1978; Silver & Wortman, 1980). In Study 2, we demonstrated that participants were able to generate new perspectives on their secrets and that gaining these new insights occurred relatively quickly (after two 25-minute writing periods spanning 1 week). This effect occurred even though many participants described very disturbing and private secrets.

Whereas the results from Studies 1 and 2 clearly support the benefits of gaining new insights into secrets, Nolen-Hoeksema and her colleagues (Lyubomirsky & Nolen-Hoeksema, 1993, 1995; Nolen-Hoeksema & Morrow, 1993) have shown that if people are experiencing negative life events and choose to think about their feelings surrounding the events and the implications of those events (i.e., engage in rumination), they are more likely to become depressed and stay depressed longer than if they choose to distract themselves from the negative events. This observation seems to contradict the notion that trying to make meaning of negative life events is a buffer against suicide and other self-destructive acts (Baumeister, 1990, 1991). One way of resolving this apparent contradiction is that perhaps only successful meaning makers feel better about their troubling secrets. Silver et al. (1983) stated that

> the extent that the search for meaning results in finding meaning in an undesirable event, it is likely to be an adaptive process.... However, finding meaning does not appear to terminate the search or the ruminations. Moreover, when after an extended period the search fails to bring understanding, the continuing process of searching and repeatedly ruminating appears to be maladaptive. (p. 81)

Another way of resolving the contradiction is to differentiate between two kinds of meaning making: Making sense of an event and finding benefit in the experience (Davis et al., 1998). In a longitudinal study of people coping with the loss of a relative, Davis et al. (1998) found that making sense of the loss was associated with less distress, but only in the first year after the loss, whereas the finding of benefit was most strongly associated with adjustment 13 and 18 months after the loss, a pattern that suggests that the finding of benefit is the more long-lasting element to emotional recovery. Perhaps researchers could utilize an experimental design in the future to compare the effects of passive rumination with both of these types of active meaning making.

Before closing this chapter, I must mention a couple of noteworthy limitations to our research. First, both the new-insights and catharsis groups, not just the new-insights group, in Study 2 used significantly more emotion words (relative to total words) during their writing than did the control group. Also, although the catharsis group had a statistically significantly higher proportion of emotion words ($M = .03$) than did the new-insights group ($M = .02$), this difference was quite small. Thus, it is not clear whether the new-insights group actually engaged in a combination of gaining catharsis and new insights or in gaining new insights alone. Future researchers perhaps could prevent (more effectively than we did) the participants in the new-insights group from writing about emotions and then assess the effects of such a clear-cut manipulation on their affect.

Second, although the pattern of findings between Studies 1 and 2 converged concerning the effects of gaining new insights on positive affect, the pattern was somewhat different for the two studies concerning the effects of catharsis on negative affect. This difference could have been the result of the fact that we studied the oral revelation of secrets to confidants in Study 1, as compared to the written revelation of secrets anonymously in Study 2. Specifically, the venting of emotions may have been linked to negative affect in Study 1 because confidants are sometimes rejecting of people who engage in such emotional expressions (e.g., see Davidowitz & Myrick, 1984). In contrast, the venting of emotions may not have been linked to negative affect in Study 2 because anonymous venting has fewer negative repercussions. Because of the different methodologies of the two studies, we cannot be sure why we obtained the different patterns for catharsis. We can only say that it did not seem helpful in either case.

CONCLUSION

Although no experimental research has been conducted on the negative health effects of secrecy, well-conducted experiments have been shown that the revealing of private traumatic information or secrets in anonymous, confidential settings can lead to health benefits, such as improved immunologic functioning (e.g., Pennebaker & Beall, 1986; Pennebaker et al., 1988; Petrie et al., 1995). It has been proposed that the reason the revealing of secrets offers these benefits is that the revealer experiences catharsis, gains new insights into the secrets (i.e., makes meaning out of them), and no longer has to expend cognitive and emotional resources actively hiding the secrets (Pennebaker, 1989, 1990; Pennebaker et al., 1990). Along these lines, Polivy (1998) noted that expressing emotions behaviorally, or gaining catharsis, is helpful more often than not. However, as described in this chapter, there is much contradictory evidence concerning whether catharsis is indeed helpful (e.g., Bushman et al., 1999), just as there has been mixed evidence regarding the benefits of high levels of insightful thinking (e.g., Nolen-Hoeksema et al., 1997; Pennebaker et al., 1997).

We (Kelly et al., 2001) conducted two studies in which we teased apart the effects of gaining new insights and catharsis to see which makes people feel better about their secrets. In Study 1, undergraduates indicated whether they had gained new insights or catharsis from revealing their secrets to their confidants in the past. As it turned out, gaining insights was associated with feeling positive about the secrets, whereas gaining catharsis was associated with feeling negative about them. In Study 2, undergraduates were randomly assigned to write about their (1) secrets while trying to gain new insights, (2) secrets while trying to gain catharsis, or (3) previous day. The new-insights group felt significantly more positive about their secrets than did the other groups. Moreover, they came to terms with their secrets during the writing to a greater extent than did the catharsis group. Not coming to terms with their secrets was associated with participants' feeling negative about them. By obtaining these results, we (Kelly et al., 2001) showed that focusing on getting a new perspective on secrets is a superior means of making oneself feel more positive about them. This strategy seems not only to be useful at increasing positive affect, but also seems to encourage the person to come to terms with the secrets, and thus diminish his or her negative emotions surrounding the secrets. By contrast, solely focusing on stirring up and releasing negative emotions may put the revealer at risk for feeling worse about the secret. Integrating our findings with those of Pennebaker et al. (1997) and Nolen-Hoeksema et al. (1997), who obtained mixed results regarding the benefits of high levels of insightful thinking or analysis, we suggest that attempts at meaning making are valuable to the extent that the person is able to come to terms with their secret or trauma. Continued dwelling on a secret without such closure may backfire, just as venting the negative emotions surrounding a secret without gaining new insights may backfire.

CHAPTER 6

SECRECY AND OPENNESS IN PSYCHOTHERAPY

In the previous two chapters, I described the benefits of revealing secrets in a journal or diary, and in these remaining chapters, I move into a more complex analysis of what happens when revealing secrets to another person, starting with one's therapist. Psychotherapy clients could be expected to reveal their secrets completely to their therapists, no? Actually, even though they were paying a good deal of money for their treatment, 46% of a sample of clients in long-term therapy (Hill et al., 1993) and 60% of a sample of short-term therapy outpatients (Kelly, 1998) reported keeping some major secret from their therapists.

These findings are puzzling given that many theorists from the different mainstream approaches to psychotherapy, such as the psychoanalytic, family, and group therapy traditions, have emphasized the importance of high levels of revelation from clients in psychotherapy (e.g., Foa, Rothbaum, Riggs, & Murdock, 1991; Fong & Cox, 1983; Freud, 1958). For example, Freud (1958) routinely explained to his patients that it was crucial for them to reveal as much about themselves as possible in psychoanalysis, no matter how ridiculous, unacceptable, or anxiety provoking those revelations seemed to them. He referred to this directive as the fundamental rule of psychoanalysis (see Hoyt, 1978).

Being open (i.e., truthful and revealing) is thought to allow clients to release harmful pent-up emotions and gain an understanding of themselves and their problems (Hill & O'Grady, 1985; Hill et al., 1993; Jourard,

1971a,b; Martin, 1984; Stiles, 1987). Presumably, the more disclosing clients can be about their thoughts and feelings, the more their therapists should be able to help them. Fong and Cox (1983) noted that "until clients can expose their innermost 'secrets' and make themselves vulnerable to the counselor, the real work of counseling cannot begin" (p. 163). Likewise, Jourard (1963) suggested that a requirement for mental health is the ability to reveal one's inner self to at least one other person and that disclosing secrets increases self-knowledge and psychological health. It follows that revealing oneself, in time, to a trusted therapist would potentially have great therapeutic effects. Along these lines, many therapists today require a great deal of revelation from their clients, arguing that for clients to benefit from therapy, the clients must first work through painful personal experiences (e.g., Arnow, 1996; Courtois, 1992; Horowitz, 1986; Liotti, 1987; Rando, 1993; Reichert, 1994).

In fact, psychotherapy techniques from a wide range of approaches are aimed at promoting clients' self-disclosure (Sloan & Stiles, 1994). For instance, if a client states that she is too ashamed to reveal a troubling indiscretion from her past, the therapist may try to help her disclose by describing what the therapist anticipates is an even more embarrassing act. The rationale for such an intervention is that if the client hears the description of a situation that is worse than her own, then she may have an easier time describing her relatively minor indiscretion.

However, Bok (1982) has argued that the common, negative view of silence and of secrecy in general may encourage people to make revelations about themselves indiscriminately in social interactions. For example, such revelations in group therapy can backfire and result in clients' experiencing acute anxiety attacks or expressions of hostility from other group therapy members, or in extreme cases even making suicide attempts (Lieberman, Yalom, & Miles, 1973). Thus, the question remains, Are the clients who resist their therapists' attempts at eliciting self-disclosure or those who keep relevant secrets harming themselves?

In this chapter, I first provide an overview of the theories and traditions from the psychoanalytic, family, and group therapy literatures that have led many therapists to believe that clients' secret keeping undermines the therapeutic process. Along the way, some alternative perspectives within each tradition on the role of clients' openness are discussed. I then review the empirical research on whether clients' openness is associated with favorable therapy process ratings and outcomes and conclude by discussing the limitations of such evidence and offering suggestions for future research.

THEORETICAL PERSPECTIVES
ON THE ROLE OF CLIENTS' OPENNESS

PSYCHOANALYSIS

Freud focused his theorizing on the concept of censorship, which encompasses both unconscious and conscious forms of inhibition; he tended to use the terms repression and suppression interchangeably (see Wegner, 1992, for a discussion of this point). This is perhaps because he assumed that one's personality was almost entirely unconscious, and so conscious inhibition did not require much discussion. Therefore, when I discuss the psychoanalytic emphasis on patients' openness, I refer to patients' revelations of both secrets and repressed material together.

Benefits of Confession

Since the turn of the 20th century, psychoanalysts have viewed secrecy as problematic and accessing repressed material as being very helpful to patients. Psychoanalysis relies on the search for unspeakable, sealed-off trauma; "... behind an emotion expressed, behind a symptom manifested, there lurks a contrary, repressed emotion" (Abraham, Torok, & Rand, 1994, p. 18). Freud based his fundamental rule of psychoanalysis on a number of case observations that patients' revealing of their secrets allowed them to relive their repressed or buried traumatic experiences and that this reliving was typically followed by a reduction in the patients' symptoms (e.g., Breuer & Freud, 1975).

Jung (1933) also encouraged patients to face those things that they typically repressed or kept hidden from themselves. He made patients' revelations of previously hidden material the focus of his psychoanalytic sessions, encouraging his patients to engage in a thorough confession of the facts and suppressed affect surrounding their emotional experiences (Jung, 1933). Jung stated that "... every personal secret has the effect of sin or guilt" (p. 34). He believed that if patients could be more conscious of what they were concealing, then they would be harmed less by the buried material. For example, if a patient admitted during his analysis that he sometimes felt like killing his beloved mother, then he would be less susceptible to blurting out unintended insults about her mothering skills when visiting her during the holidays.

Even though Freud and Jung encouraged their patients to reveal their secrets in treatment when the patients felt ready to do so, these famous analysts observed that their patients resisted complete openness (Kaufman, 1989). Freud thus inferred that patients are instinctively driven both to be cured through revealing themselves completely and to avoid being cured through keeping their unconscious images buried in the deeper regions of their minds (Freud, 1958). This phenomenon has been described as "a tension between the urge to retain and urge to expel" (Hoyt, 1978). The patients fear penetration and yet they long for extraction of the secret (Rosenfeld, 1980). When patients refuse to explore their secrets in psychoanalysis, they are perceived to be defensive and resistant (Rosenfeld, 1980; Minoff, 1992).

Psychoanalysis developed as a means of overcoming such resistance to the revelation of hidden or repressed material (Bernfeld, 1941). Analysts believe that by examining the manner in which patients disclose a secret, they can gain insights into the patients' psychological development and conflicts (Schoicket, 1980). Psychoanalytic sessions are devoted to trying to remove obstacles to confession (Bernfeld, 1941). But at the same time, analysts avoid rushing or outwardly forcing patients to reveal their deepest secrets (Rosenfeld, 1980). The analyst says and does things to reduce the patient's discomfort or shame about the previously suppressed information (Weiss, 1995). Freud drew an analogy between the psychoanalyst's intense efforts to draw out hidden information and a criminal investigator's procedures to extract a confession (Welsh, 1994). The analyst hypothesizes about what the patient's secret might be, comments on the resistance in the patient, and makes an interpretation about the hidden content to the patient (Bernfeld, 1941). The analyst also uses the primary psychoanalytic techniques of dream analysis and free association (i.e., in which the analyst presents a series of words and the patient says what immediately comes to mind) to elicit the revelation of hidden, unconscious material (Handelman, 1981).

If patients are not willing or able to share their secrets, psychoanalysts believe the energy that the patients spend keeping secrets repressed might become represented in compulsive behavior or other symptoms (Abraham et al., 1994; Freud, 1958; Hesselman, 1983; Margolis, 1966; Reik, 1945; Wergeland, 1980). For instance, a patient's denial or repression of a trauma may contribute to the development of psychological disorders such as dissociative identity disorder (multiple personality disorder), bipolar disorder, anorexia, and melancholia (Abraham et al., 1994). Some psychoanalysts believe that only through the confession of secrets can the treatment of these disorders succeed and symptoms be reduced (Abraham et al., 1994).

A number of case studies have been cited to support these claims. For example, in one well-known case of a woman named Dora who suffered from migraine headaches and depression, Freud identified and reconstructed her traumatic childhood experiences (Mahony, 1996). He believed that the source of Dora's illness was her childhood masturbation, and he elicited her confession that she had masturbated. Her symptoms subsequently diminished. Another case involved a 41-year-old man who suffered from alcoholism and drug abuse. His analysis included a focus on uncovering his previously withheld sexual history and extracting his confession of gay sexual feelings for the analyst (Wallerstein, 1986). After 7 years of analysis, the patient reached his treatment goals: his addictive behaviors were gone, and he was leading a satisfying life with his wife and children.

Why Revealing Is Critical for Therapeutic Progress

Psychoanalysts have offered several interconnected explanations for why revealing secrets is essential for therapeutic progress. First, revealing the secret is believed to allow catharsis or a discharge of pent-up emotions such as shame, guilt, and anger that previously inhibited creative growth (Hoyt, 1978). Hymer (1982) speculated that the benefits of revealing private information outweigh the risks: "The initial embarrassment of confessing is frequently outweighed by the relief that comes with the verbalization of the darker, secretive aspects of the self" (p. 131).

Second, while helping the patients to overcome anxiety and guilt, confession also theoretically gratifies the patients' masochistic needs for punishment (Gillman, 1992; Reik, 1945). Patients seem compelled to resolve unfinished business by reenacting past traumatic events (Dushman & Bressler, 1991). Traumatized patients "fear the return of the trauma, yet they tend to retraumatize themselves through repeated actions symbolizing aspects of the trauma" (Bergmann, 1992, p. 452). Confession allows an emotional reliving of the original trauma, and thus presumably provides partial gratification of the patients' drives and impulses to punish themselves (Reik, 1945). Dushman and Bressler (1991) conducted a case study of a 17-year-old male who used drugs and was in psychodrama group treatment. They observed that he was able to find closure on a friend's death through revealing this secret in treatment. The group provided him with a safe environment to recover from his guilty feelings about having survived his friend and find meaning in his own survival.

Third, the disclosure of secrets may help patients develop their identities (Hymer, 1982). The revealing of a secret presumably makes it less foreign to their sense of who they are and dispels their uncomfortable moral burden of deceptiveness (Schwartz, 1984). Thus, the revealing allows an integration of the positive and negative aspects of themselves (Hymer, 1982; Schwartz, 1984). In one case study, a psychiatric inpatient hid from other patients the fact that he had killed one of his parents (Schwartz, 1984). The patient later reported feeling isolated from the other patients on his ward as a result of this concealment. Schwartz (1984) recommended that therapy patients reveal their secrets to other patients when they feel ready to do so.

A common theme to all these explanations is that revealing secrets to a noncondemning analyst instead of to rejecting parents is a corrective emotional experience (Margolis, 1974). In contrast to past experiences, the analyst presumably will not reveal the secret, will not take sides, and will not use the information against the patient (except where bound by the legal limits of confidentiality). Through confessing the buried impulses and the mechanisms driving toward repression of these impulses, a better adjustment to reality may replace the process of repression. Confession offers a more realistic meaning for the repressed wishes and the possibility for greater self-understanding (Reik, 1945).

In sum, psychoanalysis developed as a means of helping patients reveal themselves to the analyst and confess their secrets, and the revelation of secrets has become the cornerstone of modern psychoanalysis (Castets, 1988). Drawing largely from case studies, psychoanalysts have contended that keeping secrets in treatment prevents patients from benefiting from the treatment. In these case studies, patients typically have recovered following an important confession or retelling of previously suppressed or repressed material.

Alternative Perspectives

New avenues for research exploration often can be gleaned from case studies. However, it is very difficult to draw conclusions or generalize from such studies. Although Freud considered himself a scientist (Barron, Beaumont, Goldsmith, & Good, 1991), Bernfeld (1941) has noted that the case study methods of psychoanalysis deviate greatly from the scientific method of observation. In particular, compared with other research designs, such as correlational or experimental designs, case studies are especially vulnerable to the biases of the investigators. Because psychoanalysis grew out of the notion that very high levels of patient revelation are essential for therapeutic progress, perhaps psychoanalytic researchers have expected to find that secrecy in sessions is problematic. For example, Coons (1986) surveyed psychotherapists treating patients with dissociative identity disorder and found that the therapists rated secrecy as a major hindrance to improvement. Thus, it is possible that psychoanalytic researchers may not have documented the times when revealing a secret went awry because that result was so different from their expectations.

One psychoanalytic researcher concluded, "Practical experience ... suggests that total disclosure is not necessary" (Hoyt, 1978, p. 238). Some psychoanalysts have proposed that there are even times when keeping secrets may be beneficial. Margolis (1966) suggested that retaining secret thoughts and feelings leads to a healthy sense of separateness, individuality, and ego identity. He also indicated that people learn about their uniqueness through recognizing that they have the power to divulge or withhold information. Likewise, Hoyt (1978) argued that secrets are important for establishing interpersonal boundaries. With the knowledge of a secret comes a certain amount of power, and others may abuse the power accompanying secret knowledge (Hoyt, 1978).

A problem with very high levels of revelation in psychotherapy is that, although analysts are depicted typically as noncondemning, neutral listeners who will help the patient with the secret and will not utilize information against the patient (Margolis, 1974), this depiction is not always accurate. Hoyt (1978) and Hoffman (1983) warned that when countertransference (i.e., the thoughts, feelings, and impulses that the therapist has toward the clients) occurs, the analyst may not provide the nonjudgmental environment that patients so desperately need when the patients are revealing painful or shameful deeds. Furthermore, Silver (1983) has indicated that it is risky to agree to unconditional secrecy when treating clients who have a borderline personality disorder, because such collusion may interfere with the building of a trusting relationship. Confidentiality may have to be broken in the event that the borderline client attempts suicide or performs other dangerous acts (Silver, 1983). Another harmful effect may occur if the patient becomes too ashamed or embarrassed about the revelation and decides to terminate therapy prematurely (Hoyt, 1978).

In sum, the case studies from the psychoanalytic tradition lend only initial, tentative support for encouraging very high levels of revelation from clients. Furthermore, some psychoanalytic theorists have offered examples of when secrecy in psychotherapy may actually be productive.

FAMILY THERAPY

Detriments of Secrecy

Although psychoanalysts were the first modern-day psychotherapists to emphasize the importance of uncovering secrets in therapy, family therapists may have had the most to say about the negative effects of secrecy. The strain of keeping a secret is often considered by family therapists to be the source of clients' problems, and symptoms are thought to be mere by-products of the secret keeping (e.g., Saffer et al., 1979). For example, a child may exhibit symptoms as a diversion from the family's denied or secret problems (Eaker, 1986). The parents may bring a child into therapy because it is easier to blame or scapegoat the child than it is to face their own problems (Pincus & Dare, 1978). Indeed, there have been documented occasions when secret keeping seemed to be linked to psychotic symptoms in children (Saffer et al., 1979).

Secrets are thought to control family members and keep them bound to one another by making the members feel an unhealthy sense of obligation to the family (Avery, 1982). It has been suggested that when one family member wants to separate from the secretive family, these families are often driven into therapy (Gutheil & Avery, 1977). Hence, some therapists have construed the main purpose of therapy as helping the family with their secrets while also helping them to stay together (Avery, 1982).

The notion that secrecy in families is dysfunctional has received some empirical support. Vangelisti (1994) showed that there is a negative relationship between family members' reports of the number of secrets that their family keeps in relation to other families and the members' levels of satisfaction with their family. However, the actual estimated number of secrets that family members reported was not correlated with their family satisfaction (Vangelisti, 1994). Vangelisti (1994) concluded that dissatisfied family members may be inclined to believe that their families are unusually secretive, even if the families are not actually unusually secretive.

As described in Chapter 1, nearly every family has secrets (Vangelisti & Caughlin, 1997). The types of family secrets that have received the most attention in the literature include secrets about incest (Swanson & Biaggio, 1985), extramarital affairs (Shlien, 1984), the sexual orientation of one or more family members (Murphy, 1989), and death (Paul & Bloom, 1970). In the paragraphs to follow, I describe the rationales for emphasizing the revealing of these various types of secrets in family therapy. I have organized the material this way because the rationales vary to some extent based on the types of secrets the family is keeping.

Secrets surrounding incest are considered particularly troubling for the family. Incest victims have reported that they fear being abandoned (Kaufman, Peck, & Tagiuri, 1954), not being believed (Butler, 1978), being punished (Herman, 1981), and being blamed for complying with the incestuous activity (Geiser, 1979; Goodwin, 1982; Justice & Justice, 1979; Meiselman, 1978). In cases in which a father has molested his daughter, secrecy is thought to isolate the family from the outside world, thereby contributing to the father's abusive dominance in the family (Hoorwitz, 1983). Repression or denial are typical responses to the incest experience (Lindberg & Distad, 1985; Russell, 1986), and such responses allow the incest to continue (Hays, 1987). The child feels isolated and different from other children her age (Luebell & Soong, 1982). There is tremendous pressure on her to maintain secrecy (Swanson & Biaggio, 1985). The daughter understands that revealing her secret could destroy her family and could mean her being removed from it (Swanson & Biaggio, 1985).

Despite these fears, Swanson and Biaagio (1985) argued that the victim must reveal the secret during therapy sessions. A critical part of therapy is to diminish the daughter's sense of isolation by encouraging her to break the silence surrounding the incest trauma (Black, 1981; Hoorwitz, 1983). The victim also ultimately must discuss the incest with someone other than the therapist so that she can rid herself of her feelings of isolation (see Herman, 1981; Meiselman, 1978; Tsai & Wagner, 1978). Group therapy for adult survivors of incest often requires not only disclosing the secret of the incest to the therapist and other group members (Hays, 1987) but also confronting the family with the secret in an effort to rebuild oneself (Swink & Leveille, 1986).

Some family therapists have suggested that even though the initial relief of revealing of family secrets in therapy may be followed by feelings of guilt and an increase in symptoms, the revealer ultimately will enjoy symptom reduction. Three documented cases involving family sexual secrets showed this pattern (Saffer et al., 1979). In each case, an adolescent was concealing information about the inappropriate sexual conduct of one or more family members, and in each case the adolescent was encouraged by the therapist to reveal this secret. After the adolescents complied, they experienced some immediate abating of their symptoms of paranoia, acting out, and severe depression. However, these symptoms then increased during the days immediately following the disclosure. After more time had passed, their symptoms lessened once again. Saffer et al. (1979) suggested that this pattern was due to the fact that the patients initially felt that they had been disloyal to the family by revealing their secrets and then the patients regained a sense of equilibrium after coming to terms with this sense of disloyalty, even though their families dissolved.

In cases in which one spouse has had an extramarital affair, many marriage and family therapists have indicated that it is critical for the infidel to confess to the other spouse (e.g., Brown, 1991; Pittman, 1989; Shlien, 1984). As described in Chapter 1, their reasoning is that it is not the extramarital sex that causes problems but rather the secrecy surrounding the sex (Pittman, 1989). Once the person has had the affair, it takes energy to keep the secret by omitting truths or telling lies, and these deceptive efforts may destroy a person's sense of self-worth (Shlien, 1984). The guilt and shame of the secret affair may simply become torturous for the person who is having the affair (Shlien, 1984).

In addition, the "other woman" (or the "other man") also may be hurt by the secrecy surrounding the affair (Richardson, 1988). Richardson (1988) conducted interviews with 65 women who were involved with married men and found that the relationships typically were maintained by both parties' efforts to keep the affairs hidden. This secrecy resulted in both positive and negative feelings by creating intense feelings of togetherness for the couple, but it also undermined the woman's sense of power within the relationship (Richardson, 1988).

Some marital therapists have asserted that secret extramarital affairs should be revealed because hiding the affair means keeping a piece of oneself from one's spouse (Brown, 1991, p. 138). Brown (1991) postulated that when clients bring up the affairs to their therapists, such as in a private session away from their spouses, it is apparent to the therapists that the affairs are still having an impact. The therapists presumably need to be aware of the affairs to try to understand their impact on the marriage (Westfall, 1989), and then hopefully the therapists can assist the clients in sharing the affair with the spouse (Brown, 1991).

One case study involved a couple who vaguely expressed their goal of improving their marriage. In an individual therapy session with the husband, the therapist learned indirectly about the affair (Brown, 1991). Just before the next session, it was the wife who canceled their treatment, and this abrupt termination was interpreted to mean that the wife and husband were trying to avoid facing the affair. It was thought that both could have benefitted from an open discussion of the infidelity (Brown, 1991).

The literature on revealing one's gay or lesbian identity to others suggests that having an open identity across all domains of one's life is associated with increased self-esteem (e.g., Cass, 1979; Hencken & O'Dowd, 1977; Ponse, 1978). In particular, coming out to one's parents is thought to be central to a lesbian's self-acceptance (Sophie, 1988). When a daughter hides her lesbian identity from her parents, "what closeness exists is considered pseudocloseness, because a relevant piece of information is missing" (Murphy, 1989, p. 49). Through revealing her lesbian identity, the daughter can dispel this sense of isolation from her parents (Roth, 1985).

However, many gay men and lesbians who have revealed their sexual orientation to their parents have reported that their parents disapproved of this fact (Chafetez, Sampson, Beck, & West, 1974; Jay & Young, 1979; Mendola, 1980). For example, in a survey of 20 lesbians in committed relationships who had come out to their parents, Murphy (1989) found that 70% of the women reported that their parents disapproved of their sexual orientation. At the same time, the women in that study also reported feeling a sense of relief that they did not have to conceal such an important aspect of their lives. Thus, Murphy (1989) concluded that the disappointing effects of coming out were outweighed by the positive aspects of having parents know about the nature of the couple's relationship.

Murphy (1989) recognized the costs to revealing one's sexual orientation to important others such as one's parents. She recommended that in therapy with lesbian couples, the therapist should help clients balance the effects of secrecy against the consequences of coming out in what she referred to as "identity management." In particular, Murphy suggested that therapists should help the couple prepare for the effects of coming out to parents and then help the couple grieve over the loss of "heterosexual privilege" in the family of origin.

Secrets about death and loss of a family member (e.g., through divorce) also are considered to be highly detrimental to family functioning. For example, after conducting two family therapy case studies, Evans (1976) concluded that the dysfunctional secret surrounding the death (or impending death) of a family member contributed to the development of symptoms in one child in each family. The secret seemed to intensify feelings of alienation among the members of each family. The interventions aimed at bringing the secret out in the open and resolving it seemed to lead to substantial improvements in the clients' functioning (Evans, 1976).

Paul and Bloom (1970) postulated that families in crisis, such as in the case of an imminent death, necessarily have secret or denied emotions that members often project onto one scapegoated family member. They proposed that such secrets need to be addressed directly in therapy (Paul & Bloom, 1970). A case of several families treated in multifamily group therapy illustrates this phenomenon (Paul & Bloom, 1970). For one family in the group, the suicidal thoughts of the son, John, were viewed by therapists as part of the effort to keep the secret of his father's terminal illness from the father: "It became apparent that the strain of hiding his serious illness from Mr. Henry had produced frantic behavior in the family, leading to reinforced scapegoating of John" (p. 43). With the therapist's encouragement, the family told the father of his illness. Although John's self-esteem improved after the disclosure, the family abruptly terminated treatment, and it was the parents who initiated the termination. The authors indicated that if the family had remained in treatment, they ultimately might have developed more functional and open patterns of communication.

In another case study, an asthmatic 10-year-old son revealed in play therapy his secret wish that his divorced father would come back to the family or would at least befriend his mother (Eaker, 1986). Shortly after such discussions, the boy's symptoms lessened. However, his 12-year-old brother subsequently developed some misbehaviors at home and at school. Despite these mixed findings, Eaker concluded that although families may resist revealing their secrets, they often are helped by such open discussion (Eaker, 1986). Play therapy is seen as a "cushion" that can allow the family to tolerate the anxiety associated with the revealing, for many families drop out after secrets emerge in standard family therapy (see Winnicott, 1980).

Researchers who have studied families with a member who has AIDS have found that the families expend a great deal of energy keeping the secret because of the social stigma associated with the disease (e.g., Bor, Miller, Scher, & Salt, 1991; Greif & Porembski, 1988; Miller, Goldman, & Bor, 1994). Two case studies of families dealing with HIV-infected members showed that, regardless of how the disease was contracted (i.e., because of hemophilia or sexual promiscuity), both families worked very hard to hide the disease (Miller et al., 1994). Moreover, extensive interviews of 11 significant others of person who died of AIDS showed that all 11 reported that there was some attempt to keep the AIDS a secret from others. Forty-four percent of the families of the AIDS victims reported that it was stressful for them to maintain the secrecy (Greif & Porembski, 1988). It seemed that the burden of the secret over time left these significant others feeling isolated from their own support networks (Greif & Porembski, 1988). Thus, Bor et al. (1991) suggested that to address feelings of loneliness and isolation, the therapist should attend early on in treatment to the secrecy of the illness and who could be told about the illness.

Greif and Porembski (1988) provided a more cautious perspective on revealing the secret of AIDS by suggesting that despite the potential strain of secret keeping, secrecy may be the best way for the person with the disease to cope with his or her immediate crisis. Dealing with the disease itself is so stressful that the patient may not have the resources to cope with the added strain of managing other people's reactions to the disease.

In sum, as with the psychoanalytic literature, there is a preponderance of theoretical work that suggests the revealing of secrets is a critical part of family therapy. Yet the evidence supporting this claim has been composed almost entirely of case reports, which offer limited generalizability. In the next section, I suggest some alternative ways of looking at the functions of secrecy in family therapy.

Alternative Perspectives

Some therapists have put secret keeping in the family in a positive light by describing shared family secrets as ones that strengthen the family boundaries from the outside world (Karpel, 1980). It is believed that the occasions in which the therapist must insist on disclosure of a secret occur when she or he learns that one family member is keeping a secret for the sake of another member (Karpel, 1980; Palazzoli & Prata, 1982). Such concealment places the therapist in an ethical dilemma that involves betraying the trust of the person kept unaware (Karpel, 1980; Palazzoli & Prata, 1982). These therapists systematically refuse to allow secret revelations, unless the revelations are made in the presence of the entire family in treatment. The content of the secret is not considered important, nor is the fact that there is a secret, but rather that the therapist is being offered a coalition against someone else in treatment, an undertaking that presumably can undermine treatment completely (Palazzoli & Prata, 1982).

Kaslow (1993) also has taken a stance that is contradictory to most family therapy perspectives on secrecy and on secret affairs in particular. She has complained that in some marriages full disclosure between the dyad is unduly expected or demanded. Thus, having an extramarital affair may seem like the only way for one partner to assert a sense of identity that is separate from that of the other partner (Kaslow, 1993). Kaslow has asked difficult questions of therapists, such as: Who are therapists to claim that they know some absolute truth about the benefits of revealing secrets? Should clients not be permitted to decide that for themselves?

A number of women have reported that their secret affairs actually added to their happy marriages and reawakened important aspects of their identities (Heyn, 1992). If a therapist requires that no secrets be kept between the couple, such a requirement may cause the partner who is having the affair to flee treatment rather than admit to the affair (Kaslow, 1993). Therefore, it has been suggested that the therapist should take a neutral stand in helping a client decide whether revealing a secret is in the client's best interest (Moultrop, 1992).

Some family therapists have postulated that keeping secrets is part of healthy family functioning, such as when parents appropriately keep private details of their sex lives from the children (Grolnick, 1983; Imber-Black, 1993), and some have even prescribed secret keeping for family members who have no secrets (Adams, 1993). Adams (1993) suggested that such withholding could revitalize romantic relationships by adding a sense of intrigue to them and could allow for differentiating relationships that are too enmeshed.

How the family interacts over a secret is considered more critical in determining its function in the family than the actual content of the secret (Imber-Black, 1993). One case study involved parents who were keeping the secret that the child's biological father had committed suicide (Adams, 1993). Because of the parents' fears of disclosure, the therapist intervened with questions targeting the functioning of the secret (e.g., who knew and who did not know the secret), rather than the revelation of the content itself. The recommendation was that the timing of the revelation would be best left up to the family (Adams, 1993).

In sum, although family therapy theorists generally have taken a negative stance toward keeping secrets in therapy, there are several note-worthy exceptions. Some therapists have even prescribed secret keeping and boundary setting in families where there is too little secrecy.

GROUP PSYCHOTHERAPY

Therapeutic Effects of Revealing Secrets

Yalom (1985) argued that actively hiding information from the thera-pist or other group members can take energy away from constructive revelation and group interaction. A premise of group psychotherapy is that over time when people are able to be open and honest with one another they can learn about themselves through getting feedback about how they come across to other people (Yalom, 1985). Theoretically, if they expend effort hiding a secret, they may become less spontaneous in their interactions with other group members and participate in the group on only a superficial level (Yalom, 1985). Moreover, revealing in group ther-apy is thought to allow clients to release and accept their feelings of shame surrounding their secrets (Asner, 1990; Silverstein, 1993; Winter, 1985). For example, in a psychotherapy group composed of six Jewish members, the members shared their secrets about the perceived stigma of being Jewish, and this sharing of shame seemed to build a sense of trust among the members (Klein, 1976). Keeping secrets also is thought to lead to subgroup formation and the premature termination of group members (Silverstein, 1993). In a case study of Jews and Arabs and their relationships in psycho-therapy training groups, the secrets the ethnic subgroups kept among themselves seemed to undermine the progress of the entire training group (Rippa, 1994). Presumably, a group becomes "stalemated" until a group member who has been keeping a secret from the group finally reveals it (Hough, 1992).

Hough (1992) stated that the "destructiveness of secrets in group psychotherapy is well known" (p. 107). As such, the revealing of secrets is often the focus of group psychotherapy (Bloch & Reibstein, 1980), espe-cially for problems such as incest abuse (Hays, 1987; Sturkie, 1983), alcohol-ism (Bingham & Bargar, 1985), bulimia (Asner, 1990), and dissociative disorders (Buchele, 1993). For example, Bingham and Bargar (1985) pro-posed that a central task in the group treatment "of the latency-age child from an alcoholic home is to encourage the child to share the dreaded family secret with other people in a supportive and trusting atmosphere" (p. 15).

In the group treatment of persons with bulimia, sharing secrets may attenuate the strong feelings of alienation and shame that often accompany bingeing and purging (see Asner, 1990). Case studies have pointed to secrecy and the "bad self" as one of six themes that emerge in group psychotherapy for women with bulimia (Weinstein & Richman, 1984). Across three groups, Weinstein and Richman (1984) found that of the 16 women who attended at least 20 meetings, 6 had totally stopped binge eating and 8 had reduced the frequency of bingeing. All group members reported improvements in self-concept, ability to identify feeling states, and experiencing a sense of control over their lives. The authors suggested that it was the elaboration of these themes, the foremost of which was secrecy, and their expression in the group that were therapeutic for these women.

Often clients reveal secrets in individual therapy sessions that they feel too ashamed of to share with the group. Wright (1990) described a case of a woman who remained silent during the first 2 years of group therapy, even though she had shared private material during individual therapy sessions. She ultimately emerged as a very powerful and articulate group member who simultaneously became successful in her management career. Wright (1990) attributed this development to providing her with the time she required to feel safe enough to share secrets with the other group members, and he noted that individual and group therapy work well together to prepare a client for essential revealing in the group context.

Alternative Perspectives

Some group psychotherapists believe that the content of the communication of secrets is generally irrelevant and that the goal of therapy must be to enhance mature communications among group members, not merely to provide an atmosphere for revelation of secrets and probing the unconscious (Kirman, 1991). Too much probing in group therapy may be counterproductive for psychiatric inpatient adolescents in particular (Amini, Burke, & Edgerton, 1978). Amini et al. (1978) observed 11 male and 11 female inpatients who attended numerous meetings with other patients and staff in which tensions between patients and staff were openly expressed. After 3 months, the adolescents reported that they felt overexposed and overunderstood. This need for secrecy and privacy seemed to be a function of the adolescents' stage of development and needing a sense of independence from adults (Amini et al., 1978).

Five time-limited (10 sessions) psychotherapy groups for women who were survivors of incest abuse provided additional examples of group members that may have been overexposed (Herman & Schatzow, 1984). During the middle sessions, the group leaders encouraged members to discuss in greater detail their incest experiences. Their aim was to help members resolve issues of secrecy, shame, and stigmatization associated with incest, but the effectiveness of this approach was questionable. At 6-month follow-up, although most of the women reported that they had higher self-esteem, some of them reported that sex was worse for them.

Revealing private information can have negative effects beyond what may occur during the group therapy sessions. Davis and Meara (1982) warned that it is difficult to ensure group confidentiality because group members are not bound by the same legal and ethical rules as are therapists. Group members may reveal the details of another group member's sexual encounters, private fears, and personal traumas to people outside of the group. Hence, group members may be hurt by their revealing secrets to other members (Davis & Meara, 1982).

In sum, as demonstrated above, a number of group therapists believe that it is important for clients to reveal their secrets to the group when they feel ready to do so. When group members do keep secrets, their withholding sometimes is seen as a form of acting out in the group sessions (Silverstein, 1993). Thus, the expectations therapists sometimes place on their clients may set clients up to feel what Bok (1982) has called a counterproductive "compulsion to confess" (p. 79). Members may come to feel guilty about violating the expectations for participation when they do choose to keep secrets, which could have negative effects on the members.

SUMMARY

The various theoretical approaches to psychotherapy offer different yet overlapping explanations for why revealing secrets in therapy is beneficial. Psychoanalysts believe that revealing secrets allows patients to avoid the neurotic symptoms associated with expending energy to keep undesirable impulses suppressed (e.g., Abraham et al., 1994). Confession allows a release of pent-up energy, or catharsis, and alleviates feelings of shame and guilt while presumably satisfying one's masochistic impulses (e.g., Gillman, 1992; Reik, 1945). Family therapists believe that addressing secrets helps the family avoid scapegoating a particular family member and allows them to deal with dysfunctional interactions among family members (e.g., Paul & Bloom, 1970). Addressing secrets can help alleviate the symptoms (e.g., hostile outbursts, depression, and suicide attempts) exhibited by the scapegoated family member that may have been caused by the strain of keeping the family secrets. In particular, in cases of revealing incest or other types of abuse, the victim can feel protected and less isolated from other family members and the outside world (e.g., Black, 1981; Hoorwitz, 1983). In group therapy, revealing secrets allows group members to have meaningful interactions with other group members and can provide them with a sense that they are not alone in their troubles (e.g., Yalom, 1985).

As noted above, the majority of the studies that have pointed to the importance of being open in therapy have been case studies. These case studies offer a good starting point for subsequent research, but they are too vulnerable to the biases of the researchers (who are likely to expect that secret keeping is problematic) to represent a conclusive perspective on secret keeping in therapy. I believe that it is now time to reevaluate the general efficacy of high levels of revelation in therapy and to assess when such revealing leads to positive or negative outcomes.

EMPIRICAL FINDINGS ON THE ROLE OF CLIENTS' OPENNESS IN THERAPY

A *Consumer Reports* (November, 1995) survey of roughly 4000 psychotherapy clients showed that the clients who "formed a real partnership with their therapist—by being open, even with painful subjects, and by working on issues between sessions—were more likely to progress" (p. 739). This finding resonates with the widely accepted belief that high levels of clients' openness are therapeutic. In the following paragraphs, I provide a close look at the empirical evidence on this position by reviewing the research on clients' disclosure and covert processes in psychotherapy.

CLIENTS' DISCLOSURE

Clients' disclosure is defined as the clients' revealing of thoughts, feelings, perceptions, or goals in therapy (Stiles, 1995; Stiles & Sultan, 1979). Researchers have frequently measured clients' disclosure by having observers rate these intentions and then tallying the percentage of utterances during the therapy session that qualify as disclosure (e.g., Stiles, 1995; Stiles & Sultan, 1979). Stiles and colleagues (McDaniel, Stiles, & McGaughey, 1981; Stiles & Shapiro, 1994; Stiles & Sultan, 1979) showed that across all types of psychotherapy, clients typically had disclosure intent for 40–60% of their utterances. This high percentage makes the therapy client role distinct from other expository roles in which disclosure occurs less frequently, such as the medical patient and the courtroom eyewitness roles (McGaughey & Stiles, 1983; Premo & Stiles, 1983; Stiles, Putnam, & Jacob, 1982).

The high percentage also supports the claim that "disclosure is at the heart of psychotherapy" (Stiles, 1995, p. 71). High levels of clients' disclosure are seen as a very promising indicator of good therapy process

(Stiles, McDaniel, & McGaughey, 1979). It is believed that by disclosing in the first person (i.e., using "I" statements), clients come to understand their own points of view and to take responsibility for their feelings and actions (Stiles et al., 1979).

There is surprisingly little research on the relation between clients' disclosure in psychotherapy and improvement rates. The research is scant on this relation because investigators often have used clients' disclosure itself as a measure, as opposed to a predictor, of outcome (e.g., Halpern, 1977; Kremer & Gesten, 1998; Strassberg & Anchor, 1977).

Perhaps surprising too is the fact that the research that has specifically studied levels of clients' disclosure in psychotherapy has not supported the assertion that more disclosure is associated with improved therapy outcomes. For example, in a study of 18 hospitalized schizophrenics, the patients who made fewer self-disclosures during a 10-week period of group therapy sessions actually showed greater posttherapy improvements in their intelligence test and Minnesota Multiphasic Personality Inventory (MMPI) scores (Strassberg et al., 1975). These patients also reported a greater reduction in symptoms than did their more disclosing counterparts (Strassberg, Roback, Anchor, & Abramowitz, 1975).

In another example, Stiles and Shapiro (1994) studied 39 clients who participated in the 16-session Sheffield Psychotherapy Project (Shapiro & Firth, 1987) and found that increases in clients' disclosures across a cognitive–behavioral phase of treatment were significantly correlated with increases in their depression. They also found that overall, after a combination of both interpersonal and cognitive–behavioral phases of treatment, there were no significant relations between (1) the percentage of clients' disclosures in sessions and (2) changes in symptomatology and depression scores from intake to termination (Sloan & Stiles, 1994; Stiles, 1995; Stiles & Shapiro, 1994).

Likewise, McDaniel et al. (1981) studied 31 male college students in time-limited psychotherapy and found that there was no relationship between the percentage of clients' disclosures in sessions (as rated by trained coders) and clients' improvement rates. These outcome ratings were made across intake, termination, and 1-year follow-up by the clients, their therapists (intake and termination only), and independent clinicians (McDaniel et al., 1981). In addition, in an investigation of the ongoing psychotherapy of 11 clients (seen at a university psychology department clinic or in private practice), Stiles (1984) found that the percentage of clients' disclosures was not correlated with the clients', therapists', and external raters' perceptions of session depth and value. The three raters also observed that the sessions that were unusually high in disclosure (relative to the clients' usual levels) were rough, unpleasant, difficult, and dangerous (Stiles, 1984).

Researchers studying encounter groups have shown that revealing powerful negative emotions to other group members can backfire with devastating effects. Lieberman et al. (1973) conducted what has been called "the best-executed study" on encounter groups among those studies conducted in the 1960s and early 1970s (Hartley, Roback, & Abramowitz, 1976). At the height of the encounter group movement, they studied 15 encounter groups composed of undergraduates led by well-trained, established facilitators with varying theoretical approaches. The groups were all limited to 30 hours and the members were assessed for their psychological functioning at the beginning of the groups, at group termination, and at 6- to 8-month follow-up. Their psychological functioning was assessed based on questionnaires given to the leaders, participants, co-participants, and observers and based on interviews with participants. Using a criterion of downward change on three or more measures, the researchers discovered that 16% of the group members showed negative change, including 8% that were considered "casualties" who showed more psychological distress and/or used more maladaptive defenses as a direct result of the group experience. One member even committed suicide after the second group therapy session. A main finding was that encouragement of confrontation and expression of anger were associated with negative outcomes for the targets of those attacks (Lieberman et al., 1973).

How can the fact that high levels of clients' disclosure are not linked to favorable therapy outcomes be explained? One possible explanation stems from the fact that the clients who are the most distressed tend to disclose the most (McDaniel et al., 1981; Stiles, 1984; Strupp & Hadley, 1979). Stiles (1995) has argued that because the most distressed clients tend to get the least out of therapy (see Garfield, 1994; Stiles, 1987), the benefits of high levels of disclosure are not apparent.

Another explanation is that it may be the quality (i.e., the intimacy and relevance), as opposed to the quantity, of clients' disclosures is related to improvement. There again, though, the evidence does not support the claim that more disclosure is better for clients. In a study of 53 clients, it was discovered that therapists' perceptions of their clients' "willingness to share material of a personal and intimate nature" were positively related to the therapists' ratings of the clients' improvement (Strassberg, Anchor, Gabel, & Cohen, 1978). However, an independent coder's ratings of the intimacy of clients' actual self-disclosure in the sessions were not significantly related to the therapists' ratings of the clients' improvement (Strassberg et al., 1978). Thus, it seems that therapists may perceive that intimate self-disclosure is related to outcome more than it actually is.

Another possibility is that therapy clients experience delayed benefits to disclosure that have not yet been documented in the client disclosure literature. Along these lines, Foa et al. (1991) observed a pattern of delayed benefits of exposure therapy when they compared the effectiveness of exposure therapy with other treatments for reducing posttraumatic stress disorder (PTSD) in female rape victims. The treatments used were prolonged exposure (PE), stress inoculation training (SIT), and supportive counseling (SC). The rationale behind using PE is that the fundamental task of any therapy for fear or anxiety is to identify the stimuli that elicit the fear and then provide corrective information to alter the memory structures (Foa & Kozak, 1986; Foa & Rothbaum, 1989). Exposure therapy theoretically allows habituation to the fear and may be especially useful when the disorder involves excessive avoidance of the problem (Foa & Kozak, 1986). Foa and Rothbaum (1989) offered the following illustration of the treatment of PTSD in rape victims:

> Seven sessions are devoted to re-experiencing in imagination the rape scene. Clients are instructed to try to imagine as vividly as possible the assault scene and describe it aloud. The exposure is paced to allow the most anxiety-provoking details only during the later sessions. The narrations are repeated in their entirety several times for 60 minutes per session and tape-recorded for playback at home at least once daily (p. 223).

Also it turned out in Foa and coworkers' (1991) study, SIT seemed superior immediately after treatment, but at the follow-up assessment, PE evidenced more lasting improvement. These researchers explained this pattern of results by stating that the procedures utilized in PE are expected to produce high levels of arousal initially because patients are asked to repeatedly confront the rape memory, and then these procedures are likely to cause permanent positive changes in the rape memory.

Likewise, in their experiments with undergraduates, Pennebaker and his colleagues (Harber & Pennebaker, 1992; Pennebaker, 1990; Pennebaker & Beall, 1986; Pennebaker et al., 1988) observed that even though participants often reported feeling worse after anonymously writing about traumas, they later felt better as a result of the revelation. Pennebaker (1990) suggested that to be reminded of pain may be painful initially, but then the writing may lead to the lasting relief associated with facing a trauma. It is important to keep in mind, however, that neither Pennebaker's nor Foa's experiments specifically involved a comparison of high levels of client disclosure with low levels of disclosure in therapy.

Summary

To date, there is no direct evidence that greater clients' disclosure in therapy is linked with posttherapy benefits. At this point, the most parsimonious interpretation of the findings on clients' disclosure is that greater disclosure is not associated with therapy benefits, even though this issue needs far more exploration. In the future, researchers will need to tease apart the effects of high levels of distress and high levels of disclosure on clients' improvement rates and will need to explore the long-term effects of clients' in-depth disclosures in therapy.

COVERT PROCESSES

Hidden reactions are those hidden thoughts and feelings that clients have in response to therapists' interventions, and things left unsaid are those thoughts and feelings that clients have during sessions that they do not share with their therapists (Hill et al., 1993). They are both covert responses to the therapy itself. Unlike hidden reactions and things left unsaid, secrets arise over a relatively long time period and do not necessarily stem from events within the therapy sessions (Hill et al., 1993). Secrets are major life experiences, facts, or feelings that clients do not share with their therapists (Hill et al., 1993). Because both hidden reactions and things left unsaid are very similar processes, I present the findings pertaining to them together in this chapter, followed by a separate discussion of secrets.

Hidden Reactions and Things Left Unsaid about Therapy

Researchers have shown that clients frequently conceal their reactions from their therapists and that the most of these hidden reactions are negative (Hill, Thompson, & Corbett, 1992; Regan & Hill, 1992; Rennie, 1985, 1992; Thompson & Hill, 1991). For example, using a qualitative methodology, Rennie (1985, 1992) discovered that clients acted cooperative and amiable, even when they were secretly questioning the therapists' interventions and feeling resentful toward the therapists. The clients did not reveal such negative reactions because they thought it was not their place to question the experts, felt it was immature to criticize the therapists when the therapy was generally appreciated, or were concerned that criticism might threaten the relationship with the therapists (Rennie, 1985, 1992).

It is commonly believed that therapists need to encourage clients to reveal private information that the clients might be disinclined to reveal (e.g., Hill et al., 1993; Stiles, 1995) and that therapists need to have greater awareness of clients' hidden negative reactions to therapists' interventions (e.g., Hill, Helms, Spiegel, & Tichenor, 1988a). If therapists are aware of such hidden reactions, then presumably they can make helpful adjustments to their interventions (e.g., Hill et al., 1988a; Rhodes, Hill, Thompson, & Elliott, 1994). Rhodes et al. (1994) conducted a qualitative study of

19 therapy cases and obtained results that were consistent with this idea. Clients recalled an event in therapy in which there was a major misunderstanding and described how it was or was not resolved (Rhodes et al., 1994). A good relationship, clients' willingness to assert negative feelings about being misunderstood, and therapists' facilitation of a mutual repair effort through maintaining a flexible and accepting stance were factors that were associated with resolution. In contrast, a poor relationship, therapists' unwillingness to discuss or accept clients' assertion of negative reactions to being misunderstood, and therapists' lack of awareness of clients' negative feelings were associated with unresolved misunderstandings and clients' terminating therapy (Rhodes et al., 1994).

Despite the intuitive appeal of a very open therapist–client relationship, only one (Wright, Ingraham, Chemtob, & Perez-Arce, 1985) of a recent string of correlational studies on covert processes in therapy (e.g., Hill et al., 1992, 1993; Kelly, 1998; Regan & Hill, 1992; Thompson & Hill, 1991) produced findings that are consistent with the results from the qualitative Rhodes et al. (1994) study. Fifteen graduate students participated in two experiential training groups that met for an hour and a half each week for 13 weeks as part of a course in group psychotherapy (Wright et al., 1985). After each group therapy class, the students rated their perceptions of the session. The more that members of a group therapy class withheld from other group members and the group leaders, the less satisfied they were with the group sessions. However, the reader should be alerted to the fact that the two first authors (i.e., Wright and Ingraham) were the two group leaders in that study, who had hypothesized that the participants would report less satisfaction in group meetings in which the participants held things back. As conscientious group leaders, the authors used the weekly feedback to try to enhance the subsequent sessions. Thus, because of the possible demands on the students to fulfill their instructors' expectations, these findings would need to be replicated in studies where the demand characteristics are less prominent before researchers could conclude that concealment in group therapy is associated with less satisfaction with the sessions.

In another study, Regan and Hill (1992) observed that the more things that the clients in time-limited therapy left unsaid with behavioral/ cognitive content (e.g., "I wasn't able to express all my feelings articulately," p. 169), the less satisfied the clients were with the amount of progress they had made in their sessions. However, there was a positive relation between the proportion of things with emotional content that clients left unsaid in therapy (e.g., "I was feeling anxious about being videotaped and having to review the videotape at the end," p. 169) and the clients' satisfaction with therapy and change (Regan & Hill, 1992). Furthermore, the therapists were aware of only 17% of the things clients left unsaid in sessions. When the therapists could identify what clients left unsaid, the therapists rated the sessions as being rougher, and the clients were less satisfied with the treatment (Regan & Hill, 1992).

The findings from several investigations involving therapists' and clients' reviews of video- or audiotapes of a just-concluded therapy session have pointed to a clearer conclusion concerning whether therapists' recognizing clients' hidden negative reactions is beneficial to clients (Hill et al., 1992, 1993; Thompson & Hill, 1991). Such recognition of negative reactions does not seem to be helpful.

In one of the studies, Hill et al. (1992) showed that clients in time-limited therapy reported that they hid more negative reactions (e.g., scared, confused, misunderstood) than any other kind of reaction. Although the therapists did guess that the clients were hiding reactions from them, the therapists typically could not identify when the clients were hiding their reactions or what the reactions were (Hill et al., 1992). Likewise, 65% of a sample of long-term therapy clients reported that they left something unsaid in therapy; yet only 27% of the therapists were able to match what the clients left unsaid (Hill et al., 1993). Perhaps most interesting is the fact that both Hill et al. (1992) and Thompson and Hill (1991) found that when therapists recognized the hidden negative reactions of their clients, the therapists themselves and the clients rated subsequent therapist interventions as less helpful than when the therapists did not recognize these reactions.

It is noteworthy that the therapists from two of these studies were able to match the clients' supported reactions (i.e., understood, hopeful, relief), which were not hidden, at a better-than-chance rate (Hill et al., 1992, 1993). Furthermore, Thompson and Hill (1991) found that the therapist's accurate perceptions of positive client reactions were related to the therapist's ability to generate helpful interventions. Hence, the findings from these studies taken together support the notion that it is fruitful for therapists to recognize positive, overt reactions from their clients. However, the findings clearly do not support the idea that therapy is enhanced by the therapists' recognizing covert, negative reactions from their clients. As Hill (1992) succinctly put it, "clients often hide negative reactions; and when therapists are aware of negative reactions, there may be negative effects on the therapy" (p. 689).

What causes therapists to be less effective after recognizing negative client reactions? Thompson and Hill (1991) suggested that therapists' becoming anxious after such recognition may be somewhat debilitating to them. Supporting this suggestion are the findings from a study involving graduate student counselors with varying levels of experience (Russell &

Snyder, 1963). Russell and Snyder (1963) showed that regardless of their level of experience, the counselors became more anxious when interacting with clients who acted negative and hostile than they did with clients who acted positive and friendly. I suggest that the therapists' subsequent ineffectiveness may stem from their responding to the clients in ways that reduce the therapists' own anxiety rather than in ways that help the clients. For example, a client angrily tells her therapist that she sees him as unsupportive and condescending for not backing her efforts at becoming a famous actress. He may respond by saying that the sessions are a good place for her to learn to manage her anger, and these words may make her even angrier because she perceives them to be an invalidation of her complaint.

Researchers in fact have shown that psychotherapists tend to avoid hostility that is directed at themselves more than when it is directed at others and that following therapists' avoidant reactions, clients are more likely to drop the hostile topic or change the object of the hostility (Bandura, Lipsher, & Miller, 1960). Given these findings and the ones described in the previous paragraphs, the statement that "perhaps counselors operate more effectively if they operate under a slight delusion that clients are reacting positively to them" (Regan & Hill, 1992, p. 173) seems to be an appropriate conclusion.

Secrets

As mentioned earlier, Hill et al. (1993) found that about half (46%) a sample of individual therapy clients who had received an average of 86 sessions reported that they were keeping secrets from their therapists. The length of time that the clients had spent in therapy was not related to the number of secrets they were keeping (Hill et al., 1993). Because so many of the clients reported keeping secrets from their therapists, Hill et al. (1993) recommended that "therapists might attend to methods to enable clients to feel more comfortable and less embarrassed about revealing secrets" (p. 285). However, secret keeping was not significantly related to the clients' satisfaction with therapy; and symptomatology was not assessed, so there was no evidence that clients who kept secrets actually had greater symptomatology.

In another study mentioned in previous chapters, I (Kelly, 1998) assessed the relation between secret keeping in therapy and symptom reduction, using a sample of 42 clients who had received an average of 11 therapy sessions. Much like the clients in the Hill et al. (1993) study, just over 40% of the clients reported keeping relevant secrets (i.e., ones that they perceived to be related to their presenting problems) in therapy. Most important is the finding that, after I statistically adjusted for clients' social desirability and self-concealment scores, keeping relevant secrets in therapy was associated with a reduction in the clients' reports of symptoms since the intake. (I adjusted for self-concealment scores to see whether keeping a particular secret from the therapist was associated with a reduction in symptoms above and beyond the effects of the client's general tendency to keep secrets.) This result supports the idea that clients who in practice do conceal some unfavorable aspects of themselves from their therapists may benefit more from therapy than those who do not (Kelly, 1998). I suggest that it is possible that these benefits occur because the clients who do keep secrets may have an easier time imagining that their therapists see them favorably (Kelly, 1998, 2000a,b). See the next chapter for an elaboration of this point.

SUMMARY

On the whole, the research on clients' disclosure and covert processes in therapy does not offer much support to the notion that a high degree of clients' openness is therapeutic. In a study of schizophrenics, researchers showed that more disclosure in group therapy was associated with less improvement on the MMPI and on measures of intelligence and self-reported symptomatology (Strassberg et al., 1975). In another study, more disclosure either was not associated with symptom reduction or was associated with an increase in depression (see Stiles & Shapiro, 1994). In addition, higher levels of clients' disclosure have been associated with negative therapy process ratings (Stiles, 1984). Likewise, even though in some case studies, therapists' lack of awareness of clients' negative feelings have been problematic (e.g., Rhodes et al., 1994), researchers conducting correlational studies generally have demonstrated that therapists' awareness of clients' negative covert processes is associated with negative therapy ratings from both the clients and therapists (e.g., Hill et al., 1992; Regan & Hill, 1992; Thompson & Hill, 1991). Moreover, I (Kelly, 1998) recently showed that clients' keeping relevant secrets from their therapists was associated with a reduction in symptoms, after the analyses adjusted for clients' social desirability and general self-concealment scores. Hence, the best conclusion that can be drawn from all this research is the qualified statement that higher levels of clients' disclosure are not helpful in therapy. The statement is qualified by the fact that there are gaps in the literature concerning whether (1) a greater depth of clients' disclosure is associated with therapy benefits and (2) there are long-term benefits associated with more disclosure in therapy. The statement also is qualified by the fact that in a number of these studies, researchers primarily used clients' self-reports to measure outcome. Even though it seems reasonable to ask clients about their perceptions of themselves if the aim of therapy is to promote positive self-concept change, it is still possible that clients either deliberately or inadvertently misrepresent their views of themselves on questionnaires.

CONCLUSION

Many theorists from various approaches to psychotherapy believe that high levels of revelation from clients, particularly carefully timed revelations, are important for therapeutic progress. This emphasis on very high levels of openness in therapy has its origins in Freudian psychoanalysis and may have been perpetuated by the humanistic/encounter group movement in the 1960s.

However, it is far from clear from the research on clients' disclosure and covert process that high levels of clients' openness are beneficial to clients (e.g., Hill et al., 1993; Kelly, 1998). There are even some occasions when the benefits of revealing secrets in therapy might outweigh the costs. For example, some case studies have shown that clients' families dissolved after the clients revealed a family secret in treatment (e.g., Saffer et al., 1979). Moreover, confidentiality is not a guaranteed part of treatment, particularly in family and group therapy contexts (see Davis & Meara, 1982), and clients may be wise to protect their self-interests of privacy (e.g., in cases of pending divorce and child custody battles) (McCarthy, 1995). In addition, the revelation of shameful secrets may cause some clients to flee therapy prematurely before deriving many therapeutic benefits (e.g., Kaslow, 1993). Again, though, these too are case studies, which offer limited generalizability, so it is unclear when and which clients should hold back from revealing negative material in therapy. Also, there have been no follow-up studies comparing cases in which clients did or did not disclose important secrets in therapy. It is possible, for example, that the clients whose families dissolve because of the revelation of a secret are better off than clients who live under the shroud of secrecy.

Perhaps future researchers could examine the characteristics of clients to see which clients fare best when they are very open with their therapists. One example of work that already has been done is the study by Amini et al. (1978), which demonstrated the negative effects of too much probing for psychiatric inpatient adolescents who may need more privacy than adults. Another promising line of research is that on counseling men (e.g., Good, Dell, & Mintz, 1989; Robertson & Fitzgerald, 1992). These researchers have gathered evidence that a task-oriented, as opposed to a more open, expressive, and feeling-oriented, approach to treatment could be more efficacious with individuals with a masculine gender role orientation.

In closing, I suggest that psychotherapy may create difficult situations for clients who are inclined to keep information private. The clients are likely to perceive that their therapists want them to divulge completely, yet hiding some negative aspects from the therapist may be healthier for them (Kelly, 1998). Specifically, it may allow them to maintain their own sense of personal boundaries and privacy (Hoyt, 1978; Margolis, 1966, 1974). Perhaps therapists who encourage clients to make careful decisions about what to reveal and what not to reveal in therapy are providing an opportunity for the clients to practice judicious revelation that could be invaluable to them in dealing with people outside of therapy.

CHAPTER 7

WHY OPENNESS MAY NOT BE THERAPEUTIC
A SELF-PRESENTATIONAL
VIEW OF PSYCHOTHERAPY

As outlined in the previous chapter, psychotherapy researchers have demonstrated not only that clients withhold personal information and reactions from their therapists but also that such discretion is associated with positive therapy process ratings and outcomes. The question I address in this chapter is, how can these puzzling findings be explained?

One obvious reason for the clients' concealment is that clients want to avoid making a bad impression on their therapists and might feel too ashamed or embarrassed to reveal their secrets (see Hill et al., 1993; Kelly, 1998). If the clients were to tell their therapists abhorrent things about themselves, the clients would run the risk of constructing unwanted images of themselves. For example, recall the case of a New York City woman who abused her 6-year-old daughter Elisa Izqueido, to the point of killing the child in 1997. It is reported that on one occasion, when Elisa had gone to the bathroom on the floor, the mother had turned her upside down to use her hair to mop up the excrement. If the mother were to tell her therapist about such an event, she may come to imagine, or accurately perceive, that the therapist sees her as a horrifyingly abusive, self-centered (or antisocial) person who is in need of deep-seated personality change. In everyday interactions, people normally refrain from telling others highly objectionable information about themselves because of fears that they will receive negative evaluations from others (see Kelly & McKillop, 1996). Presumably, in therapy, clients have the chance to reveal personal information without the fear of receiving negative judgments about themselves as people (e.g., Rogers, 1951, 1957). However, I contend that the same concerns that people have about looking bad in front of others when they say unfavorable things about themselves are likely to apply to interactions with a therapist. The concerns may even be accentuated because of the therapist's being an expert, knowledgeable audience (see Kelly, McKillop, & Neimeyer, 1991; McKillop & Schlenker, 1988).

After all, therapists are trained to diagnose their clients' pathologies, and they often make broad-based diagnoses such as labeling the clients as having narcissistic, borderline, or psychotic tendencies (see American Psychiatric Association, 1994). These diagnoses may not seem evaluative to the therapists, because they are trying to help their clients, but the clients would probably find such diagnoses to be very negative and demoralizing. In their study of brief therapy, Regan and Hill (1992) showed that therapists did indeed form diagnoses or explanations for their clients' behaviors that were very negative (as rated by judges) and hid these conjectures from the clients. Yet ironically, therapists secretly may deem the clients who express worries about being judged to have paranoid tendencies.

When one considers the fact that therapists form negative opinions about their clients, the findings that clients frequently hide negative material from their therapists and that high levels of clients' openness are not linked to greater therapy benefits (e.g., Hill et al., 1992, 1993; Kelly, 1998; Regan & Hill, 1992) begin to make sense. I suggest that the findings can be explained by conceptualizing psychotherapy as a self-presentational process. Specifically, clients may come to benefit from therapy by perceiving that their therapists have favorable views of them. Part of creating these favorable impressions can involve clients' hiding some undesirable aspects of themselves from their therapists, because if the clients are too revealing, they might perceive that their therapists view them unfavorably.

The components of this self-presentational perspective are as follows: (1) Clients present themselves in various ways to their therapists, (2) therapists then offer feedback to their clients *based on those self-presentations*, (3) this feedback can lead to the clients' altering their self-beliefs to be in line with the feedback, particularly because the feedback is from an expert audience, and (4) this shifting of self-beliefs followed by similar self-presentations and feedback may eventually lead to changes in the clients' self-concepts (i.e., in their relatively stable collections of self-beliefs) (Kelly, 2000a). At the heart of this perspective is the suggestion that clients may benefit from therapy through presenting themselves to their therapists in a manner that is believable to the clients and consistent with how they wish to be seen by the therapists (e.g., as decent people who are courageous enough to deal with their problems). The clients may then come to see themselves in these desirable ways by getting the impression that their therapists do see the clients in these ways.

More precisely, self-concept change should be enhanced when the clients find their self-presentations to be believable and when they *think* that their therapists find them to be believable. It really should not matter for clients' self-concept change whether the therapists do in fact find the clients' self-presentations to be believable (Kelly, 2000b). Nevertheless, there is still a good, separate argument for the suggestion that clients' self-presentations should be believable to their therapists. This argument comes from the evidence that extremely positively biased self-perceptions are not associated with favorable mental health (see Taylor & Brown, 1994). Having therapists find the self-presentations believable is likely to provide some indication that the clients' self-presentations are not too extreme or maladaptive, even if the therapists' actually believing the self-presentations may not be crucial for clients' self-concept change (see Kelly, 2000b).

In formulating this theoretical perspective, I have drawn from self-identification theory (Schlenker, 1980, 1986; Schlenker & Weigold, 1989, 1992; Schlenker, Britt, & Pennington, 1996) and from social psychological research on self-concept change. In this research, people have been induced to describe themselves in particular ways, such as extraverted or introverted, and then have reported changes in their self-beliefs to be consistent with their self-presentations (e.g., Fazio, Effrein, & Falender, 1981; Gergen, 1965; Jones, Rhodewalt, Berglas, & Skelton, 1981; Kelly et al., 1991; Kulik, Sledge, & Mahler, 1986; Rhodewalt & Agustsdottir, 1986; Schlenker, Dlugolecki, & Doherty, 1994; Schlenker & Trudeau, 1990; Tice, 1992).

There are two major sections of this chapter. In the first major section, I lay the empirical and theoretical foundation for the proposed view of psychotherapy. I describe the psychotherapy research findings that clients do try, either consciously or unconsciously, to manage the impressions that therapists have of them. This research is included because in order to embrace the notion that clients may benefit from presenting themselves in believable and desirable ways, one needs to see the evidence that clients do vary their self-presentations in therapy, depending on their goals for the interactions. I then present the social psychological research on self-concept change to illustrate how the clients' impression-management attempts can be a part of healthy client self-concept change. In the second major section, I indicate how the proposed self-presentational view of psychotherapy can explain previously confusing findings in the psychotherapy literature. In addition, I provide guidelines concerning (1) what might be optimal levels of self-revelation from clients and (2) how therapists might appropriately respond to these revelations. I conclude by addressing some alternative points of view and limitations of this theoretical perspective, as well as by offering new research directions.

SELF-PRESENTATION RESEARCH

CLIENTS' SELF-PRESENTATIONS

I take a broad view of self-presentation, defining it as showing oneself to be a particular kind of person for various audiences (See Schlenker, 1986). The types of self-presentations people perform are influenced by their goals for interacting with others, and the subsequent real or imagined feedback from others is thought to be an integral part of how people come to view themselves (Kelly et al., 1991; Schlenker, 1980, 1986, 1987; Schlenker et al., 1996; Schlenker & Weigold, 1992). For example, an adolescent client who has been physically abused by her father and who also has been engaging in shoplifting may discuss the abuse but may not tell her therapist about the shoplifting. Her private goal is to have her therapist see her as the survivor of abuse, not as a criminal. Researchers have shown in fact that counselors' judgments of clients are affected by the clients' initial self-presentations (Schwartz, Friedlander, & Tedeschi, 1986) and that such initial impressions are stable and may influence the course of therapy (see Wills, 1978).

This view of self-presentation contrasts with the more narrow traditional view of self-presentation as a way of strategically describing oneself to others in order to get one's needs met by them (Jones & Pittman, 1982). It also contrasts with the way the term has been used in the psychotherapy literature, where clients' self-presentations have been construed as counterproductive efforts to manipulate or influence their counselors (e.g., Friedlander & Schwartz, 1985; Haley, 1963; Strong, 1968). In that literature, therapists have been advised to offset such attempts because it is believed that if they are manipulated or controlled by their clients' self-presentations, then they will not be able to help the clients (Friedlander & Schwartz, 1985; Haley, 1963; Kiesler, 1981; Strong & Claiborn, 1982; Strong, 1987).

When self-presentation is viewed in this broad way, the implications are different for psychotherapy than would be the case with the more traditional view of self-presentation as a form of deliberate manipulation (see Friedlander & Schwartz, 1985, for a discussion of the latter). According to this broad view, clients cannot avoid trying to construct desirable images of themselves in the presence of their therapists; it happens automatically, much like communication itself (see Schlenker & Weigold, 1989). Clients may invest different levels of effort in constructing their desirable identities, may have varying degrees of awareness of their self-presentational motives, and may have additional motives for why they fail to disclose information to their therapists. Nonetheless, self-presentational motives are likely always to be present in the counseling relationship (see Schlnker & Weigold, 1989). For example, a man who is being treated for his shyness with women may be reluctant to bring up details about his having grown up in fear of his mother's cruel disciplinary tacts. He may fear that the therapist will weigh those details too heavily in developing a treatment plan (a non-self-presentational concern). At the same time, he may unconsciously wish to avoid having the therapist view him as weak or pathetic (a self-presentational concern).

In general, people put more effort into creating desirable impressions when the audience is significant (i.e., expert, powerful, attractive) and psychologically close to them (see Leary & Kowalski, 1990; Nowak, Szamrej, & Latane, 1990). People perceive clinical and counseling psychologists to be more knowledgeable about human behavior, expert, intelligent, caring, supportive, and helpful than their own peers (Kelly et al., 1991; McKillop & Schlenker, 1988). Therefore, it is not surprising that researchers have demonstrated in several in-the-field experiments that clients do try, either consciously or unconsciously, to manage the impressions that their therapists have of them (Braginsky & Braginsky, 1967; Braginsky, Grosse, & Ring, 1966; Kelly et al., 1996; McArdle, 1974).

For example, in early experiment with psychiatric inpatients, the instructions to a mental health assessment were manipulated so that a group of "short-timers" and a group of "old-timers" (i.e., patients who were most and least motivated to be discharged, respectively) believed that their mental hospitalization status would potentially be determined by the test, whereas a control group of old-timers received no such instructions (Braginsky et al., 1966). As it turned out, the experimental group of old-timers presented themselves as mentally ill and unprepared for discharge, whereas the short-timers presented themselves as self-insightful and ready for discharge. The control group of old-timers did not present themselves as poorly as the other old-timers nor as well as the short-timers.

In a similar experiment, hospitalized chronic schizophrenics were randomly assigned to groups who were led to believe that either their continued eligibility for open-ward status or their appropriateness for continued hospitalization would be determined by an interview (Braginsky & Braginsky, 1967). During the interview, the patients who believed that their open-ward status was in question presented themselves as healthy, whereas the patients who believed that their hospitalization status was in question presented themselves as mentally ill. Moreover, these self-presentations were convincing to a group of experienced psychiatrists

(Braginsky & Braginsky, 1967). The findings from this study and the Braginsky et al. (1966) study are relevant to the proposed view of psychotherapy, because they demonstrate that even patients with severe psychiatric disorders can and do vary how they present themselves to their therapists, depending on their goals for the interactions.

More recently, my colleagues and I conducted an in-the-field experiment in which we asked 92 therapy outpatients to complete intake forms that would be reviewed by either (1) their counselor, (2) their counselor who requested that they reveal their innermost thoughts in completing the forms, or (3) researchers who would not know who completed the forms (Kelly et al., 1996, Exp. 2). We found no significant differences in the outpatients' reports of well-being across the three conditions. Specifically, the outpatients in all three groups reported on average that they were depressed and had low self-esteem. However, the outpatients in the counselor conditions had higher social desirability scores than did those in the anonymous condition, suggesting that the clients attempted to look like good people to their counselors (Kelly et al., 1996, Exp. 2).

Moreover, at the end of that experiment, we asked the outpatients in all three conditions to rate anonymously how representative of themselves their self-descriptions had been. Interestingly enough, those who had described themselves as depressed tended to rate those self-descriptions as less representative of themselves than did the outpatients who had described themselves as nondepressed (Kelly et al., 1996, Exp. 2). Based on this finding, I (Kelly, 2000a) suggested that even when clients present themselves in a way that could be considered appropriate for the client role (i.e., as depressed individuals), they still are motivated to see those self-presentations as being unrepresentative of themselves. Hence, the findings support the idea that clients are quite similar to the general population in that people predominantly prefer to construct beneficial self-images and avoid detrimental ones (se Baumeister, 1982; Jones, 1990; Schlenker & Weigold, 1992; Tesser, 1988). A restriction to this claim is that a couple of the clients in that sample reported very high levels of depression and very low levels of self-esteem, and they rated these presentations as highly representative of themselves. Thus, there may be some clients who have such firmly entrenched depressive self-views that they would view feeling good about themselves as atypical, and those clients might be most resistant to change (see Swann, 1996).

SELF-CONCEPT CHANGE

What makes the fact that clients vary how they present themselves to their counselors so critical is that these self-presentations are likely to play a pivotal role in the way that the clients come to see themselves (Kelly, 1968). For example, imagine a client who sometimes experiences intense feelings of grief, anger, and hopelessness when thinking about his ex-wife's taking sole custody of their children and who at other times feels that he is recovering from these negative emotions. He may not be sure whether he is making progress in therapy. During his therapy sessions, he may emphasize the periods of relief and tell his therapist that he thinks that he is making good progress. Theoretically, the client should come to see himself as less grief-stricken and angry in part because he comes to perceive that the therapist sees him as making progress (see Quintana & Meara, 1990; Schlenker, 1986; Schlenker & Trudeau, 1990; Schlenker & Weigold, 1989).

Clients who incorporate desirable images into their self-beliefs should become even more likely to describe themselves in these favorable ways in the future. Such self-presentations followed by additional desirable feedback from the therapist—and additional internalization of that feedback—may ultimately lead to changes in the clients' self-concepts (see Schlenker, 1986; Schlenker et al., 1994). It is through this process of self-concept change that clients may come to benefit from therapy (see Kelly, 2000a). This idea is consistent with research that suggests that positive views of oneself promote psychological well-being, the ability to care about others, and the ability to engage in productive work (Taylor & Armor, 1996; Taylor & Brown, 1988, 1994; Taylor & Gollwitzer, 1995).

This characterization of how clients may experience self-concept change is compatible with the notion that the self-concept has some flexibility, as it has been depicted in the social psychological literature. Baumeister (1998) noted that although a person can have only one self, he or she can have multiple self-concepts across time. The self-concept may be seen as having a relatively solid nucleus of strong self-beliefs with a permeable periphery of weaker, more situationally dependent self-beliefs (Rosenberg, 1979; Schlenker, 1985, 1986; Schlenker & Trudeau, 1990). These flexible boundaries of the self-concept account for the idea that people can choose from a range of self-presentations that all would be considered representative of themselves (Schlenker, 1986; Schlenker et al., 1994; Schlenker & Trudeau, 1990).

Psychologists have long theorized that people form their self-concepts in part through presenting particular self-images to others and then receiving reactions to these images (e.g., Baldwin, 1992; Cooley, 1902; James, 1890; Mead, 1934; Goffman, 1959; Schlenker, 1980, 1986; Schlenker & Weigold, 1992). Whereas there is a fair amount of evidence that self-concepts are relatively stable and resistant to change (e.g., Maracek & Mettee, 1972; McFarlin & Blascovich, 1981; Sullivan, 1953; Swann, 1987, 1996; Swann &

Ely, 1984; Swan & Hill, 1982; Swann & Predmore, 1985; Swann & Read, 1981), there also is evidence that following their self-presentations, people do shift even strong self-beliefs (i.e., ones that people perceive themselves to hold consistently) in the direction of the self-presentations (e.g., Schlenker & Trudeau, 1990). In addition, research supports the idea that such temporary shifts in people's self-beliefs can affect their behaviors, which then can have an impact on their self-concepts (e.g., Fazio et al., 1981; Schlenker et al., 1994).

This process whereby people incorporate aspects of their self-presentations into their own identities often is referred to within the social psychological literature as *internalization* (e.g., Tice, 1992). Its meaning is similar to the way the same term has been used in the counseling literature to describe clients' incorporating feedback from others into their own self-images (e.g., Quintana & Meara, 1990). I review the research on this phenomenon next and discuss how the findings help explain how self-concept change may take place in clients.

Effects of Self-Presentations on Self-Beliefs

In a well-known series of experiments, Jones et al. (1981) studied the effects of strategic self-enhancement or self-deprecation on subsequent ratings of self-esteem. In the first two experiments, participants were induced to present themselves in either a self-enhancing or self-deprecating manner during an interview. The participants in the self-enhancing condition later showed increased self-esteem, whereas the participants in the self-deprecating condition showed decreased self-esteem. Likewise, in the third experiment, participants who played a self-enhancing role for the interview subsequently showed an increase in their self-esteem. However, this shift only occurred for participants who had the freedom to respond in-role to interview questions. It did not occur for participants who gave preplanned, in-role answers. In contrast, participants who played the self-deprecating role during the interview subsequently showed lowered self-esteem only in the condition in which they had been given a clear choice concerning whether to engage in the interview. Schlenker (1986) suggested that "participants in the Jones et al. (1981) study may simply have shifted their self-feelings in the direction of their behavior whenever the behavior seemed to be representative of the self" (p. 39). Schlenker proposed that the believability of one's self-presentations in general enhances the internalization of those presentations.

Applying this idea to counseling, I content that the likelihood that the client will come to internalize the therapist's feedback is enhanced when a client performs self-presentations that are within a range of self-presentations that the client finds to be believable. (It would probably help if the therapist also could find the client's self-presentations to be believable; what really matters, though, is that the client is able to believe the therapist's feedback.) Believability is likely to be important because if the client tells himself that he lied to the therapist and that the therapist would not view him in a desirable way if the therapist knew more accurate information about him, then the client should not be able to place much weight on what he perceives as the therapist's uninformed opinions of him (see Schlenker, 1986; Swann, 1996). By contrast, if the client feels that his self-presentations have generally been honest and accurate (despite his having kept some secrets), then he can internalize what he sees as the therapist's informed and favorable opinions of him (see Schlenker, 1986).

Another experiment showed that self-presentations affect subsequent self-appraisals, behaviors, and recall of events that are relevant to the self-presentations (Schlenker et al., 1994, Exp. 1). Participants were either instructed to present themselves as sociable during an interview or were given information about the importance of sociability but were not interviewed. All the participants then waited in a room with a confederate who later judged how socially each participant behaved (e.g., whether the subject initiated conversation, how much he or she spoke). For the final portion of the experiment, participants assessed their own sociability and a recall measure concerning experiences that had had (outside the laboratory) that were relevant to sociability. As it turned out, the participants who presented themselves as sociable later behaved more sociably, rated themselves as more sociable, and recalled more past experiences in which they had behaved sociably than did the participants who were not interviewed. Another noteworthy finding was that no differences emerged for assessments of features other than sociability, such as self-esteem, intelligence, leadership abilities, or affective states. Therefore, an important contribution of this study was that it demonstrated not only that self-presentations have an impact on self-evaluations and behaviors but also that these effects specifically correspond to the self-images that are portrayed in the self-presentations. The effects are not the result of a mere shift in affect or self-esteem (Schlenker et al., 1994).

In yet another experiment, participants were asked biased questions that elicited either introverted or extraverted responses (e.g., "What things do you dislike about loud parties?"; Fazio et al., 1981). After the interview, participants interacted with a female confederate who would later make judgments concerning how introverted or extraverted each participant appeared (e.g., how close he or she sat to the confederate, whether he or she initiated conversation). For the final portion of the experiment, participants rated how introverted or extraverted they perceived themselves to be. Results from both their own self-ratings and from the confederate's behavioral ratings of them supported the idea that participants internalized their earlier self-presentations. The authors interpreted their findings in terms of self-perception (Bem, 1972) and self-fulfilling prophecy (Merton, 1948). Specifically, they indicated that once an individual behaves in a particular manner, that person looks to her behaviors to determine her internal state and internalizes the very traits that the audience expected her to possess (Fazio et al., 1981). The authors concluded that such a change in her self-concept is apt to affect her behavior in future and different situations that do not even involve the original audience.

Audience Effects

Not only do one's self-presentations to various audiences influence one's self-beliefs but also the feedback from those audiences seems to play a central role in such shifts (Gergen, 1965). In one early study, participants were interviewed under the pretext that they would be helping to train interviewers who would later conduct large-scale personality surveys (Gergen, 1965). The participants were instructed either to present themselves accurately or to try to make a good impression. During the interview, they either received reflective reinforcement (e.g., "very good," "yes, I would agree") or did not receive reinforcement. After the interviews, participants in the reflective-reinforcement condition described themselves significantly more positively following their self-presentations than did participants in the no-feedback condition. Also, participants who had been instructed to try to make a good impression during the interview became even more positive in their self-descriptions following the interview than those who had been instructed to be accurate. Gergen (1965) concluded that these results support the contention that affirming social feedback is effective in elevating people's self-evaluations.

Even the mere presence of an audience can augment the internalization of one's self-presentations (Tice, 1992). In two studies, Tice (1992) demonstrated that participants who were induced to describe themselves in particular ways (i.e., as emotionally stable or emotionally responsive in Study 1 and as introverted or extraverted in Study 2) for an audience tended to bring their self-beliefs more in line with their self-descriptions than did participants who described themselves anonymously. This shift in self-beliefs extended to changes in the participants' behaviors. Moreover, these behavioral changes occurred even when participants were unaware that they were being observed (Tice, 1992, Study 2). In Study 3, participants were asked to describe themselves as introverted to a clinical psychology graduate student whom they would meet or whom they would not meet. In addition, they were instructed to draw on their own past experiences (self-reference group) or to read from a script of responses that was generated by the self-reference group (yoked group) in their portrayals of themselves as introverted. As it turned out, the participants who expected future interaction with the clinical graduate student internalized their self-presentations more than those who did not. Moreover, the participants who were in the self-reference group, as compared with those in the yoked group, experienced internalization to a greater extent, and the combined effect of these two manipulations on internalization was larger than either effect alone (Tice, 1992).

Researchers have demonstrated that the type of audience (i.e., clinical psychologists vs. untrained peers) has a differential impact on the internalization of self-presentations (McKillop & Schlenker, 1988). Participants were asked to present themselves in either a depressed or nondepressed manner for a videotaped interview and were informed after the interview that the audience who would be viewing their videotapes would either be clinical psychologists or general psychology students (McKillop & Schlenker, 1988). The participants who thought that clinicians would view their sessions became more depressed following a depressed presentation and less depressed following a nondepressed presentations. However, these shifts did not occur in the conditions in which participants thought that the untrained peers would view their session. The authors explained the fact that the clinical psychologist audience had a greater impact on participants' internalization than did the peer audience by saying that "the expert audience caused participants to focus their attention more on their prior self-presentation which, in turn, enhanced its impact" (p. 7).

The idea that audiences play a key role in the construction of the self-concept has particular relevance for counseling, which can be conceptualized as a process in which therapists use their role as an expert on human behavior to induce change in their clients (Strong, 1968). In one study, clients did seem to come to internalize the positive dispositions that they perceived that their counselors held toward them (Quintana & Meara, 1990). Forty-eight short-term therapy clients rated their counselors' dispositions toward them (e.g., "he/she shows understanding of my views and has empathy for me"), their dispositions toward the counselors (e.g., "I freely, openly disclose my inner self when he/she is listening"), and their dispositions toward themselves (e.g., "I tell myself things to make me feel bad, guilty, or unworthy") both after their first and last counseling sessions. After the initial session, clients' ratings of their dispositions toward themselves were quite different from (i.e., more negative than) their ratings of the counselors' dispositions toward them. But by the end of their treatment, clients shifted their self-views in the direction of

their therapists' favorable dispositions toward them, rating their dispositions toward themselves and their counselors' dispositions toward them to
be very similar. Quintana and Meara (1990) suggested that when clients
seek therapy, they may be looking for an interpersonal relationship that
will provide what they are not providing for themselves (e.g., self-
affirmation and self-empathy). They concluded that at termination, the
clients provided for themselves some of the positive actions and attitudes
that counselors had been providing for them. The findings from this in-
the-field study are especially important because most of the internalization
research has been conducted in the laboratory with undergraduates. These
findings support the possibility that the internalization processes observed
in the laboratory may indeed generalize to therapy contexts.

Summary

I have reviewed seven sets of findings on self-presentation to help
provide insights into how self-concept change may take place in clients.
First, psychotherapy researchers have shown that patients vary how
they present themselves to their therapists according to their goals for
the interaction (e.g., Braginsky & Braginsky, 1967; Braginsky et al., 1966;
McArdle, 1974). They present themselves as good people to their counselors at intake (Kelly et al., 1996, Exp. 2), and even when they appropriately (given their role as clients) present themselves as depressed, they
still view those presentations as relatively unrepresentative of themselves
(Kelly et al., 1996, Exp. 2). Second, it has been demonstrated in the laboratory that self-presentations have effects on subsequent self-appraisals,
such that participants change their self-beliefs to be in line with their self-
presentations (Schlenker et al., 1994; Fazio et al., 1981; Gergen, 1965; Kelly et
al., 1991; Jones et al., 1981; McKillop & Schlenker, 1988; Tice, 1992). Third,
these internalization effects have been shown to be enhanced when participants see their self-presentations as believable (see Jones et al., 1981;
Schlenker & Trudeau, 1990). Fourth, these effects extended to subsequent
behaviors with a new audience (Schlenker et al., 1994; Tice, 1992) and to
recall of events relevant to the self-presentations (Schlenker et al., 1994;
Fazio et al., 1981). Fifth, these internalization effects are specific to the types
of presentations performed and do not seem to be the mere result of shifts
in affect (Schlenker et al., 1994; Tice, 1992). Sixth, the presence of different
types of audiences (e.g., clinical psychology graduate student vs. a private
audience) has been shown to have different effects on the internalization of
people's self-presentations (McKillop & Schlenker, 1988; Tice, 1992). Finally, clients do seem to come to internalize the positive dispositions that
they perceive that their counselors hold toward them (Quintana & Meara,

1990). These findings taken together support my contention that clients may experience desirable changes in their self-concepts by presenting themselves to their therapists in a way that is both believable and consistent with how the clients wish to be seen by the therapists, as specified by the proposed self-presentational view of psychotherapy (Kelly, 2000a). This contention must be seen as tentative, however, because the experiments (i.e., involving random assignment to experimental and control groups) in which the internalization of one's self-presentations have been observed have not yet been tried in psychotherapy contexts.

SELF-PRESENTATIONAL VIEW OF CLIENT CHANGE

Although the findings that high levels of openness in therapy are associated with negative therapy process and outcome ratings are not consistent with popular mainstream theories, such as the psychoanalytic and client-centered approaches, they are consistent with the proposed self-presentational perspective. In particular, even though the therapy setting often is intended as a haven for extensive revelation (e.g., Freud, 1958; Fromm-Reichmann, 1950; Lodge, 1995; Rogers, 1951, 1957), many clients in practice do keep secrets from their therapists (Hill et al., 1993; Kelly, 1998). This practice may actually enable them to construct more desirable images of themselves before the credible, knowledgeable therapist audience (see Kelly, 1998). Likewise, therapists in practice do hide their negative clinical conjectures from their clients (Regan & Hill, 1992). Therapists have been rated as more effective when their clients do not know what are the intentions behind their therapists' interventions (Hill et al., 1993; Martin, Martin, Meyer, & Slemon, 1986; Martin, Martin, & Slemon, 1987). My contention is that therapists may be especially effective when instead of revealing their intentions, they spend more time reflecting desirable images of their clients and showing them that they are "on the client's side" (see Elliott, 1985).

Some may think that I am advocating deliberate manipulation attempts in therapy. However, what I am doing is describing what goes on in therapy: some censorship on the part of both clients and therapists. I am suggesting that these practices are not necessarily harmful and they may even be productive. In this section of the chapter, I identify the recent theoretical trends in the psychotherapy literature as a backdrop for understanding what the proposed self-presentational view of psychotherapy contributes to the psychotherapy literature. I then describe the self-presentational view and demonstrate how this view can explain previously counterintuitive findings from the psychotherapy literature. I offer several practical suggestions for how therapists and clients might interact and address some limitations and alternative perspectives to this view.

COMMON FACTORS IN PSYCHOTHERAPY

Psychotherapists today are faced with many choices for how to proceed with their practice because there are roughly 400 or more variants of psychotherapy available (Kazdin, 1986). There has been a recent trend for psychotherapists to use a mixture of approaches, with more therapists' identifying themselves as eclectic than any other orientation (Lambert & Bergin, 1994). This trend may have been spawned by meta-analytic studies that showed that therapy is more beneficial than no treatment and that no one approach is clearly superior to another (Lambert, Shapiro, & Bergin, 1986; Landman & Dawes, 1982; Smith, Glass, & Miller, 1980).

Researchers have moved away from trying to sort out which of these many therapies are the best, and some have tried instead to assess the "common factors" that may underlie the effectiveness of all types of therapies. These factors include the creation of hope, opportunity for ventilating feelings, interpretation of one's problems, support, advice, experimenting with new behaviors, and modification of cognition (see Frank, 1973; Garfield, 1980, 1991). In addition, some researchers have proposed that instead of thinking about therapy as an application of techniques to clients' problems, therapeutic processes may be best understood as reciprocal interactions between the therapist and client (e.g., Strong, 1995; Weinberger, 1995).

A meta-analysis of 24 studies of the therapeutic alliance, or working bond between clients and their therapists, showed that the quality of the alliance was a good predictor of clients' improvement, especially when the clients rated both the bond and the outcome of their therapy (Horvath & Symonds, 1991). Likewise, a review of what psychotherapy researchers across 50 publications believed to be effective elements of therapy showed the most frequently proposed factor (56% of all authors) was the development of the therapeutic alliance (Grencavage & Norcross, 1990). Similarly, in their review of the effects of a variety of therapist variables on counseling outcome, most of which showed no consistent relations to outcomes, Beutler, Machado, and Neufeldt (1994) concluded that "a warm and supportive therapeutic relationship facilitates therapeutic success" (p. 259).

Moreover, in their meta-analysis of paradoxical interventions, Shoham-Salomon and Rosenthal (1987) found that interventions such as symptom prescription were significantly more effective when the therapist used a positive connotation than a negative connotation. For example, a therapist who praises her depressed client for his tolerance of solitude and willingness to sacrifice for the good of others is more likely to help the client than a therapist who tells the client that he is using his depression as a passive–aggressive way of making others feel guilty (see Feldman, Strong, & Danser, 1982).

In his study of brief counseling, Elliott (1985) found that clients rated their therapists' encouraging a new perspective on the clients' problems as being particularly helpful, along with the therapists' offering understanding, assurance, personal contact, and so forth. Elliott (1985) concluded that what the clients deemed to be helpful went beyond the therapists' accurate following of client material to include the clients' experiencing the therapist as being "on the client's side" (p. 319).

I suggest that these central findings concerning what is helpful in counseling (i.e., the therapists' offering a new perspective on the clients' problems and a warm, supportive relationship—showing clients that the therapists are on their side) all support the notion that it is crucial for therapists to convey that they view their clients in ways that the clients would find to be desirable. This idea is the basic tenet of the proposed self-presentational view of psychotherapy. The notion that therapy should be conceptualized as an interactional process (e.g., Strong, 1995) also is entirely consistent with the proposed view of psychotherapy.

THE PROPOSED SELF-PRESENTATIONAL VIEW

The findings that clients who successfully conceal their negative reactions tend to rate their sessions as more helpful (e.g., Hill et al., 1992) and that clients who keep relevant secrets from their therapists experience greater symptom reduction (Kelly, 1998) are congruent with the proposed self-presentational view of psychotherapy. If the therapist knows extremely objectionable things about the client, then the client could come to imagine or in some cases accurately perceive that the therapist is reflecting undesirable images of the client during therapy sessions. Supporting this idea is the finding that several of the clients in the Kelly (1998) study indicated that the reason they did not share their secrets was that they were afraid the therapist would see how little progress they had made. What was especially interesting about the Kelly (1998) study is that a number of the clients' secrets involved lies about verifiable facts, such as their continuing to have a sexual relationship with an abusive former partner, yet they still experienced more symptom reduction than did the clients who were not keeping any relevant secrets. It may be that those clients saw their presentations as more representative of themselves, even though they lied about some things, than did clients who were completely truthful about their shortcomings. People tend to see more desirable self-presentations as more truthful (Schlenker, 1980, 1986), as did the undergraduate and client participants in the Kelly et al. (1996) experiments who rated their more depressed self-descriptions as relatively atypical of themselves.

As described earlier, the components of the self-presentational view of psychotherapy are as follows: (1) Clients perform various self-presentations in therapy; (2) therapists then offer feedback to their clients based on those self-presentations; (3) this feedback can lead to clients' internalization of their self-presentations; and (4) this internalization process followed by similar self-presentations and feedback eventually may lead to changes in their self-concepts (Kelly, 2000a). In addition, the internalization effects resulting from counselor feedback may be enhanced by the perceived expertise of the counselor (McKillop & Schlenker, 1988). Hence, in the proposed view of psychotherapy, I emphasize the importance of clients' making good decisions about what to reveal to their therapists that will enable the clients to construct believable and desirable images of themselves before this expert audience.

In the proposed view of psychotherapy, I have identified both the self-presentations and the corresponding feedback as important to self-concept change, even though the relative contributions of each to self-concept change are not known (see Kelly, 2000b). Emphasizing both, as opposed to only the self-presentations, provides a parsimonious yet comprehensive accounting for the evidence. Any theory of psychotherapy should account for the interactional nature of the relationship between the therapist and client, including the feedback from the therapist (Strong, 1987). Even though clients keep some undesirable information from their therapists, they also tend to disclose their problems such as feelings of low self-esteem and depression (e.g., Kelly et al., 1996). Because the clients are performing so many negative self-presentations to an important audience, one might expect that they would emerge from therapy worse off than if they had received no treatment. However, researchers using meta-analytic techniques (e.g., Smith et al., 1980) have shown that the average treated therapy client is better off than 80% of the comparable untreated clients (i.e., those on a waiting list for treatment). Why do clients fare so well in therapy despite their many negative self-presentations? I argue that it is the real or imagined favorable feedback from the therapists, along with corresponding favorable changes in the clients' self-presentations, that can explain how clients come to experience positive self-concept change (Kelly, 2000a).

Explaining Previous Findings

This self-presentational view of psychotherapy provides an explanation for many of the puzzling findings that have surfaced in the psychotherapy literature. First, it may help to explain the findings that therapists and clients typically do not agree about how the clients are faring in therapy (e.g., Caracena & Vicory, 1969; Fish, 1970; Hansen, Moore, & Carkhuff, 1968; Hill, 1974; Hill et al., 1988b; Kurtz & Grummon, 1972; Tichenor & Hill, 1989; Truax, 1966; see Lambert & Hill, 1994, for a review). This perplexing set of results makes sense when one considers that clients may tend to view therapy as more helpful when their therapists are giving them favorable feedback (as specified by the proposed view of therapy). In contrast, the therapists may be more inclined to view therapy as effective when their clients are in the midst of divulging painful or troubling personal information (as specified by the more traditional approaches to therapy).

Along these lines, when Eugster and Wampold (1996) identified what therapy process variables (e.g., patient and therapist involvement in a session, patient and therapist comfort, etc.) 114 therapists and 119 of their patients perceived to be important in their separate evaluations of how useful or good a psychotherapy session was, the researchers discovered that there were significant differences between the two groups. For the therapists, it was their perceptions of their own expertness that were most closely associated with their ratings of how good a session was. However, for the patients, it was their perceptions of how much the therapists seemed to like them and seemed to act outside of the constraints of the therapist role (i.e., the therapist real relationship) (Gelso & Carter, 1994) that were most closely related to how good the patients thought a session was. At the same time, the therapists' perceptions of the therapist real relationship were negatively associated with their evaluations of a session when all the process variables were considered simultaneously. What this pattern suggests is that therapists may be underestimating how much liking their clients plays a role in helping them. It is possible that if therapists change their ideas about what is helpful to clients, there will be greater congruence between therapists' and clients' ratings of therapy outcome.

Second, Hill and colleagues (Hill et al., 1992; Regan & Hill, 1992; Thompson & Hill, 1991) have demonstrated that therapists and clients rate therapists' interventions as less helpful when the therapists accurately perceive their clients' hidden (usually negative) reactions or things left unsaid. This counterintuitive set of findings may be explained both by the fact that clients who express negative reactions to their therapists tend to be less well liked (Russell & Snyder, 1963) and by the fact that clients who are less well liked by their therapists tend to have poorer therapy outcomes (Ehrlich & Bauer, 1967; Nash et al., 1965; Stoler, 1963). In essence, when clients express negative reactions, their therapists may like them less and therefore the therapists may be less inclined to express desirable views of the clients. These clients may benefit less from therapy because they are missing out on the most crucial element of the proposed view of psychotherapy: getting desirable feedback about themselves from their therapists.

The notion that clients should be concerned about creating desirable images before their therapists challenges traditional forms of psychotherapy that conceptualize "working" or "experiencing" in therapy as involving clients' revealing previously hidden private information (e.g., Klein, Mathieu, Gendlin, & Keisler, 1969; Klein, Mathieu-Coughlan, & Kiesler, 1986; Stiles et al., 1979). However, this idea is quite consistent with the rationale behind solution-focused therapies, which depict the delving into client problems as an unnecessary part of treatment (e.g., Chevalier, 1995; Fish, 1996; O'Brien & Pilar, 1997; Okun, 1997). It also is consistent with other cognitive–behavioral approaches in which the therapists emphasize the positive aspects of their clients in an effort both to reinforce (or shape) the clients' optimistic statements about themselves. These efforts are designed to enhance the clients' feelings of being capable of solving their problems (e.g., Kyrios, 1998). The proposed view of psychotherapy may be seen as offering a deeper level of understanding these processes of change, because it addresses the prospect that the clients' perceptions of *how their therapists view them* may come to influence how the clients view themselves.

Certainly, clients do need to reveal personal information to be able to receive helpful interpretations of their difficulties. At the same time, the fact that some clients keep secrets from their therapists may not be problematic. The following are descriptions of what might be appropriate levels of revelation from both clients and therapists.

What Clients May Benefit from Revealing

An example of a series of self-presentations that a client might happen to make that would be both believable and desirable is a case of a 31-year-old married male client who is dealing with the problem of sexual compulsion. He has been extremely promiscuous, including having a one-time sexual encounter with a 12-year-old girl. The man does not tell his female therapist about the sex with the girl, because he fears that the therapist will view him unfavorably. However, he does discuss his feelings of being out of control of his sexual impulses, giving examples of numerous sexual affairs and offering the therapist enough information to provide useful, believable interpretations of his difficulties. By hearing disclosures about his sexual behavior only with adult women, the therapist may be better able to reflect desirable images (i.e., of a client who is a good person who is struggling to control his sexual impulses) to the client.

As therapy gets under way, the client is likely to receive both helpful and nonhelpful interventions. If he happens to acknowledge how much he has gained from receiving the helpful interventions even though he also acknowledges the times when he feels that he is not making progress, the therapist should be able to continue to reflect desirable images to the client. I am speculating that this result would take place both because she likes her client more (see Ehrlich & Bauer, 1967; Nash et al., 1965; Stoler, 1963) and because she feels less anxious about her ability to help the client (see Russell & Snyder, 1963; Thompson & Hill, 1991) than if he just complained about the lack of progress. A client who presents himself in this way may come to internalize the view of himself as one who is making good progress. In contrast, if such a client happens to emphasize the times when he feels that he is not making progress and finally admits to the statutory rape, *he may perceive that the therapist sees him as a therapeutic failure and child molester, and thus may come to see himself this way.*

How Therapists May Benefit Their Clients

Therapists are likely to help their clients by assessing early on in therapy what kinds of images the clients perceive to be desirable. The therapists then can encourage the clients to make desirable statements about themselves. Simultaneously, the therapists can encourage the clients to reveal some of their problems, so that the clients will see their therapists as having informed, believable opinions of them. The therapists can respond to those revelations with interpretations that convey a new perspective on the clients' problems (see Elliott, 1985; Hill, 1992) and can reflect desirable (see Shoham-Salomon & Rosenthal, 1987) and believable images back to the clients. For instance, the therapist of the 31-year-old male client who is dealing with feeling out of control of his sexuality may ask how the client likes to be seen by others. The client may respond by saying that he likes to be seen as a leader who gets what he wants, as one who can take care of others, and as someone who is accommodating and flexible. He also may indicate that his lack of control over his sexual impulses makes him feel as though he is a weak, immoral person. The therapist might interpret this revelation by stating that expressing his

---

*It may seem unethical to indicate that it is acceptable for clients to hold back information from their therapists. Imagine, for example, if he continues to have sex with children. In that case, the therapist could have prevented the very negative outcome by eliciting the client's disclosure of the statutory rape and reporting it to the authorities. However, many therapists already do prompt clients to avoid revealing acts that the therapists would have to report to the police by informing the clients at the outset of therapy about the legal limits of confidentiality (see Roback & Shelton, 1995).

sexuality may stem from the lesson he learned as an attractive adolescent that strong men get what they want through physical means, including offering sexual gratification to women. The therapist also might state that it is because of the success of his seductiveness as an adolescent that he continues to be seductive as an adult and at the same time he now has the flexibility to change his behavior.

The therapists may enhance positive self-concept change by explicitly, as opposed to subtly, giving believable and desirable feedback to clients. Therapists already do this in practice in the form of interpretations, and research on brief therapy techniques shows that this is one technique that has been linked with positive outcomes (Hill, 1992).

An implication of applying these principles to psychotherapy is that therapists could offer therapy on a relatively short-term basis, because such therapy would not necessarily involve the delving into buried material such as unconscious intrapsychic conflicts and repressed memories. A practical consideration for therapists today is that even though there are many long-term approaches to therapy and even though some clients may need longer-term treatment, research shows that the average client who begins treatment (such as a client who has prepaid mental health insurance) is likely to receive only about six sessions (see Garfield, 1994). Moreover, when clients and their therapists are asked to indicate how many sessions the clients will need, the clients' estimates are lower, and it is these lower estimates that are the better predictor of how many sessions the clients actually receive (see Garfield, 1994).

BOUNDARY CONDITIONS

In this section, I describe several key boundary conditions to the proposed self-presentational view of psychotherapy to help the reader determine when it makes the most sense to think of therapy in these self-presentational terms. After reading the example about the child molester, the reader might misconstrue what I am saying to mean that therapists should encourage clients to hide essential information from them that may be necessary for their treatment. For example, my theoretical perspective may be mistakenly seen as encouraging people with personality disorders to practice manipulating their therapists as they do others. I am not suggesting that clients should set out deliberately to hide information from their therapists that could be essential to their recovery. Rather, I am suggesting that *if the clients feel that the revealing of a specific piece of information about themselves would make it very difficult for them to imagine that the therapist still sees them favorably, even if the therapist offers them support, then it is acceptable for the clients to discuss the themes as opposed to the details of those revelations.* That way, the clients will still be able to talk about relevant information without making the sessions so embarrassing that they may not want to return to face their therapist. For example, a client who is struggling to overcome her debilitating fear of germs may benefit from describing her oven-cleaning, floor-scrubbing, and hand-washing behaviors in an effort to work through these rituals, as long as describing these rituals would not make it difficult or impossible for the client to imagine that the therapist views her favorably. In contrast, a client like Jeffrey Dahmer who has dissected people and animals for pleasure may want to discuss his "sadistic urges" and leave out the ghastly details. The problem with revealing these details is that such revelations are likely to leave the client feeling that the therapist sees him in undesirable ways, given that society in general condemns such individuals.

The proposed view of psychotherapy seems to place a fair amount of responsibility on the client to decide what he or she is comfortable revealing. The fact is that clients already do censor their revelations in practice (Hill et al., 1993; Kelly, 1998), and there is some evidence that clients who engage in such censorship do better in therapy (Kelly, 1998). The therapist can facilitate the client's decision making by reminding the client that it is his or her choice to reveal private information and that complete openness is not a requirement of successful therapy. It might make the clients who do hide information from their therapists feel relieved that they are not necessarily undermining their treatment.

At the same time, there are likely to be some clients who begin therapy with very negative self-views surrounding specific transgressions or humiliating events, and who over time could come to believe that their therapists would still have favorable impressions of them, even if the therapists knew about these transgressions. Such clients might benefit tremendously from disclosing these events and then hearing the therapists' challenges of their negative self-views surrounding the events. An example might be a woman who enters therapy feeling extremely ashamed and guilty about having shaken her crying baby brother when she was 10, leaving him with mild brain damage. She does not reveal this event until after a year of psychotherapy, whereupon the therapist reframes the event in a believable way by telling her, "You weren't capable of thinking like an adult when you were 10, and you need not hold yourself accountable for what you did as a kid. In fact, that event may have played a role in why you have developed to be so kind and considerate of others now."

What should therapists do when clients choose to reveal information about themselves that the clients find to be desirable but that therapists and others would find to be abhorrent or maladaptive? An example might be a client who feels that she would enhance her existence by taking revenge on all the men who ever abused her. Another example might be a former police officer who believes that he knows what is best for the city and is considering shooting all the local drug dealers. Should therapists be restricted to reflecting what their clients believe to be desirable? Or should therapists try to change these potentially destructive beliefs? A potential solution lies in the therapist's ability to reframe the clients' articulated desirable self-images in such a way that the clients still find them to be desirable and believable, and that the therapist perceives as not being problematic. For instance, the therapist might accurately perceive that what underlies the desire to kill the drug dealers is the wish to become a respected, powerful hero. The therapist can convey his respect for the client by saying, "You have been a wonderful leader who has protected the community for many years. At the same time, being a great citizen involves your upholding the law. How can you put your energies into helping the community within the limits of the law?"

Rogerian therapists have encountered similar challenges with the notion of their offering unconditional positive regard to antisocial clients who may express the desire to harm others. Rogers's (1951, 1957) theory accounted for such concerns by assuming that human nature is essentially good and if clients were truly left to their own accord, they would not choose to do such things. I also think that it would be unlikely for clients to articulate such antisocial goals to their therapists. However, rather than my assuming that this censorship stems from the fact that humans are essentially good, I am postulating that the great majority of clients would have some idea that their therapists would not view such a statement in a positive way. Because therapy is an interactional process, the clients' initial expressions of desirable self-images would already be affected by what the clients anticipate that the therapists would view as favorable. Thus, it would be a small minority of clients who would articulate such destructive tendencies or maladaptive self-beliefs. In such cases, the therapists would most likely need to concentrate on modifying the grossly impaired judgment or potential dangerousness of the clients.

How can therapists inoculate clients against receiving feedback about themselves from other important audiences outside the therapy context that contradict the desirable feedback from their therapists? For example, if a therapist reflects images to a female client that she is effervescent and intelligent, yet the client's boyfriend sees her as somewhat frivolous and simpleminded, then the client may have a difficult time maintaining the benefits of the favorable feedback from the therapist. She may come to see that she feels better about herself after being with the therapist than with her boyfriend, and thus may want to break off the relationship with the boyfriend. In such cases, the effectiveness of therapy might be enhanced either by including the fiancé in the therapy and helping him provide her with desirable feedback or by supporting the client's decision to disentangle herself from relationships with people who view her in ways that she finds to be particularly undesirable.

One last boundary condition is that the clients are most likely and perhaps are only likely to benefit from their desirable self-presentations when those presentations are within a range of self-presentations that are believable (see Schlenker, 1986). For instance, imagine a client who tells his therapist that he is no longer snorting cocaine, yet he comes to therapy with dilated pupils. The client is not likely to benefit from that declaration because both he and the therapist will know that it is not true. But if that same client says that he has recently snorted a few lines but is really trying hard to give it up (and he sees that statement as being truthful at least some of the time), he is likely to fare better than if he flatly states that he does not think that he will ever be able to stop (a statement that he also sees as being truthful at least some of the time).

ADDRESSING ALTERNATIVE PERSPECTIVES

In this section, I address a number of anticipated counterarguments and limitations to the proposed self-presentational view of psychotherapy.

Having One True Self

The suggestion that clients' concealing some undesirable aspects of themselves may be helpful to them seems to be an endorsement of dishonesty that may impede the therapeutic process. One might argue that if a client really thinks that his or her "true self" is undesirable, then he or she should be as revealing as possible with the therapist to allow the therapist to help negate those self-beliefs. However, a core assumption that I am making in proposing this self-presentational view of therapy is that clients have multiple self-beliefs that all fall within a fairly wide range of believable self-views, as opposed to "one true" self-concept. Many of the ways that they describe themselves to their therapists fall within this range of believable self-presentations (see Schlenker, 1986; Schlenker et al., 1994; Schlenker & Trudeau, 1990). The findings from a study in which four clients interacted with four experienced therapists and presented themselves very differently to the therapists (Fuller & Hill, 1985) are congruent with this idea:

> [T]he helpees presented different problems to the four counselors which in effect made them appear to be different persons in each pairing. Undoubtedly, each person has a range of possible behaviors and behaves in a specific way depending on what he/she perceives to be appropriate in that situation. (p. 337)

As such, it does not seem unreasonable to suggest that clients present those aspects of themselves that are consistent with how they would like to see themselves.

Recognizing the Concealment

Even though therapists and clients do conceal the unfavorable reactions that they are having from each other, they might have concerns that the other person will be able to recognize the concealment. This concern is offset by research that shows that even highly trained psychiatrists are generally very poor, at least initially, at determining when others are concealing thoughts and feelings from them (see Ekman, 1991; Ekman & O'Sullivan, 1991). Moreover, as mentioned earlier, therapists in both long-term (e.g., Hill et al., 1993) and short-term therapy contexts (e.g., Regan & Hill, 1992) can identify what their clients leave unsaid only a small percentage of the time. Therapists are typically able to guess accurately *that* their clients are hiding reactions from them, but they are unlikely to be able to detect what their clients' specific hidden reactions are or when they are having them (Hill et al., 1992). Therefore, I suggest that even though their concealment may be detected as a general or nonverbal level, clients and therapists should not feel overly concerned that they will be "found out" about a specific omission, simply because it is difficult to detect things that go unsaid.

Not Caring What the Therapists Think

One might argue that some clients, such as those who are highly reactant (i.e., motivated to restore their freedom) (Brehm & Brehm, 1981; Dowd, Milne, & Wise, 1991) or high in private self-consciousness (i.e., "tuned out" to the expectations of others and behaving in a way that is consistent with internal motivations) (Buss & Briggs, 1984; Carver & Scheier, 1985), are not likely to be influenced by what their counselors think of them. However, Baumeister (1982) gathered a substantial amount of evidence that although reactant people often appear to be behaving in a manner that is consistent with their internal standards, many times they are actually behaving in a manner that is intended to create the public impression that they are independent and autonomous (see Baer, Hinkle, Smith, & Fenton, 1980; Heilman & Garner, 1975; Heilman & Toffler, 1976). Likewise, Schlenker and Weigold (1990) found that participants who were high in private self-consciousness were highly responsive to feedback from a partner (who regarded them as dependent or independent) and publicly changed their attitudes in an effort to make themselves appear autonomous. In contrast, participants who were high in public self-consciousness shifted their attitudes to conform to whatever the expectations of the partner were (i.e., they altered their attitudes to appear to be independent or dependent, depending on the expectations of the partner). Schlenker and coworkers (1996) interpreted these findings to mean that audiences matter for everyone, although different people have different goals when relating to others.

Gaining Catharsis

One also could argue that clients need the opportunity to ventilate pent-up negative emotions (i.e., experience catharsis) as a means of feeling better about their problems. This expression may include the clients' telling their therapists how much they resent the therapists and disapprove of the therapists' attempts to help them. However, as described in Chapter 5, the therapeutic effects of catharsis have not been supported generally (see Bohart et al., 1976; Ebbesen et al., 1975; Kelly et al., 2001; Stone et al., 1995; Tesser et al., 1978).

Contradicting Assumptions of Openness

The notion that clients might benefit from censoring particularly heinous details from their revelations in therapy seems to contradict psychodynamic approaches to trauma that involve remembering and working through images of very negative or traumatic experiences. It also seems to contradict some cognitive–behavioral therapies that require the revelation of what can be excruciating or humiliating details. For example, as described earlier, in exposure therapy, clients who have experienced traumas are asked to "relive" the trauma in an effort to modify the memory structures that may serve as blueprints for the client's fear behavior (Foa & Kozak, 1986; Roa & Rothbaum, 1989). Foa and colleagues have demonstrated that exposure therapy resulted in reduced anxiety-related symptomatology (Foa et al., 1991; Kozak, Foa, & Steketee, 1988) and in more organized thoughts surrounding a rape trauma, which were negatively correlated with depression (Foa et al., 1995). At the surface, these findings seem to disaffirm the proposed view of psychotherapy, but I suggest that there is no real contradiction because the successfully treated women in these studies probably were able to continue to imagine that their therapists viewed them favorably after their revelations. A central principle of the proposed view of psychotherapy is not that deliberate censorship on the part of the clients is necessary, but rather that such censorship is recommended if revealing a certain piece of information about themselves would make it difficult for the clients to imagine that their therapists still see them in desirable ways.

Truly Knowing the Clients

Some clients may feel bad or guilty about leaving out objectionable details about themselves. They might feel as though the therapists could not really know them unless the therapists knew about these very negative things. However, does truly knowing someone mean knowing the worst things that they have ever felt or done? In most circumstances other than in therapy settings, people would feel that if others knew such bad things, those others would actually get the wrong impression of them. People tend to believe that more favorable things about themselves are more, not less, truthful (see Kelly et al., 1996; Schlenker, 1980, 1986).

One reason why clients might feel guilty about not telling their therapists everything may be that they assume that the therapists have the expectation of full disclosure, rather than that the clients have some justifiable worry that they can only be truly known with full disclosure. Virtually all the clients in my study on secret keeping in psychotherapy (Kelly, 1998) indicated they believed that the therapists expected full disclosure from them. In nontherapy relationships in which there is no expectation of full disclosure, it would be unlikely for the clients to worry about whether they would still be accepted if the others knew about their "skeletons in the closet." For instance, imagine a 57-year-old married woman who enters therapy for the treatment of depression and feelings of alienation from her colleagues. After a few sessions, she begins to ruminate over whether she should tell her therapist about the time in high school when she experimented with sex acts with multiple partners and even spent a night in jail for indecent exposure. She feels both ashamed about this promiscuous phase and guilty about not disclosing this information to her therapist. She has never told her husband about the experience because they have had a long-standing agreement that their previous sexual histories are private matters that do not need to be discussed. In the context of her marriage, she considers it to be her right to keep such information private; she feels reasonably close to her husband and does not ruminate over what he would think of her if he knew about the previous promiscuity. But in the therapy setting, her belief that the therapist expects revelation might cause her to feel bad and exert energy in hiding that information from the therapist.

It is understandable that clients would believe that therapists expect full disclosure. After all, as discussed earlier, modern psychotherapy has grown out of Freudian psychoanalysis, wherein the fundamental rule of psychoanalysis required patients to be as open about themselves as possible (Freud, 1958; Hoyt, 1978). In addition, most counseling psychology graduate programs have been heavily influenced by Rogers's approach to therapy (Hill & Corbett, 1993), in which the therapeutic ideal involves high levels of openness on the part of both clients and therapists (Rogers, 1951, 1957). My intention in proposing the self-presentational view of psychotherapy is to stimulate a rethinking of common assumptions about how psychotherapy leads to change. Specifically, I believe that if clients and therapists could change their expectations that therapy be a place for full disclosure, then clients might not have those bad feelings about whether the therapists would still accept them if the therapists knew about the most negative things.

Manipulating the Therapist

The assumptions underlying the proposed self-presentational view of psychotherapy are directly opposed to the common notions of client self-presentations as maladaptive manipulations (e.g., Strong, 1987). According to Strong's (1987, 1995) interpersonal influence theory of counseling, the beginning of therapy is based on patients' perceptions of their own ineffective self-presentations. The therapist's role is to cause a change in the client's understanding of his or her environment in order to promote a change in the client's self-presentations. In inducing such change, the therapist needs to avoid being manipulated and to offer clients a validation of the clients' most feared selves: to give clients unexpected responses while also supporting them (Strong, 1987, 1995). However, there is no evidence to back the idea that giving clients feedback that they would fear or find to be undesirable is helpful, and there is a good deal of evidence that providing clients with feedback that suggests that the therapist is "on the client's side" is helpful (see Elliott, 1985).

Just Providing Social Support

Yet another concern may be that this view of psychotherapy is a euphemistic reframing of the idea that therapists are merely available to provide social support, just as friends do. In actuality, friends often do not provide effective social support when people really need it, such as when victims disclose details surrounding the death of a loved one (e.g., Davidowitz & Myrick, 1984). Moreover, as Swann's (1996) research has demonstrated, people's romantic partners and close friends often make attempts to confine them to acting in a manner that is consistent with the views that the friends already have of them. These views may be undesirable to the individuals, thus leaving them feeling trapped and unable to improve themselves. Because of the therapists' training in providing desirable and believable feedback, they should be better able to offer such feedback consistently than friends should be. Given the status associated with the expert role of the therapist, the therapists' feedback should have an even greater effect on internalization of these positive self-images than should friends' feedback (see McKillop & Schlenker, 1988).

Having a Weak Empirical Foundation

Finally, there are some constraints to the empirical foundation of the proposed view of psychotherapy. As mentioned earlier, the internalization experiments from the social psychology literature have yet to be attempted in psychotherapy contexts. Moreover, because most of the studies from the clinical–counseling literature on clients' openness have been correlational in nature and conducted in short-term therapy contexts, the conclusions that can be drawn from them are restricted. For example, because of the correlational design of my secret keeping in psychotherapy study (Kelly, 1998), I could not establish that keeping relevant secrets in therapy *caused* the symptom reduction in clients. I merely showed that there was a relationship between these two variables. Also, because the clients in my study were in relatively short-term therapy, it is not known whether this relationship would hold up in long-term therapy contexts (Kelly, 1998). In essence, more research is needed to see if the proposed view of psychotherapy predicts future psychotherapy outcomes in both short- and long-term therapy settings. Experiments could involve randomly assigning clients to therapists who either encourage the revelation of highly objectionable material or explain that such material is private and up to the client's discretion to reveal. The experimenters could then assess the extent to which clients do indeed reveal or conceal very undesirable information about themselves to their therapists. The clients' perceptions of the desirability of the therapists' feedback also could be measured to see how those perceptions are related to both short- and long-term changes in the clients' self-images.

Such studies would provide answers to some of the questions surrounding the intriguing phenomenon of one's making multiple self-presentations to important audiences over time. To date, multiple self-presentations followed by audience feedback and internalization of that feedback over time have not been adequately assessed by self-presentation researchers (McKillop, 1991). These studies could assess how crucial it is for one's self-presentations to be believable when interacting with respected audiences, namely the therapists. It has been postulated that believability is important in predicting whether one will internalize one's self-presentations (e.g., Schlenker, 1986), but the parameters of this believability have not been clearly delineated in the context of multiple, complex self-presentations. The fact that one study (Kelly, 1998) showed that clients who actually lied to their therapists about verifiable facts fared well in terms of their experiencing symptom reduction begs the question of what kinds of complex sets of self-presentations are seen as most believable and most likely to be internalized. Are these self-presentations ones that are completely free of lies or ones that include them? The interaction of clinical–counseling and social psychological research offers enormous potential for understanding self-concept change more fully.

CONCLUSION

Many therapists encourage their clients to discuss undesirable aspects of themselves in therapy in an effort to help the clients change those aspects. Yet given the social psychological research on self-concept change (e.g., Fazio et al., 1981; Jones et al., 1981; Rhodewalt & Agustsdottir, 1986; Schlenker & Trudeau, 1990; Tice, 1992), I suggest that this process of extracting undesirable information actually may be encouraging clients to solidify these negative images of themselves. Clients attempt to manage the impressions therapists have of them and they view more depressed self-presentations as less representative of themselves (e.g., Kelly et al., 1996). They also seem to come to internalize the images that they perceive their therapists have of them (Quintana & Meara, 1990). Assuming that the goal of therapy is to induce positive self-concept change and that the self-concept change processes observed by social psychologists generalize to psychotherapy contexts, it may make sense for counselors to reflect images of their clients that the clients would find to be desirable and representative of themselves.

There certainly will be times when clients reveal undesirable information about themselves to their therapists. I am not suggesting that the therapists' responding in a normalizing, accepting manner is harmful. The therapists should accept and reframe the clients' problems, just as the research suggests (e.g., Elliott, 1985; Shoham-Salomon & Rosenthal, 1987). What I am adding here is the suggestion that when clients reveal terrible things about themselves, such as their having savagely beaten their children or cruelly neglected their pets, the clients are likely to imagine that their seemingly accepting therapists are judging them negatively. In fact, therapists do make very negative clinical conjectures about their clients' pathologies (Regan & Hill, 1992). Because therapists tend to use the details of the clients' problems to develop themes or explanations for the problems during the course of therapy, perhaps the clients themselves could focus on the themes to their problems. This option might be preferable to the clients' running the risk of perceiving that they have horrified their therapists with the details of their sometimes abhorrent actions.

In a nutshell, instead of suggesting that clients deliberately should hide information from their therapists to make a good impression, I note that clients do conceal information as part of either conscious or unconscious attempts to construct desirable images before the therapists. There is evidence that such discretion does not necessarily undermine their treatment (and it may even enhance their treatment). In those cases when clients believe that their therapists could not view them favorably after hearing particularly heinous revelations, I suggest that it is acceptable for the clients to discuss themes as opposed to details of those revelations. At the same time, there may be some clients who enter therapy with very negative self-views surrounding specific transgressions or humiliating events and who may come to believe that their therapists would still have favorable impressions of them even if the therapists knew about these events. I suggest that these clients might benefit immensely from telling the therapists about these events and then hearing the therapists' challenges of their negative self-views surrounding the events (Kelly, 2000a). Rather than my suggesting that clients show only positive self-images to their therapists, I propose that it is acceptable for clients to use some discretion based on their perceptions of the therapists' responses (Kelly, 2000a,b).

So, what is the main contribution of this reconceptualization of psychotherapy? For some therapists, such as some cognitive–behaviorists, adopting this new perspective would not change anything that they do in therapy. These therapists already spend time reinforcing the favorable statements that clients make about themselves. Yet for other therapists, such as some classically trained psychoanalysts, adopting this view would dramatically alter their efforts at eliciting the patients' expression of repressed or buried negative material. I see the major contribution of this proposed view not so much as offering a new set of techniques for intervention, but rather I see it as offering a new understanding of how psychotherapy works. Specifically, in the proposed view, I emphasize the role of the therapists' opinions of their clients in effecting client change. I also see this proposal as a challenge to the idea that therapy is a place where clients are supposed to be completely revealing of themselves. If both therapists and clients could change their expectations that revelation is required of the clients, then the clients could potentially benefit even more from psychotherapy. This idea gets back to what I described in Chapter 1 as the distinction between secrecy and privacy. If clients can view the material that they keep from their therapists as private material that the therapists do not expect access to, then the clients may not feel bad about keeping such information from their therapists.

In closing, I suspect that social psychologists (e.g., Arkin & Hermann, 2000) are likely to accept the notion that the "masks" people wear when interacting with others are a very important part of who they are and will become. In contrast, clinical and counseling psychologists (e.g., Hill, Gelso, & Mohr, 2000) may reject much of the evidence that people's self-concepts are influenced by what they show others. For example, Hill et al. (2000) stated that "we believe that one of the most important things that can happen in therapy is for therapists to accept clients deeply for themselves *as they are*" (p. 498). Besides rejecting my position, Hill and coworkers' comment also implies that self-concepts are more stable than they actually may be, given that people seem to have multiple self-concepts over time (see Baumeister, 1998).

Perhaps social psychologists and clinical-counseling psychologists will seem to have in common a greater sense of optimism about the psychotherapy process than what I have described here. For example, Arkin and Hermann (2000) recommended that clients fully describe their very negative behaviors, so that their therapists can help them see their behaviors as separate from the broader implications of who they are. Likewise, Hill et al. (2000) seemed to suggest that therapists can and do truly hold their clients in high regard, even when the clients reveal heinous details. I have seemed somewhat less optimistic in suggesting that being judgmental is part of human nature and that clients are rightfully sensitive to the possibility that their therapists may form very negative clinical conjectures about them if the clients say really heinous things about themselves (see Regan & Hill, 1992). The key message from my proposal is that at its core psychotherapy is an interpersonal endeavor that is not exempt from social processes that characterize normal discourse. In particular, people put on masks when interacting with others. These "masks" have important implications for how they perceive that others see them and for how they see themselves. I am optimistic that once this perspective is acknowledged, scientists can exploit what is known about self-presentation to enhance their understanding of psychotherapy and potentially increase its effectiveness (Kelly, 2000b).

DILEMMAS TO REVEALING SECRETS AND THE ROLE OF THE CONFIDANT

Now I move away from a discussion of revealing secrets in therapy to the broader dilemmas associated with revealing secrets to confidants in general. In Chapter 4, I noted that some critics thought that the ending of the film "Secret and Lies" seemed false, because it is unlikely that people would so readily accept some secrets that they previously considered loathsome. In particular, the movie simplistically depicted uneducated people with racist beliefs readily embracing a family member from a different race. What the movie illustrated is that the responses of the confidant should largely determine whether someone will benefit from revealing a secret; all was well in the end because the family could accept the secret. However, in real life, some confidants cannot be expected to accept some secrets, and they might even be obligated to reject the revealer.

For this reason, I believe that pop star Michael Jackson made the right decision never to admit to having behaved inappropriately with a 13-year-old roughly a decade ago. If he did admit to any sexual misconduct, then (among other problems) the people who spend time with him like Elizabeth Taylor would be put in an awkward position; they would seem as though they were defending a child molester. In the absence of a confession, his friends and fans can avoid being compelled to act on what would become public knowledge and avoid having to reject the pop star. Likewise, I think Hillary Clinton made the right decision never to admit knowing about the Monica Lewinsky affair as it was happening. If she had, people might see her lack of intervening on behalf of the young intern as a sign of weakness or immorality.

What strings these examples together is that revealing secrets typically has a social context in which the revealer is held accountable for the disclosed information, unlike the revealing that went on in the writing experiments described in Chapters 4 and 5. As John Steinbeck (1961) wrote, "The king told his secrets down a well, and his secrets were safe. A man who tells secrets or stories must think of who is hearing or reading, for a story has as many versions as it has readers" (p. 89). Unfortunately, researchers studying disclosure have not paid enough attention to the role of the confidant (see Kelly & McKillop, 1996). For example, even though Pennebaker (1990) acknowledged the importance of having an accepting confidant when disclosing private information, at one point he approvingly described a psychiatrist's advice to a traumatized woman "to tell her story to *everyone* she met" (p. 37, italics added). I contend that such a recommendation can backfire with stigmatizing secrets and that the health benefits of revealing most likely would be wiped away if one were to reveal to an indiscreet, judgmental, or rejecting confidant. The experiments on the health benefits of revealing were extremely important in capturing the mechanisms that can lead to recovery from troubling secrets. However, the reader must keep in mind that the participants in those experiments were assured that their responses would remain confidential and anonymous. Thus, it is difficult to extend the findings from such experiments to everyday situations. "In the laboratory we have inadvertently provided people with a safe, nonjudgmental haven for disclosure" (Pennebaker, 1990, p. 65). Such protection allowed participants to avoid the usual worrying about whether their confidants would tell all their peers about their wrongdoings, shortcomings, or private embarrassments, or would reject them outright (Kelly & McKillop, 1996).

Along these lines, there is evidence that although supportive social networks often reduce distress in individuals experiencing stressful life events, unsupportive or critical social networks can increase it (e.g., Abbey, Abramis, & Caplan, 1985; Holahan, Moos, Holahan, & Brennan, 1997; Kennedy, Kiecolt-Glaser, & Glaser, 1990; Lepore, 1992; Major et al., 1990; Major, Zubek, Cooper, Cozzarelli, & Richards, 1997; Manne, Taylor, Dougherty, & Kemeny, 1997; Rook, 1984; Vinokur & Van Ryn, 1993). Moreover, disclosure is not necessarily associated with positive outcomes for the revealer (e.g., Cutrona, 1986). As Lepore, Ragan, and Jones (2000) put it, "Disclosure seldom occurs in a social vacuum, and its effects may be contingent on the social context" (p. 500).

Despite the health benefits of anonymous and confidential revealing described in Chapter 4, some research has not supported the idea that sharing emotions (i.e., joy, affection, sadness, fear, anger, and shame) with others is helpful or curative (Rime et al., 1991a). In that series of studies, although an overwhelming majority of the participants reported being highly motivated to share their emotions with others (especially their most disruptive emotions), the amount of social sharing participants had engaged in was not associated with their recovery over time from the disruption caused by the emotion (Rime et al., 1991a). Moreover, as described in Chapter 1, Finkenauer and Rime (1998a) found that shared and nonshared events did not differ on ratings of recovery.

In this chapter, I describe the trade-offs associated with revealing secrets to other people. It can feel good initially to unburden secrets, and there is evidence that a revealer can become more physiologically relaxed even when there are dire consequences to revealing, such as when a criminal discloses crimes to a police officer (see Pennebaker, 1985). However, once the revelation has occurred, the revealer has to live with the consequences. The following quote from the confession of the infamous serial killer Edmund Emil Kemper illustrates this dilemma:

> I went in to some detail today on these cases, and I wish I hadn't now. (Referring to statements made earlier in the day during a telephone conversation he had with police officers after surrendering.... While waiting for units to arrive and take him into custody, Kemper spoke erratically, offering to the officers fragmented details as evidence that he was, in fact, the "Co-Ed Killer.") It's been bothering me more and more, just thinking about it, and then talking about it today with someone else. It just really didn't have an effect then. I told the officers that when I am talking about something like that, from being in Atascadero for so long, and talking about very serious things and very tender things, bothersome things, I get kind of calloused, you know, where I don't show emotion. I just talk, getting the thing out, and later on it hits me. I spent the whole afternoon in there trying to decide whether I was gonna climb the bars and jump off or hang myself.... You know, I was really very seriously depressed about the whole damn thing, so I was hoping that—I suppose you're going to have something to go on prior to going back and really getting something laid out. (Edmund Emil Kemper, III, http://serial-killers.virtualave.net/kemper.htm. Retrieved November 21, 2000.)

I not only explore the negative and positive consequences of revealing personal secrets in this chapter but also discuss how the confidant's qualities and responses to a revelation can have a great impact on the revealer. The chapter ends with a description of the characteristics of the ideal confidant.

NEGATIVE CONSEQUENCES OF REVEALING SECRETS

SECRET IS REPEATED TO OTHERS

One of the biggest problems associated with revealing personal secrets is that confidants often cannot be trusted to keep the secrets or to protect the revealer's identity. In a recent pair of studies, college students reported that when someone had disclosed an emotional event to them, they in turn revealed the emotional disclosure to others in 66 to 78% of the cases (Christophe & Rime, 1997). This high rate of revealing occurred despite the fact that the participants were intimates of the original revealers in 85% of the cases (Christophe & Rime, 1997). In addition, when the original disclosure was of a high emotional intensity, as compared with when it was of a low or moderate emotional intensity, the participants indicated that they had shared it with others even more frequently and had told more people. On the average, they told more than two other people. In another study, Christophe and Di Giacomo (1995) found that in 78% of the cases in which the original event was disclosed to others, the name of the original revealer was explicitly mentioned. These researchers recommended that if people do not want others to learn about their emotional experiences, then they should avoid sharing the experiences with others altogether.

It is important to note, however, that a limitation to these studies is the participants were asked about their having heard emotional episodes, as opposed to secrets. The participants were not explicitly asked if they had actually been sworn to secrecy when listening to the emotional episodes. It is possible that explicitly telling a listener that confidentiality is expected would discourage the person from repeating the secret. In addition, due to the reciprocal nature of revealing personal information, it is likely that intimates know personal information about each other that could be used as a form of assurance that neither will disclose the others' secrets.

Petronio and Bantz (1991) conducted a study that more directly assessed the lack of discretion surrounding the revelation of secrets per se. They found that although the phrase "don't tell anybody this" is intended to keep one's confidant from revealing one's secrets, that may not be the case (Petronio & Bantz, 1991). A large group of undergraduates completed questionnaires consisting of scenarios that varied in terms of how private (high, moderate, or low) the information transmitted was and whether the phrase "don't tell anybody this" was used in revealing the information (Petronio & Bantz, 1991). A substantial percentage of both revealers and confidants indicated that they expected the confidants to repeat that information to others, which suggests that revealers are aware of potential ramifications from disclosure. What was most interesting about these findings was that whether or not the phrase "don't tell anybody this" was used, confidants were more likely to repeat information than the revealers expected when that information was either highly or moderately private. Again, these findings reinforce the idea that revealing one's secrets may be ill-advised because the confidant may repeat the secret to others, especially when the secret is "juicy."

REVEALER'S IDENTITY CAN BE UNDERMINED

The danger to having others know one's stigmatizing secrets is that his or her very identity may be undermined by such exposure. For example, if a man reveals an especially humiliating secret (or his confidant reveals it) to his friends, then his friends become witnesses and reminders of this humiliation. The following example is a true story, but the names and some of the details have been changed to protect the identity of the real-life "Jeff": At age 30, Jeff still struggles to get the love of his life out of his mind 3 years after she abruptly abandoned him. The abandonment was particularly painful, because it came suddenly only 21 days after she moved into his apartment. He had returned home to find her clothes gone, with no note of explanation. When he was later able to track her down, she had moved to a new city and told him that she was not ready for a deep commitment. She said that perhaps when they were both 40 there could be some sort of rekindling of the relationship. Jeff still recounts those excruciating details to his work associates, whom he considers to be close friends. Those who met her agree with Jeff that she is one of the most beautiful, intelligent, and mesmerizing women they ever met. One of the friends, Alex, noted that after seeing that Jeff was capable of being in a relationship with such an extraordinary woman, he became convinced that Jeff was "capable of attracting even supermodels." When Jeff tells his story to new close friends, he quotes Alex on this point.

Somehow these revelations to his friends do not seem to make Jeff feel any better, even 3 years after the breakup. As compelling as it is to tell others about personal struggles and emotional events in general, in this case the problem has now become the revelations themselves. Because his friends now know about this failure experience and because their opinions matter a great deal to him, Jeff feels that he has to win her back to show them that he is not a failure and that he truly is capable of attracting the very most desirable women. If he had never admitted that he was so devastated by that experience and had never mentioned what happened, it is possible that he would have recovered by now. In essence, just the sight of his friends reminds him of the rejection, and it is the friends' seeing him as a failure that is so troubling. As Jeff explained to me, even if he acts as though he is interested in a new woman, he imagines they know that he is still suffering.

Jeff recently made a new friend who has never met this woman and who, despite hearing about the painful breakup, expresses his belief that Jeff is masterful at wooing women and that Jeff actually is over the woman. It is this friend toward whom Jeff gravitates for his salvation, because this friend has managed to discount the revelation given his own lack of belief in any such romantic things.

What Jeff's story illustrates is that a problem associated with telling others especially humiliating events and receiving undesirable feedback from them is that as described in the previous chapter, people may form their identities through interacting with others (e.g., James, 1890; Cooley, 1902; Mead, 1934; Goffman, 1959). They incorporate their public self-portrayals into their private self-beliefs in a process known as internalization (Tice, 1992). Researchers have shown that public expressions can influence private self-beliefs regarding depression (Kelly et al., 1991), sociability (McKillop, Berzonsky, & Schlenker, 1992), independence (Schlenker & Trudeau, 1990), and global self-esteem (Jones et al., 1981; Rhodewalt & Agustsdottir, 1986).

Although social psychologists know that internalization occurs, they have offered at least three different major explanations for why it occurs. The explanation I emphasized in the previous chapter is what Schlenker et al. (1994) referred to as *public commitment to an identity*. Specifically, after people perform various self-presentations, they then incorporate either real or imagined feedback from the audience (e.g., therapist or confidant) to construct their self-images because publicly claiming to be particular kinds of people obligates them to behave consistently with those identities (e.g., Schlenker, 1980; Schlenker et al., 1994). If people fail to be consistent in their self-descriptions and actions, they may face the very negative consequences of being seen as unreliable, hypocritical, or self-deluding, or as liars (Kelly, 2000b). Along these lines, Schlenker et al. (1994) found that participants who described themselves as sociable to one person actually behaved more sociably with a new person. Schlenker and co-workers argued that the new person would give feedback that is consistent with more sociable self-descriptions, and thus the actor would become more sociable to be consistent with the feedback.

A second explanation comes from self-perception theory (Bem, 1972). People look to their self-portrayals to infer their attitudes about themselves, especially when the self-portrayals are not incompatible with their prior self-beliefs surrounding their self-portrayals or when the prior self-beliefs are weak. A third explanation is the biased-scanning version of self-perception theory. When people describe themselves in certain ways, they search for information in their memories to support their freely chosen self-descriptions (Jones et al., 1981; Rhodewalt & Agustsdottir, 1986). The major distinction between these two explanations is that the former describes the creation of new self-beliefs, whereas the latter describes how some existing self-beliefs are made more salient than others (Schlenker et al., 1994).

I contend that the first explanation for internalization, the public commitment view, is the best one so far because it seems to provide the best fit with existing evidence. For example, after reviewing approximately 50 naturalistic studies, Shrauger and Schoeneman (1979) concluded that "people's self-perceptions agree substantially with the way they perceive themselves as being viewed by others" (p. 549). Furthermore, researchers have shown that once people have committed themselves to particular identities, their peers tend to give them feedback that constrains them to being consistent with those identities (e.g., see Swann, 1996).

Also supporting the public commitment view is evidence that the real or imagined presence of an audience is a crucial element of internalizing one's self-portrayals (Baumeister & Tice, 1984; Schlenker et al., 1994; Tice, 1992). Tice (1992) found that self-portrayals had a greater impact on the participants' self-concepts when they were performed publicly rather than privately. Although she suggested that the presence of an audience made even more salient the participants' self-focus and corresponding memory search for consistent information about themselves (Tice, 1992), Schlenker et al. (1994) obtained evidence that directly contradicted this biased-scanning view. Schlenker and coworkers asked participants to engage in biased-scanning tasks in which they listed memories that were either congruent or incongruent with their earlier self-portrayals. As it turned out, the participants simply internalized their public self-portrayals, regardless of the biased-scanning procedures.

It seems that the public commitment view offers the best-supported explanation thus far for why people's identities may be undermined by revealing too much to others. By revealing too much, they may constrain themselves to being consistent with their earlier undesirable self-portrayals, just as Jeff constrained himself to being the failure who could not hold on to the love of his life.

These constraints associated with revealing too much may extend to all domains of one's life, including therapy (as discussed in the previous chapter) and the work setting. Revealing personal information in the work setting may be threatening to one's identity or career if the revealed information is contrary to how one wants to be seen at work. For example, if a woman makes the painful choice to announce to her co-workers that she has been raped, then she may come to see herself as a victim because she may perceive (either accurately or inaccurately) that her co-workers see her as a victim. Or if she tells her colleagues that she has been punching in early before her lunch hour is over, then the colleagues might report her to the boss. As described earlier, most confidants probably cannot be trusted to be completely discreet, especially about highly loaded or emotional events.

Not only is this kind of exposure hard on most people, but also rejection-sensitive individuals, or those who are attuned to and hurt by negative evaluations from others, may be especially vulnerable to the negative effects of such exposure. Support for this idea comes from the same researchers (Cole et al., 1996a) who showed that being out of the closet was associated with reduced risk for cancers and infectious diseases among a sample of gay men (see Chapter 2). When these researchers studied a sample of rejection-sensitive gay men in particular, they actually found the opposite pattern. Specifically, among initially healthy HIV-positive gay men, those who were rejection-sensitive experienced a significant acceleration in how quickly they developed a critically low CD4 T-lymphocyte level, an AIDS diagnosis, and died from the HIV infection (Cole, Kemeny, & Taylor, 1997). However, the accelerated HIV progression was not observed in the rejection-sensitive men who concealed their homosexual identity, suggesting that being in the closet actually may protect such individuals from negative health effects (Cole et al., 1997). What is especially interesting about these findings is that the study was conducted in Los Angeles, a place known for its large gay population and where gay men may be accepted to a greater extent than they are in more socially conservative cities. It could be that this buffering effect of staying in the closet may be even more pronounced among rejection-sensitive men who live in cities with a population that has greater anti-gay sentiments.

LISTENER FEELS BURDENED

Although the undermining of one's identity seems to be at the heart of the problems associated with revealing secrets, a primary reason people give for not sharing their traumatic or negative secrets is that they are concerned that they will upset others if they do reveal their secrets to them (Pennebaker, 1993; Pennebaker et al., 1989). Coyne et al. (1987) found that people who lived with a depressed person reported that they were upset by the depressed person's complaints of worthlessness and expressions of worry. Furthermore, when people observe the distress of others, they often respond with increased physiological and psychological arousal (Lazarus,

Speisman, Mordkof, & Davison, 1962; Learner, 1980), sharp changes in mood (Tannenbaum & Gaer, 1965), and unpleasant ruminations related to the distress (Horowitz, 1975; Horowitz & Wilner, 1976; Wilner & Horowitz, 1975).

It seems that when telling traumatic secrets, the revealer becomes more relaxed, whereas the listener becomes more physically aroused or distressed (Pennebaker et al., 1989; Shortt & Pennebaker, 1992). A group of Holocaust survivors who revealed their traumatic secrets experienced decreased skin conductance levels (SCLs) as they talked, whereas the undergraduates who were listening experienced increased SCLs (Pennebaker et al., 1989; Shortt & Pennebaker, 1992). Harber and Pennebaker (1992) argued that learning about a terrible trauma is difficult for the listener because it can threaten the listener's assumptions about the orderliness of the world. Listeners often react to such threats by attributing personal responsibility for a trauma to the victim, or blaming the victim, to lend credence to their own beliefs that the world is fair and just (Coates, Wortman, & Abbey, 1979).

Unfortunately, the people who most desperately need supportive feedback, such as those who are extremely depressed or who have suffered a major loss, are the least likely to receive the support (Silver, Wortman, & Crofton, 1990). If victims of negative life events "maximize their chances for personal adjustment by openly expressing their distress, they may risk alienating their social network" (Silver et al., 1990, p. 401). Those who express their struggles actually elicit more rejection from others than do people who act as if they are coping quite well (Coates et al., 1979), and people respond negatively to depressed individuals (see Gurtman, 1986, for a review). For instance, in one experiment, depressed people elicited depression, anxiety, hostility, and rejection from others with whom they interacted for only 15 minutes (Strack & Coyne, 1983).

Most important, people tend to be avoided by confidants altogether after revealing traumatic secrets to them (e.g., Coates et al., 1979; Lazarus, 1985). For example, cancer patients live with constant fear, but they do not share their fear with family, friends, and health care staff because these individuals do not respond well to such revelations (Spiegel, 1992). The patients therefore end up withdrawing from others and feeling isolated (Spiegel, 1992). This isolation is potentially extremely problematic for the victim: Weaker social support has been found to be associated with less protection from stress and from its related physical problems (see Broadhead et al., 1983; Kessler & McLeod, 1985; Kessler, Price, & Wortman, 1985; Levy, 1983; Mueller, 1980; Turner, 1983; Wortman, 1984; Wortman & Conway, 1985, for reviews). Moreover, as mentioned in Chapter 1, the need to belong seems to be a fundamental human motivation (see Baumeister &

Leary, 1995). Any severe threat to one's network of social attachments is likely to be both physically and psychologically detrimental to him or her.

In addition to fearing rejection, people also anticipate that others will give unhelpful responses to their revelations, such as unwanted advice or comments to the effect that the listener knows how the victim feels (Lehman, Wortman, & Williams, 1987; Pennebaker, 1993; Pennebaker et al., 1989; Wortman & Lehman, 1985). A number of researchers have observed that when people do disclose private information surrounding a trauma to others, they tend to receive unhelpful comments (Davidowitz & Myrick, 1984; DiMatteo & Hays, 1981; Helmrath & Steinitz, 1978; House, 1981; Lehman, Ellard, & Wortman, 1986; Lehman & Hemphill, 1990; Maddison & Walker, 1967; Peters-Colden, 1982; Thoits, 1982; Wortman, 1984). Potential confidants interrupt victims' disclosures and switch the topic of conversation to something other than the trauma. They also tend to impose upon the victim their own interpretation of the trauma (Coates et al., 1979). In one survey, people who experienced a death in their immediate families were asked to report the kinds of responses they received from others while they were grieving (Davidowitz & Myrick, 1984). Eighty percent of the responses they reported were ones that they considered unhelpful; the responses included such statements as, "You shouldn't question God's will," and "Be thankful you have another son."

These types of responses are intended to discourage open discussion and to encourage recovery, yet they actually isolate the victim, dismiss the victim's feelings as being insignificant, and imply that the victim should be getting over the trauma more quickly than the victim is (Lehman et al., 1986). By encouraging someone in distress to look on the bright side, a confidant may be conveying to the person that the person's feelings and behaviors are not appropriate (Kessler et al., 1985). Moreover, when confidants offer advice, they may be implying to the victims that the victims are incapable of helping themselves (Brickman et al., 1982).

Despite the fact that confidants make such poor attempts at providing support, people do know what responses would be helpful to hypothetical victims (Lehman et al., 1986). However, they respond to the victim in ways that dismiss the severity of the victim's distress in order to diminish their own stress levels that have been generated by the victim's troubles (Lehman et al., 1986). Cialdini et al. (1987) showed that even when undergraduate participants were made to feel heightened empathy toward a victim who was videotaped receiving electric shocks, the participants apparently were selfishly motivated to reduce the distress that was associated with their feelings of empathy rather than to reduce the suffering of the victim.

One limitation to the suggestion that it may not be wise to burden a listener with one's secrets is that most of the studies cited in the previous paragraphs have explored situations in which the confidant or listener was someone who did not know the victim/secret keeper well. In Strack and Coyne's (1983) depression research and in Cialdini and coworkers' (1987) empathy experiments, for example, participants rejected *strangers* whom they were told were depressed or victimized. In cases where a confidant knows a victim well, or in cases where the confidant is highly trained such as in a counseling context, the confidant may offer more supportive feedback. In such cases, the confidant typically knows positive aspects of the secret keeper to offset the negative secret or trauma, which may help the confidant avoid rejecting the secret keeper. For instance, in Coyne and colleagues' (1987) study, people who lived with a depressed person felt distressed, but they continued to take care of the depressed person.

REVEALING INFORMATION MAY MAKE IT MORE "REAL"

Another problem associated with revealing secrets is that people often are not able to articulate their deep-seated feelings and motivations accurately (see Nisbett & Wilson, 1977). Although people tend to know how they feel, they frequently do not know *why* they have these feelings (Wilson, Lisle, & Schooler, 1988). When they do attempt to reveal their feelings or problems, they may use cognitive explanations to describe these deep-seated emotions and risk presenting distorted images of the feelings or problems (Wilson, Dunn, Kraft, & Lisle, 1989). As such, their confidants are not able to understand the concerns or offer appropriate responses following the revelation. For example, a woman might tell her new boyfriend that it is fine for him to see other women, just as she intends to see other men. She may say that her reasoning is that she believes it is important for people to enjoy life fully, whereas her real motivation may be that she is worried that he will become bored with her sexually if he is constrained to monogamy. However, because he does not understand her motivation, he cannot respond appropriately and says "I wasn't raised that way and can't be in relationship with a woman who isn't faithful."

Support for the notion that attempts to explain deep-seated feelings can go awry comes from a study of dating relationships. Wilson and Kraft (1993) found that students in a dating relationship who were asked why their relationship was going either well or poorly described reasons that were inconsistent with their actual degree of happiness in the relationship. These students later changed their attitudes in the direction of their reasons. There also is evidence that if people reveal their troubling symptoms to others, those symptoms may become even more troubling and real

(Cioffi, 1996). Cioffi (1996) investigated the cognitive, behavioral, and social effects of having verbally expressed a somatic state and found that, depending on how the symptom report is elicited and the context in which it is made, the expression of a somatic state may change how that individual thinks about and remembers that state. Moreover, it affects how the individual views himself or herself and how the individual is viewed by others. In sum, people may need to be careful in sharing their private concerns about a relationship as well as their somatic complaints, because these revelations may make the negative emotional and physical experiences more real.

SECRECY MAINTAINS PERSONAL BOUNDARIES

Some researchers have argued that secret keeping is actually healthy and is an important component in the development of one's ego boundaries, or sense of identity (Hoyt, 1978; Margolis, 1966; Tausk, 1933). Learning about society's taboos (e.g., not to masturbate in public) and learning to keep such information to oneself are thought to be central aspects of this healthy development (Szajnberg, 1988). As mentioned in Chapter 1, Peskin (1992) observed that as children mature, they learn to conceal information from others and to use such information to influence or manipulate them.

Just as concealing may help people develop personal boundaries, telling others personal information can lead people to lose their independence and can leave them vulnerable to possible exploitation (Henley, 1973). In relationships, higher-status individuals know more about lower-status others than lower-status others know about them (Henley, 1973). Powerless groups, such as welfare recipients, mental patients, and prisoners, tend to have very little opportunity for privacy and often are targets of inquiry (Derlega, 1988).

In romantic relationships, when both partners maintain clear personal boundaries and keep some secrets from each other, they may create a heightened sense of mystery and intrigue in the relationship. Olson, Barefoot, and Strickland (1976) demonstrated that, at least initially, keeping a secret from a person enhanced attraction for that person. Participants followed an opposite sex individual around and kept the person under surveillance. Those participants who thought that the surveillance was not known to the target, as compared with participants who thought that their surveillance was known to the target, reported a higher attraction toward the target (Olson et al., 1976). Wegner et al. (1994) also demonstrated that keeping secrets about one's romantic relationship from other people can enhance attraction to the romantic partner. These researchers showed that mixed-sex couples who played a game of footsie with each other that they kept secret from other couples, as compared with couples who played the same game but who did not keep it a secret, reported a greater attraction for their partners (Wegner et al., 1994). However, this experiment was not designed to explore what happens to couples who keep secrets from each other, nor was it designed to explore the long-term effects of secret keeping on attraction. Although secret keeping may enhance attraction early on (Olson et al., 1976), there is the possibility that secrets could undermine the relationship in the long run by reducing the partners' trust in each other.

In a recent correlational study, Finkenauer and Hazam (2000) surveyed married couples to find out how secrecy relates to marital satisfaction. They asked married people to indicate to what extent they avoided difficult topics in their marriages, or engaged in what the researchers called *contextual secrecy*, and to what extent they suspected that their spouses were keeping information from them. One of the items assessing contextual secrecy was, "I avoid criticizing the way my partner treats me." The researchers found that contextual secrecy was positively related to one's own marital satisfaction, whereas suspecting one's spouse of secret keeping was negatively related to one's marital satisfaction. These findings converge with those from Vangelisti's (1994) study, in which she found that perceiving one's family to be high in secrecy, without actually being higher in secrecy, was associated with lower satisfaction with one's family.

SUMMARY

There are a number of negative consequences associated with revealing personal secrets. One of these consequences is that confidants may repeat the secret to others, even if they are asked not to do so. Moreover, victims of trauma fear that they will burden the listener, and in fact, they are likely to receive unsatisfactory responses when they do relate their traumatic experiences to others. This rejection and negative feedback could lead people to construct negative identities for themselves, and seeing the others in whom they confided may serve as a reminder of these negative identities. In addition, when secret keepers do try to reveal their secrets, they may not be able to articulate them in such a way that the confidant will be able to understand the secret keeper or offer helpful feedback. Finally, keeping secrets from others may help maintain healthy personal boundaries and a sense of privacy that are associated with having status or power in relation to others. One drawback to this research is that most of it has explored rejecting feedback that comes from confidants who are strangers. In the next section, I describe what happens when people reveal their secrets to appropriate, helpful confidants.

POSITIVE CONSEQUENCES OF REVEALING SECRETS

ALLOWS MEANINGFUL RESOLUTION OF SECRETS

As described in Chapter 5, if people share their secrets with others, they may gain insights regarding the meaning of those secrets and may develop a sense of control over their lives (Pennebaker, 1989, 1990; Pennebaker & Hoover, 1985; Tait & Silver, 1989). They may find meaning in the experiences by reframing them and assimilating them into their worldviews (Horowitz, 1975; Meichenbaum, 1977; Pennebaker et al., 1988; Silver et al., 1983). For example, imagine a woman who feels enraged at her husband because he has filed for divorce. She may decide to share those feelings with an appropriate confidant, who responds in a helpful way by reframing the anger as "a useful asset in making sure you will protect your interests in the divorce settlement." Part of the trouble with hiding information from others is that the secret keeper does not get the chance to hear another person's perspective on an issue (Pennebaker, 1990). The secret keeper may have a distorted perception of his or her problems and may benefit from someone else's challenge to that perception (Pennebaker, 1990).

As described in Chapter 4, there is empirical support for the idea that sharing secrets or traumas is beneficial in that it helps a person understand the trauma (Foa et al., 1995; Pennebaker et al., 1990; Silver et al., 1983). However, revealing secrets does not just offer cognitive benefits, it also can reduce shame and guilt or states of negative emotional arousal (Derlega, 1993; Stice, 1992). People who have experienced stigmatizing traumatic events, such as rape and incest, feel shame, and thus they choose to conceal these events from others (Derlega, 1993; Pennebaker, 1985, 1989; Silver et al., 1983). Unfortunately, as Pennebaker (1985) suggested, "the act of *not* discussing or confiding the event with another may be more damaging than having experienced the event per se" (p. 82). The victims may tell themselves that because of the fact that they have hidden the experience from others, the event must indeed be very negative or shameful (Derlega, 1993). As described in Chapter 3, it is possible that through this self-perception process (Bem, 1967, 1972), people may develop feelings of lowered self-worth (Derlega, 1993). It seems that not only having a painful secret but also working to hide the secret can make people feel bad about themselves.

In cases in which someone feels guilty about having betrayed someone else, such as when one marital partner has had a hidden affair, the person may feel a tremendous sense of relief upon finally sharing the betrayal with his or her spouse. Theoretically, this relief may occur even if the revelation results in the breakup of the marriage. In one study, when people who felt guilty about their actions were given the opportunity to talk about these behaviors, they reported experiencing relief from their guilt feelings (Regan, 1968). Similarly, in another study, when people were permitted to confess their guilt-inducing behaviors, they subsequently exhibited fewer remorseful behaviors (Carlsmith, Ellsworth, & Whiteside, 1968). However, these studies have not examined the long-term effects of revealing guilty secrets, and they leave open the possibility that feelings of regret could emerge at some time after revealing the secret.

Avoids Suspicions of Reciprocal Secrecy

Social psychologists have long documented the phenomenon wherein people see others as being more similar to them than they actually are and called it the *false consensus effect* (see Ross, Greene, & House, 1977). Borrowing from Sagarin, Rhoads, and Cialdini's (1998) theorizing about the negative relational effects of lying, I suggest that keeping a secret from someone may damage the relationship even if the secret is never discovered, because the secret keeper may assume that person is keeping a secret in return.

Support for this idea can be gleaned from Sagarin and coworkers' (1998) recent study in which they induced some undergraduates to lie to a partner about how they were able to solve a difficult puzzle, whereas other undergraduates simply told the partner the truth about their puzzle-solving strategies. In addition to this manipulation, half the participants in the deception condition were led to believe that their lies hurt their partners by preventing them from receiving extra credit, whereas the other participants were told that their partners received the extra credit. All the participants later were asked to rate the partners and the typical student on various traits including honesty. The participants who had lied to their partners, as compared with participants who had not lied, later rated the partners as less honest, particularly when the lie damaged the partners. These deceptive participants also rated the typical student as less honest. The authors explained the denigration of the partners by indicating that the participants in the lying condition were justifying their actions in a self-protective version of the false consensus effect, wherein they justified their dishonesty by seeing others as being similarly dishonest. However, as the researchers themselves pointed out, this study involved newly formed dyads. In long-term relationships, people who lie to their partners may continue to see their partners as honest both because they care about them and because they have had many opportunities to observe how honest their partners are. Plus, romantic couples tend to assume that their partners are honest (Derlega et al., 1993), unless they are given evidence to the contrary (see Cole, 2001).

MAKES SECRETS SEEM LESS HARMFUL

A benefit of revealing secrets is that they may seem less negative than if they are first concealed and then later discovered. As mentioned in Chapter 3, Fishbein and Laird (1979) showed that participants who revealed ambiguous information, as compared with those who concealed it, viewed that information as less negative. Moreover, people generally view openness as a sign of closeness (see Derlega et al., 1993) and may get angry at others for keeping a secret from them. Imagine the circumstance in which a woman named Elizabeth conceals the fact that she is involved romantically with her friend Mary's ex-boyfriend. Elizabeth conceals this information from Mary, even though she knows that Mary is no longer interested in the ex-boyfriend and would not mind if Elizabeth dated him. Elizabeth also realizes that there is a high probability that Mary already knows about her involvement with the ex-boyfriend because they have many mutual friends. Concealing that information is likely to be a signal to Mary that Elizabeth is not close to her, which may be more upsetting than the fact that Elizabeth is seeing her ex-boyfriend.

This phenomenon wherein personal information seems less negative when it is out in the open may help explain why people sometimes are willing to say astonishingly undesirable things about themselves, even though they are motivated to be seen in desirable ways. For example, years ago, I knew a married man who openly told his friends that he wears women's undergarments because they feel good against skin and arouse him. Even though he seemed to be giving the impression that he was impervious to what his friends thought, at some level he may have viewed his revelation as increasing the likelihood that he would be seen in a desirable way, as an open person who was so confident that he did not care what others thought about him. Indeed, in his immediate circle, his openness seemed to make the behavior acceptable, and his friends viewed him as a quirky, likable person. However, when his friends described his behavior to people outside his circle, they simply would describe his cross-dressing behaviors and omit the fact he himself was the relaxed and confident source of the information. The people outside his circle simply came to see him as "that pervert who wears women's lingerie," rather than as he wanted to be seen (i.e., as someone who is open, confident, and comfortable with his sexuality). The point I am making here is that people may find the process of revealing information to be reinforcing in the immediate context, but as time goes on and more people know about the information, its meaning may change from desirable to undesirable.

In sum, given Fishbein and Laird's (1979) finding that concealed information seems more negative than revealed information, perhaps people should be open about their transgressions early in relationships, so that the transgressions are never a secret. However, people need to know their confidants somewhat well before taking that risk because the confidants might reject them outright as a result of the revelation.

MAY ENHANCE LIKING

In the self-disclosure literature, meta-analyses have uncovered a statistically significant disclosure-liking effect: People who disclose personal or intimate information tend to be more liked than people who disclose at lower level (Collins & Miller, 1994). This effect is qualified by the content and appropriateness of the disclosure, such that disclosures that are too intimate and offered too soon may lead to perceptions of the discloser as maladjusted and less likable (Altman & Taylor, 1973; Collins & Miller, 1994). In general, there seem to be fairly strict norms about what is appropriate to reveal in various contexts (Derlega & Grzelak, 1979). It seems that disclosure will not lead to liking at extreme levels of intimacy (Archer & Berg, 1978; Brewer & Mittelman, 1980; Cozby, 1972). When disclosures are too intimate and offered too soon, people may feel obligated or pressured to reveal at an equally intimate level. Therefore, Cozby (1972) suggested that there is a curvilinear relationship between disclosure and liking, such that moderate levels of disclosure should bring the greatest liking. Along these lines, in their meta-analyses, Collins and Miller (1994) found that the strongest links between self-disclosure and liking occurred in correlational or naturalistic studies, as opposed to experimental studies. They proposed that this was because "the former were almost always concerned with disclosure processes in established relationships, whereas experimental studies were primarily concerned with disclosure and liking between strangers" (p. 470). It seems that high levels of disclosure to strangers backfired because too much information was revealed too soon.

Ajzen (1977) suggested that the reason disclosure is positively related to liking is that liking is determined by holding positive beliefs about another person. People who disclose more intimately, as compared with those who disclose less, may be viewed by others as more trusting, friendly, and warm. As logic would dictate, the more positive the beliefs, the greater the liking (Ajzen, 1977; Dalto, Ajzen, & Kaplan, 1979). Researchers have shown in a number of experiments and correlational studies that people form more favorable impressions of others who are willing to reveal personal information about themselves (e.g., Davis & Sloan, 1974; Jones & Archer, 1976; Kleinke & Kahn, 1980). For example, in one study, group therapy members who self-disclosed more, as compared with those who disclosed less, were rated as more likable by both the therapists and other group members (Weigel, Dinges, Dyer, & Straum-fjord, 1972).

SUMMARY

Some of the main benefits of revealing secrets are that it can alleviate the stress and guilt associated with hiding information from others, provide the opportunity to receive new insights or perspectives on the secrets, make the secrets seem less harmful, and make the revealer more likable. These positive consequences help explain why people so often reveal undesirable hidden information about themselves.

CONSEQUENCES OF REVEALING
MAY DEPEND ON THE CONFIDANT

Do the benefits of revealing secrets outweigh the costs of revealing in most circumstances? I suggest that such outcomes should hinge on the feedback from and qualities of the confidant. Consistent with this idea, Macdonald and Morley (2001) found that the anticipation of negative responses to disclosure, particularly labeling and judging responses, was associated with not disclosing emotional events to other people in a diary study involving psychotherapy clients. In this section, I describe the research on how the confidant may influence the outcomes of revealing potentially stigmatizing secrets, beginning with the example of sexual orientation.

Gay men who live around rejecting people or in a stigmatizing culture may not have as positive self-perceptions as they would otherwise. Frable, Wortman, and Joseph (1997) asked a large sample of predominantly white, young, educated, middle-class gay and bisexual men living in the Chicago and surrounding areas to complete a 90-minute self-administered questionnaire that included self-esteem, well-being, and symptomatology measures. The men answered questions about their experiences with gay stigma, visibility as gay men, involvement in the gay community, and commitment to a positive gay identity. The gay men in this sample, as compared with nonstigmatized samples in general, were neither particularly low in global self-esteem nor high in psychological distress on the average. However, the ones who lived around people who stigmatized gay men, as compared with those who did not, had more negative self-perceptions.

Along those same lines, Frable, Platt, and Hoey (1998) asked 86 Harvard undergraduates to keep a diary over 11 days and rate their momentary self-esteem and affect. Those participants with concealable stigmas (students who indicated that they were gay, that they were bulimic, or that their family earned less than $20,000 each year), as compared with both those whose stigmas were visible and those without stigmatizing characteristics, reported lower self-esteem and more negative affect. However, the students with concealable stigmas who had contact with similar others were the least likely to experience low self-esteem and depressed mood. Thus, Frable et al. (1998) concluded that contact with similar others may protect individuals with hidden stigmas from negative cultural messages.

When comparing 150 lung cancer patients with matched control patients from chest disorder wards, Kissen (1966) found that the cancer patients showed a significantly diminished outlet for emotional discharge or had fewer opportunities for discussing their feelings with others. Kissen (1966) concluded that among heavy cigarette smokers, a poor outlet for emotional discharge was as important for cancer development as urban residence and even more important than working in an air-polluted setting.

However, having an outlet for emotional discharge in response to a stressor may be helpful only when those people offering such an outlet are supportive. Major et al. (1990) interviewed women prior to their having a first trimester abortion and assessed their perceptions of social support from their partner, family, and friends. They also measured the women's depression, mood, physical complaints, and anticipation of negative consequences just after a 30-minute postabortion recovery period. They found that the women who had told close others of their abortion but perceived them as less than completely supportive, as compared with women who had not told or who had told and perceived complete support, had poorer postabortion psychological adjustment.

Bolger, Foster, Vinokur, and Ng (1996) also challenged the commonly held belief that when life crises occur, significant others help to alleviate distress and resolve practical problems. They interviewed 102 breast cancer patients and their significant others at 4 and 10 months after the breast cancer diagnosis. It seemed that this life crisis may have overwhelmed the significant others and detracted from their ability to provide effective support to these women. Although the significant others provided support in response to the women's physical impairment, they withdrew support in response to the women's emotional distress. The result of this pattern of support from significant others was that it did not alleviate the women's distress nor did it enhance their physical recovery. The researchers concluded that in times of extreme stress there are limits to the effectiveness of close relationships.

Researchers also have studied how social constraints on discussion of a traumatic experience can interfere with cognitive processing of and recovery from loss (Lepore, Silver, Wortman, & Wayment, 1996). Mothers who had recently lost an infant to sudden infant death syndrome (SIDS) were interviewed at 3 weeks, 3 months, and 18 months after their infants' death. Part of the interviews involved questions about the mothers' experiencing intrusive thoughts surrounding the death. Lepore et al. (1996) defined intrusive thoughts as recurring, unwanted memories, thoughts, and images of a stressor, and they conceptualized such thoughts as a sign that people are trying to make sense of the stressor. The mothers who had experienced social constraints to discussing the death (i.e., felt that others were uncomfortable, not fully supportive, or not willing to listen when they talked about the loss) were compared in their emotional adjustment to the women who had not experienced such social constraints. Interestingly enough, among socially constrained mothers, the more the women had experienced intrusive thoughts at 3 weeks after the loss, the less they talked about the infant's death at 3 months and 18 months after the loss. The reverse associations were found among unconstrained mothers. Moreover, when the researchers conducted analyses that statistically controlled for the women's initial levels of distress, there was a positive relation between intrusive thoughts at 3 weeks and depressive symptoms over time among socially constrained mothers. However, higher levels of intrusive thoughts at 3 weeks were associated with a *decrease* in depressive symptoms at 18 months among mothers with unconstrained social relationships. It seems that the cognitive processing these women experienced through intrusive thoughts about the death was only helpful when the women had supportive people to talk to about the death (Lepore et al., 1996).

This same pattern was found in studies on women with breast or colon cancer (Lepore, 1997a), men with prostate cancer (Lepore & Helgeson, 1998), and children exposed to inner-city violence (Kliewer, Lepore, Oskin, & Johnson, 1998). Lepore (1997b) suggested that, given these findings, expressing one's emotions surrounding stressful events may facilitate cognitive processing and emotional adjustment only when this expression occurs in a safe or supportive environment.

In an even more recent study, Lepore, Ragan, and Jones (2000) used an experimental design to assess the influence of talking and the social context of the talking on cognitive–emotional processes of adjustment to stressors. Two hundred fifty-six undergraduates (half men and half women) viewed a stressful 14-minute visual presentation on the Nazi Holocaust and then were assigned to one of four conditions. These were a no-talk control condition or one of three talk conditions: talk alone, talk to a validating confederate, or talk to an invalidating confederate. In the talk to a validating confederate condition, the confederate nodded, maintained eye contact, and smiled approvingly while the participant disclosed feelings and reactions to the film. The confederate also reciprocated disclosure and identified and agreed with the reactions of the participant. In contrast, in the invalidating confederate condition, the confederate avoided eye contact while the participant disclosed and when disclosing, disagreed with several thoughts and feelings expressed by the participant. Two days later, the participants were reexposed to the stressful film. As it turned out, participants in the talk alone and validate conditions, as compared with those in the no-talk condition, had a lower level of intrusive thoughts in the 2-day interim and they reported experiencing less stress when reexposed to the stressor. Lepore et al. (2000) observed that it seemed to be through experiencing fewer intrusive thoughts of the stressor that talking and validation lowered participants' perceived stress. At the same time, the participants in the invalidating confederate condition did not differ from those in the other three groups on the intrusive thoughts or distress measures. The researchers suggested that the reason this last finding seems to contradict those of Major et al. (1990) is that the confederate in this study was a peer and the participants may have dismissed the invalidating feedback, whereas the people providing support in the Major and co-workers' study were significant others, and thus their unsupportive feedback may have been more damaging. Lepore et al. (2000) concluded that talking about acute stressors can facilitate adjustment to the stressors through gaining cognitive resolution on the stressor, a process discussed in detail in Chapter 4.

In sum, the benefits associated with trying to make sense of a private disturbing event, such as the death of one's child or the diagnosis of cancer, seem to hinge on supportiveness of one's confidants. Next, I illustrate that many of the dilemmas to revealing secrets described in this chapter may be resolved by carefully choosing an appropriate confidant.

FEATURES OF HELPFUL CONFIDANTS

What makes an appropriate confidant or one to whom secret keepers would benefit from revealing? I suggest that if a troubled secret keeper has a confidant (1) who is discreet and can be trusted not to reveal a secret, (2) who is perceived by the secret keeper to be nonjudgmental, and (3) who is able to offer new insights into the secret, then the secret keeper should reveal to that person (see Kelly, 1999; Kelly & McKillop, 1996). The rationale for this recommendation is that having such a confidant would allow the revealer to gain potentially invaluable insights into the secret as well as avoid the negative consequences of revealing secrets described earlier. My rationale for depicting each of these characteristics as essential in a confidant is described in more detail in the following paragraphs.

DISCREET

Researchers have demonstrated that assuring people of the confidentiality of their disclosures, as compared with not offering such assurances, generally leads to greater disclosure of private information (Corcoran, 1988; Kobocow, McGuire, & Blau, 1983; Woods & McNamara, 1980). Trusting the confidant not to repeat the secret to others may be the most important factor in determining whether someone should reveal to that person. When a person can be assured that only the confidant will know a secret, then that person can assess how the confidant is reacting and can make a decision about whether to continue the relationship with the confidant. In contrast, in situations in which confidentiality is not guaranteed, the person loses this sense of control and may be victimized by others who are privy to the secrets (Henley, 1973). In addition, the person may begin to construct a negative identity for himself or herself by imagining, or actually hearing, the judgments others will make upon learning about the secret (see Schlenker, 1986). Given these negative possibilities, I recommend that a secret keeper avoid revealing secrets to any confidants who cannot or will not refrain from transmitting the secrets to others.

NONJUDGMENTAL

Pennebaker (1990) has stated that people are most likely to disclose their deepest secrets if they think that others will not judge them and will accept them no matter what they say: "Pennebaker's research on self-disclosure highlights the importance of a confidant who will listen without judging or withdrawing love and support" (Kennedy et al., 1990, p. 262). The idea that it is important for a confidant to be nonjudgmental is backed by Carl Rogers's (1951, 1957) theoretical work on the benefits of having an accepting therapist or close friend with whom one can sort out personal problems. Rogers (1951, 1957) proposed that the primary role of the therapist is to provide clients with a safe environment (i.e., one free from conditions of worth or judgments from the therapist) so that the clients can learn to trust their inner experiencing. He believed that if the therapist is genuinely empathic (expresses understanding) toward the client and offers the client unconditional positive regard (warmth and acceptance), then the client will develop his or her self-actualizing or growth potential.

Truax and Carkhuff (1967) and Truax and Mitchell (1971) conducted reviews on studies assessing Rogers's theoretical ideas about the therapists's role and concluded that there was strong evidence that therapist empathy, warmth, and genuineness were important in inducing client improvement. However, Lambert, DeJulio, and Stein (1978) subsequently pointed out that there was no empirical evidence that the facilitative features of the therapist actually caused client change. In addition, more recent work suggests that these features of a therapist may be more relevant for mildly disturbed individuals than for severely disturbed patients (Lambert & Bergin, 1994). Despite the fact that the debate concerning whether Rogers's proposed facilitative conditions do induce client change remains unresolved, Rogers's theoretical ideas have had a tremendous impact on the counseling field (Hill & Corbett, 1993). For example, most counseling psychology graduate programs now train their students to use the basic empathy skills (e.g., reflection of feelings, restatement of content) proposed by Rogers (Hill & Corbett, 1993).

The reason that having a nonjudgmental confidant is so helpful in the context of revealing secrets is that such a confidant provides all the benefits associated with unburdening described above (e.g., the health benefits, new insights about the secret) but none of the ramifications associated with receiving negative feedback (e.g., being rejected by and becoming isolated from others). In sharing with nonjudgmental others, the secret keeper can feel understood and accepted and can feel comforted by the fact that he or she is no longer carrying the secret burden alone (Yalom, 1985). For instance, if a young man tells his therapist that he accidentally killed a pedestrian while driving drunk and if she conveys that she accepts him despite his actions, he can feel relieved from his guilt. He can continue to construct a positive self-image by seeing himself through her eyes, rather than through the critical eyes of imagined others.

ABLE TO OFFER NEW INSIGHTS

One problem with telling a secret down a well as John Steinbeck described is that the well does not offer new helpful insights on the troubling secrets. I suggest that a key factor in making a wise decision to reveal to a confidant is whether that confidant is able to offer new insights or perspectives on a problematic secret. As described in the previous chapter, my students and I (Kelly et al., 2001, Study 1) examined undergraduates' reports of what they had gained from revealing their most private secrets to their confidants in the past. Gaining new perspectives on their secrets was associated with feeling better about the secrets now, whereas experiencing catharsis actually was negatively associated with recovery from the secrets. In addition, participants' ratings of the expertness of their confidants (i.e., their preparedness and their ability to help) were predictive of the participants' gaining insights into their secrets. In a second study, we found that participants who wrote about their secrets while trying to gain new insights into them, as compared with participants who tried to gain catharsis during their writing or who wrote about the details of their day, felt much better about their secrets after 1 week (Kelly et al., 2001, Study 2). Thus, I suggest that if the secret keeper has a confidant who is particularly insightful (such as highly skilled and well-trained counselor) and is able to provide new perspectives on the secret, then the person should reveal to that confidant.

Evidence for These Three Features

Further support for the argument that these three qualities are important in a confidant comes from that same research I conducted with my students (Kelly et al., 2001, Study 1). The undergraduate participants were provided with brief descriptions of six features of a hypothetical confidant (i.e., someone to whom they would be willing to share their most personal secrets) and asked them to rank these features in the order of importance. Specifically, participants were asked to rank six qualities according to "how important they are in determining whether or not you would tell someone your secrets in general." The qualities were: "won't judge me," "understands me," "is able to help me," "will keep my secret," "is similar to me in personal characteristics," and "has had an experience that was similar to my secret experience." This list was not meant to be exhaustive of all the desired qualities in a confidant but rather to include a number of the key confidant qualities described or alluded to in the social support literature (Barak & LaCrosse, 1975; Davidowitz & Myrick, 1984; DiMatteo & Hays, 1981; Helmrath & Steinitz, 1978; House, 1981; Kessler et al., 1985; Lehman et al., 1986; Lehman & Hemphill, 1990; Maddison & Walker, 1967; Peters-Golden, 1982; Thoits, 1982; Pennebaker, 1993; Pennebaker et al., 1989; Wortman & Lehman, 1985). Participants rated "will keep my secret" and "understands me" as the most important features of a confidant. The third most important feature of a confidant was "will not judge me," followed by "is able to help me," "is similar to me in personal characteristics," and "has had similar experiences." In essence, having a discreet confidant and being understood (and not judged) were deemed as more important than having a similar confidant.

Those same undergraduates were asked to provide descriptions of whether they gained catharsis or new insights from revealing to their actual confidants in the past and to describe how trustworthy, expert, and socially attractive (i.e., warm and likable) these confidants were. They also were asked to indicate among these features of expertness, trustworthiness, and social attractiveness, which was the most important to them in deciding whether to reveal secrets to a hypothetical confidant. We picked these three features because counseling and clinical psychologists have long identified these as being important qualities in a therapist in terms of getting psychotherapy clients to reveal themselves (see Strong, 1968). As it turns out, trustworthiness was rated as the most important feature of a hypothetical confidant. However, participants' ratings of the expertness, not the trustworthiness or attractiveness, of their *actual* confidants significantly predicted participants' gaining new insights into their secrets. As such, the findings indicate that there may be a discrepancy between what people say they want in a confidant and what is most helpful to them. Specifically, people are apt to value trustworthiness in a confidant, but a confidant who is expert (i.e., prepared and able to help) may be more likely to offer new insights into a secret, which may be most critical in recovering from the secret. As described earlier, it is through gaining new insights that one might expect the expertness of the confidant to be associated with recovery from secrets.

OPTIMAL NUMBER OF CONFIDANTS

Now that I have described the characteristics of the ideal confidant, the following question remains: How many confidants are appropriate? Stokes (1983) discovered that seven confidants may be the optimal number. He asked undergraduates in an interviewing course to solicit four participants each and to give them assessments of the extensiveness of their social networks and their satisfaction with these networks. Stokes found that satisfaction with the social networks increased up to having seven confidants, but after that having more confidants was not associated with increased satisfaction. He speculated that the added support of having more confidants may not be worth the costs of maintaining the relationships and offering social support in return.

CONCLUSION

There are a number of positive and negative consequences associated with revealing stigmatizing secrets. The negative consequences include damaging one's social reputation, being rejected by the listener, and forming a negative opinion of oneself by knowing that others are aware of the stigmatizing information. The positive consequences include hearing other people's insights on the secret, becoming more well liked, and relieving oneself of the guilty burden of secrecy. I have suggested that the outcomes of revealing stigmatizing personal secrets hinge mainly on the responses of the confidant, although researchers only recently have begun to examine the role of the confidant and more evidence is needed to support this idea. The research that is available indicates that when revealing a highly emotional or private secret, people do not adequately keep in mind that others often cannot be trusted to refrain from repeating the secret. Moreover, given that what others think matters a great deal to people and that there seems to be a fundamental need to belong, revealers may pay a price in terms of their identity and well-being. As a way of dealing with the dilemmas to revealing, I have suggested that secret keepers carefully select their confidants and search for one who is discreet, nonjudgmental, and able to offer new insights into the secrets. In the next chapter, I offer an even more complex analysis of when to reveal secrets that includes a discussion of whether the confidant expects access to the hidden information and whether he or she will discover the information anyway.

WHEN TO REVEAL PERSONAL SECRETS IN A PARTICULAR RELATIONSHIP

This final chapter opens with one more movie example that I think may have sent a counterproductive message to the public about how protecting one's privacy relates to one's integrity. In the 2000 movie, "The Contender," the vice president dies, and the president appoints a replacement, Laine Hanson (played by Joan Allen). But a political opponent in charge of approving the new appointee dredges up a history of sexual misconduct on her part, threatening to destroy her political career and tarnish the reputation of the current administration. Andrew Manning wrote in his October 2000 review that the ending is "completely unrealistic—it involves a politician being so honest that they're willing to ruin themselves for their ideals, and I find that highly unbelievable in a field where deception and pandering are some of the cornerstones of the career" (http://www.rottentomatoes. com/click/movie-1100998/reviews.php?critic=approved&sortby=default &page=10&rid=156099. Retrieved 3/16/01).

What Manning is describing here is that Hanson never denies that she is the woman in the pictures (taken when she was in college) having sex with two men as the centerpiece of a fraternity party, even though she can easily disprove the accusation by demonstrating that birth marks on her leg do not match the pictures of the woman. Her rationale (revealed to the president at the end of the movie) is that she should not even be asked such questions because they are a matter of privacy. My suggestion, however, would be to deny such rumors promptly and *then* become outraged at the inappropriateness of such questions. The same message of personal integrity can be delivered without letting people draw highly undesirable, false conclusions. I say this because just thinking that everyone is making negative judgments about one can undermine one's very identity.

Of course, that was a very straightforward, easily handled example of what to do with a troubling secret. My aim in this chapter is to offer suggestions for dealing with the sometimes very complicated situations involving secrecy that many people confront in their various relationships on a daily basis. My aim is to help people lead more physically and psychologically healthy lives; that is how central secrecy is to their existence. I encourage people to conceal and reveal information judiciously.

In the previous chapters, I described circumstances in which revealing personal secrets can lead to benefits and circumstances in which it can lead to detriments for the secret keeper. I also pointed out that the fact that high self-concealers as a group are sicker than low self-concealers may not be the result of their keeping a particular secret but rather may be the result of their being born with a genetic predisposition to be vulnerable to various illnesses. The way I see it, although self-concealers are at a disadvantage to start with, both high and low self-concealers may reap great benefits from judicious revelation. I base this proposition on the assumptions that the self-concept has an interpersonal element and that it can change over time (Baumeister, 1998). Telling someone a very stigmatizing personal secret, as compared with keeping the secret, offers greater potential for negative repercussions for one's identity and health. In the following pages, I embark on addressing the one major question on secrecy that remains unanswered: When should people reveal their personal secrets *in particular relationships* and take the risk of being stigmatized or rejected? This chapter takes the discussion from the previous chapter a step further by adding the context of a specific relationship to the complex decision to reveal.

An acquaintance of mine named Gary (not his real name) asked me for insights on an event that upset him years earlier and still perplexed him. He went to a wedding reception with his then girlfriend (who, incidentally, had a doctoral degree in psychology). When she happened to see a former lover at the reception, she whispered, "I had sex with that guy in college." Gary told me that his night was ruined by that one remark, which he viewed as either unthinkably cruel or just plain stupid. Shortly thereafter, he broke off the relationship with her because he perceived her as an insensitive person.

Just as in the example described in Chapter 1, in which Diane Zamora's confessions to her Naval Academy roommates seemed unbelievably foolish or not well thought out, this revelation too seems puzzling. Perhaps part of what the example of Gary's girlfriend boils down to is that people are motivated to protect their reputations, and a strategy for doing so is to give others one's own account of events that may make them look bad (Emler, 1990). Although social psychologists (see Emler, 1990) have argued that people normally underestimate the interconnectedness of their social networks, in this situation Gary's girlfriend may have overestimated the interconnectedness of her network and revealed something that Gary was not likely to discover on his own. She may have feared that if he did discover the information, he would feel betrayed by an omission of information that seemed relevant to their relationship. Did she really make the wrong decision as Gary's recounting of events implies? In this chapter, I offer a model for when to reveal or conceal hidden information (such as previous sexual experiences, masturbatory habits, extrarelational affairs, or hygiene rituals) in a particular relationship, and in so doing I address this and a variety of related questions that are pivotal to maintaining relationships as well as a sense of personal well-being.

The decision to reveal personal secrets within a particular relationship may most aptly be described as a trade-off between unburdening oneself of the stress and guilt of keeping troubling secrets from the relational partner on the one hand and constructing desirable images of oneself as well as avoiding rejection on the other hand. As discussed in the previous chapters, the essence of the problem with revealing personal, undesirable information is that revealers may come to see themselves in undesirable ways if other people, especially those in their immediate social networks, know their stigmatizing secrets.

The primary focus of the model for when to reveal hidden information is to help individuals construct favorable self-images, and thus enhance their well-being. The model also is intended to help them become more aware of their decision-making processes and recognize that they can control the degree of personal access they let other people have, without deception. With every step of the model, an important option is to keep the potentially stigmatizing information hidden to avoid the risks to their self-images associated with revealing such information (see Figure 1). Certainly, individuals may have additional motives besides constructing favorable views of themselves when they decide to reveal hidden information, such as deliberately wanting to get fired, become divorced, or make someone else feel superior. The model does not address these motives. Furthermore, the model does not necessarily address the broader moral implications of keeping or revealing a secret (see Bok, 1982, for a discussion of the moral implications). At the same time, however, the model may be considered morally sound because potential secret keepers and their relational partners are both likely to benefit from it. It encourages them to avoid getting into situations that will lead to the development of troubling

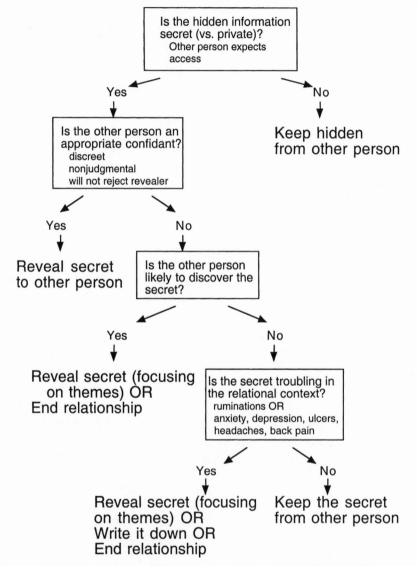

FIGURE 1. When to reveal personal secrets in a particular relationship.

secrets by making them think about the relational consequences of their secretive actions. It also encourages them to avoid revealing information that their partners cannot handle emotionally or do not need to know. Even though some of the steps in the model may seem obvious to the reader, it is my contention that many people in American society have lost sight of the importance of personal boundaries and have been lured into revealing too much information to their partners in an effort to be open and honest when building their relationships. By offering this model, I remind people of the dangers of too much revelation and provide appropriate options to complete openness.

PROPOSED MODEL FOR WHEN TO REVEAL

The first step of the model for when to reveal secrets involves deciding whether the stigmatizing hidden information is secret versus private. This decision hinges on whether the relational partner expects access to the hidden information. If the partner does not expect access to that information, then it is private and may be kept hidden. If the partner does expect access, however, then it is a secret, and the second step is to assess carefully whether he or she is an appropriate confidant. As described in the previous chapters, there is empirical support for the idea that if a troubled secret keeper has a confidant who can be trusted not to reveal a secret, is perceived as nonjudgmental, and is able to offer the secret keeper new insights into the secret, then the secret keeper should reveal to that person (see Kelly & McKillop, 1996). However, in the context of a particular relationship, these characteristics of an appropriate confidant need to be modified. Specifically, the insightfulness of the partner may not be as crucial as whether he or she will reject the revealer and end the relationship. My rationale for this claim is that the revealer can get new insights into the secret from other confidants and may not need them from a particular partner. Thus, if the partner is discreet, nonjudgmental, and not rejecting of the secret keeper, then the secret keeper should reveal the secret to him or her. The third step of the model is to consider whether the relational partner is likely to discover the secret on his or her own. In cases where the probability of discovery is high, it may benefit the secret keeper to disclose the secret, focusing on the themes as opposed to the details (see Kelly, 2000b). This focus on themes can help the revealer be honest while avoiding the stigma and humiliation that often accompany the revelation of details. If the partner is not likely to discover the secret, the fourth and final step is to determine whether the information is troubling. Because of the risks to one's identity associated with revealing stigmatizing personal secrets to inappropriate confidants, I content that people only should contemplate revealing such information if keeping the secret seems to be causing them internal stress and negative effects described by various researchers; in other words, if the secret is troubling (e.g., Lane & Wegner, 1995; Larson & Chastain, 1990; Pennebaker, 1989, 1990; Wegner, 1989, 1992, 1994). Implied in this last step is my contention that secret keeping per se is not necessarily problematic.

Note that this model concerning when to reveal secrets is different from the one described in Kelly and McKillop (1996), in which we offered suggestions for when to reveal personal secrets, such as a childhood molestation experience, that a relational partner may or may not expect to be told. This model, in contrast, includes the specific relational context of the secret information, and thus provides a more precise and comprehensive analysis of when to reveal personal secrets. In particular, it includes an analysis of whether the partner expects access to the hidden information and how likely the partner is to discover the information on his or her own, whereas the previous model did not. The term "relational partner" in this context refers to any other person with whom one has a relationship, including one's boss, spouse, or friends. In the following paragraphs, I elaborate on each of the steps to the proposed model. Each of the next four headings corresponds to the four boxes in Fig. 1, starting with the box at the top of the figure.

PRIVATE VERSUS SECRET INFORMATION

Derlega et al. (1993) have argued that in the best interests of a relationship, on the one hand, a person may want to disclose information that relates to issues of trust, trustworthiness, and caring for one's partner. An example might include having gambled away some of the couple's earnings that week or having had an extramarital affair. On the other hand, Derlega and coworkers argued, information that does not have important implications for the relationship may not be necessary to reveal (see also, Karpel, 1980). Examples of this type include secrets about one's past, such as a sexual molestation that has been reasonably resolved and does not seem to have significant effects on how the person behaves in the relationship. According to Derlega et al. (1993), the person may want to reveal the information as a means of showing trust in the partner, as well as wanting to be seen accurately by the partner, but need not feel an obligation to do so.

However, this distinction between secrets that have bearing on the relationship and those that do not is a very difficult one to make. Take the following as an example: An acquaintance, whom I will call Nancy, offered me a detailed account of the revelation of her most troubling secret. She told me that through her experiences in therapy, she finally got the courage 3 months before her wedding to tell her fiancé that she had received an abortion as a teenager. She felt that the information was relevant to their upcoming marriage and plans to have children, especially since they are both Catholic. She also felt that because it was relevant, not telling him would create mounting stress for her. Thus, she gave him the full disclosure of what was to her a traumatic experience and secretive burden. Although he seemed to respond well to the revelation initially, 2 weeks later he called off the wedding and asked her to move out of their new house. She was so shocked and distraught over this rejection that she took sedatives for several months. After she recovered, she said that she was relieved to discover sooner rather than later what an empty and unsupportive person he was. Although just months earlier she had felt that he was the love of her life and was so happy to be marrying him, now she believed that it was better to get out of this relationship than to live with the stress of that secret.

Was the abortion a relevant secret that had bearing on issues of trust in the relationship? Or was it a matter of privacy and something she would have benefitted from keeping to herself? Part of the reader's interpretation of the wisdom of Nancy's decision to reveal her abortion secret is likely to reflect the reader's core assumptions about the amount of stress that is associated with secret keeping and the extent to which suppressing information can undermine or sabotage a relationship. Classically trained psychoanalysts, for example, are likely to believe that virtually all major secrets are relevant to adult functioning and interpersonal relationships and that keeping secrets could allow the secrets to manifest themselves in recurring nightmares and other symptoms. Viewing secrets in this manner would seem to lead to the conclusion that Nancy made a wise decision to reveal the abortion secret. The reader should keep in mind, however, that psychoanalysts also might interpret Nancy's revealing her secret as an effort to sabotage the relationship and avoid dealing with her own feelings of intimacy and commitment. They might argue that revealing the secret in the therapy session is appropriate and necessary, whereas revealing to the partner is not.

The research that has the most direct bearing on Nancy's situation was the study by Major and Gramzow (1999) described in Chapter 3. They found no relationship between keeping an abortion a secret and feeling distressed (after they statistically controlled for other, more relevant factors), which suggests that keeping an abortion a secret might not be as distressing as one might think. However, even if one does assume that secret keeping is stressful and can sabotage a particular relationship, I contend that the relevant-secret versus not-relevant-secret distinction proposed by Derlega et al. (1993) does not offer a completely satisfying guide for when one should reveal a personal secret in part because it is extremely difficult to determine which secrets are relevant to issues of trust in a particular relationship. In addition, sometimes a partner will directly ask a question about a particular secret and say, "Have you ever had an abortion?" Derlega and coworkers' recommendation does not address how one should respond in such cases.

Perhaps a better guide for making the decision to reveal personal hidden information gets back to my definition of secrecy versus privacy described in Chapter 1. When making the decision to reveal hidden information, a person must first decide whether that information is indeed secret—as opposed to private—information. Specifically, the individual must ask himself or herself, "Does the other person expect to have access to this kind of information" (i.e., expect to be told the hidden information)? If the answer is no, then any fretting over a decision to reveal is moot. The person can write off that information as private and keep it hidden. In Nancy's case, her therapist encouraged her to reveal the abortion secret to her fiancé. Thus, it is possible that he reframed that once-private information as secret information, even though in actuality Nancy's fiancé may not have expected access to this information and may not have wanted her to reveal it (i.e., the information may have been private in the context of that relationship).

Such distinctions between secrecy and privacy also are essential in professional settings, where much personal information is private and is expected to be hidden. Personal revelations made at work in the name of openness and honesty often are considered inappropriate. Just as Peskin (1992) observed that the ability to conceal information to get what one desires is a sign of maturation in children, so too I argue that using discretion in the workplace is a sign of maturity and professionalism. However, people often reveal personal information at work that they probably should not reveal. In my own experiences as a professor, for example, I have been struck by the fact that students sometimes tell me that the reason they missed a class or test was that they were hung over and were throwing up! Such disclosures put me in an awkward position: Knowing that they induced their own illness makes me reluctant to give them a makeup exam because it does not seem fair to the other students who studied the night before the exam and took it on time. It is much better when they offer a simpler explanation such as, "I was sick and had to miss the test." In another example, a master's-level student once asked me to be on his thesis committee, even though I did not know the research area of his thesis very well. When I formally met with him and asked why he had picked me for his committee, he said bluntly and honestly, "I know that you are flexible when it comes to students who have already collected their data before the proposal meeting." That was the entire explanation. There was nothing substantive mentioned about why I might be an appropriate member of his committee, just the simple truth. In yet another example, a student in my undergraduate seminar told me in a private meeting that she had written the paper (for which she got an A) in one night. In all these cases, it would seem as though the students simply slipped up on their impression management tactics and just wanted to be honest. However, given the data presented in Chapters 7 and 8, it seems that at some level people always are trying to construct desirable identities, or at least avoid undesirable ones. In these cases, the students probably thought that being seen as honest was good and desirable in this professional context, just as it typically is in their personal contexts. In truth, though, I was startled by the blunt honesty and realized that I have come to expect private information to remain hidden in the workplace as part of professionalism. I viewed their disclosures as private information to which I did not expect to have access. The students may have believed that they would be viewed favorably for being so honest, but actually they more aptly might be described as being somewhat naive or lacking maturity in this instance. Thus, my recommendation to the reader is to keep in mind what the relational partner expects to have access to and what the person expects to be kept private, and to weigh that information heavily in a decision to reveal or conceal the information. This recommendation is especially salient at work where there is so much at stake and where keeping private motives hidden is often the norm. Revealing too much information can be seen as naive rather than as honest.

However, if the answer to the question of whether the other person expects access to hidden information is yes, then the information is a secret. For instance, some professors actually may expect students to give them detailed explanations for why they miss class and reward them for admitting to the complete truths. As the reader can see, such expectations are defined from the perspective of the potential confidant in a particular relationship, rather than defined according to some general rule about various social contexts. Even therapists who generally report wanting a great deal of openness from their clients do vary on what they expect their clients to reveal (Kelly, 1998, raw data). If one is uncertain what the other person's expectations about revelations are, he or she can ask about the partner's feelings about the general topic. Some couples, for example, agree that it is acceptable to engage in extrarelational sexual activities but not to tell each other about them. I contend that ascertaining whether the partner expects access to certain kinds of hidden information typically is easier than trying to figure out whether the hidden information has bearing on issues of trust or trustworthiness in a relationship because the former requires less insight from the partner. Also, as mentioned earlier, new relational partners often ask direct questions such as, "How many sexual partners have you had" or "Have you had an HIV test" which suggests that they expect to be told that information. If the hidden information is indeed a secret, as defined by the expectations of the relational partner, then the secret keeper must make some additional decisions before revealing the secret. These decisions regarding the revealing of secrets, as opposed to private information, are outlined in the following paragraphs.

DETERMINING WHETHER A PARTNER
IS AN APPROPRIATE CONFIDANT

Once a person has decided that the hidden information is a secret in the context of a particular relationship, he or she must try to gauge whether the relational partner is an appropriate confidant (i.e., who will be discreet and nonjudgmental and will not reject the secret keeper). However, anticipating whether a person qualifies as an appropriate confidant presents a challenge because it is tough to know how the person will react until after the secret has been revealed. If the secret keeper knows the partner well and has known this person for a substantial period of time, then the secret keeper will have a wealth of prior experience on which to base a prediction regarding the likelihood that the partner's response to a revelation will be positive. The secret keeper may reflect on times when he or she or others have revealed personal information to the partner and may recall whether the partner reacted in a supportive fashion as well as refrained from revealing the information to other people. The secret keeper may also recall the partner's stated opinions on topics related to the secret and use this information to predict the partner's likely response. For example, a formerly bald man would probably avoid revealing the fact that he has had hair implants to a partner who has repeatedly expressed disdain for those who have had such procedures.

In addition to relying on previous experience, individuals may test their partners' responses to a disclosure by jokingly or seemingly inadvertently introducing the topic and gauging their partners' reactions (Duck, 1988). Miell and Duck (1986) have shown that, in much the same way as politicians do, people float trial balloons before making serious and potentially damaging disclosures. For example, a husband might recount to his wife the tale of a friend's marital infidelity (taking great care not to arouse suspicion) and carefully study her reaction before deciding whether to reveal his own transgression. Or a child might ask a parent, quite transparently, what could happen to "someone" who admitted to stealing candy from the checkout line, before revealing that he or she had actually stolen the candy. Other ways of anticipating whether the relational partner will be an appropriate confidant might include paying attention to whether that person reveals personal information about other people and whether others consider this person to be trustworthy and nonjudgmental. If the partner passes these "tests," then the secret keeper should reveal to that person, knowing that there is still some risk or uncertainty in sharing with another.

Typically, such evaluations of the partner as a potential confidant take time. Timing also is important in the sense that the partner is likely to expect different levels of revelation at different times in the relationship. Models of self-disclosure indicate that the association between stage of relationship and the effects of self-disclosure is curvilinear (see Collins & Miller, 1994; Derlega, 1988). Specifically, revealing highly personal information upon meeting someone may backfire, whereas making such disclosures after getting acquainted with someone can be a way of developing intimate bonds with that person (Altman & Taylor, 1973; Wortman, Adesman, Herman, & Greenberg, 1976). As mentioned in the previous paragraphs, knowing a partner well allows the secret keeper to have enough information to determine whether the partner will keep the secret and will not judge the secret keeper for its content. However, after knowing someone a long time, revealing secrets again may backfire, because the partner may perceive that the secrets have been inappropriately withheld and may feel betrayed by the secret keeper (see Derlega, 1988). For example, if a patient who is receiving treatment to control her drinking confesses to her therapist during their last scheduled session that she has continued drinking throughout the treatment, the patient will not have the opportunity to sort out the implications of the revelation with the therapist. Moreover, the therapist may be astounded by the fact that she did not trust him enough to tell him this relevant information earlier in their sessions. I recommend that people share their secrets with relational partners they know well but not so well that it is too late to reveal to those partners.

An important paradox emerges when considering what stage of a relationship is the appropriate time for a revelation. Although people in relationships tend to trust each other more as time passes, their self-disclosure becomes more judgmental as the relationship develops (Derlega et al., 1993). Thus, each partner might be tempted to reveal very personal information during the initial, relatively nonjudgmental phase of the relationship as a way of getting closer to the other person. However, that same information that was once viewed without negative judgment may come to haunt the revealer later when his or her partner looks back on those disclosures with disdain. For example, a woman tells her new attentive boyfriend that she experimented with lesbian relationships in college but that she is decidedly heterosexual now. He seems at ease with the information and even thinks that the revelation makes her more intriguing, until a year later when she begins to lose interest in sex with him because she is so buried in work. He becomes threatened by her earlier disclosures and "accuses" her of being a lesbian. The point of this example is to encourage a secret keeper to use discretion, especially at the beginning of a relationship when the partner seems most receptive and non-judgmental. My rationale for this recommendation is that the secret keeper has not yet had enough contact with the person to be able to evaluate how he or she might respond to various revelations later.

In addition to being sensitive to the stage of the relationship when deciding to reveal to a relational partner, the secret keeper should make sure that the partner knows that the information should be kept hidden from others. Sometimes partners have a different philosophy of openness and inadvertently tell others' secrets because they themselves would not have kept such secrets in their own relationships. For example, 2 years ago, a friend told me a "secret" about his participation in a dangerous team athletic event. He had to climb a telephone pole as part of a team-building exercise with his colleagues. I thought that event actually made him look daring and brave, but he asked me not to tell anyone. Some months later, I stumbled and told the story to another friend right in front of him! He was irritated with me and I was shocked at my own slip, given how much I care about being a good confidant. I realized later that it was hard for me to remember that the story was supposed to be kept secret because it did not seem inherently like "secret material." I believed that at some level he wanted me to tell others, but I was wrong. Conversely, sometimes people tell secrets that they expect (and hope) will get spread around. One time in a professional setting a senior colleague told me in confidence that she was going to resign. I did not tell anyone that information, and she was later shocked to discover that none of my peers knew about her imminent resignation. In that case, she herself would have told others that "secret," and thus expected me to do the same. My point here is that if one wants to tell his partner a secret, then he should offer the rationale for why it should be kept secret. If the other does not seem to understand the rationale or agree that the information should be kept secret, then the revealer should expect that the other person might reveal it later. At the same time, if one is the recipient of such information that he does not agree should be kept secret, then he should say that he cannot be expected to remember in the years to come to keep the secret.

Another occurrence that enhances the chances that a relational partner will remain an appropriate confidant and continue to be discreet long after the revelation is that the partner usually discloses very personal information in return. Self-disclosure researchers often have discussed the norm of reciprocity: When someone reveals personal information to another person, it is expected that the other person will share some personal information in return or will act interested in the revelation and show understanding (Berg, 1987; Berg & Archer, 1980; Chaikin & Derlega, 1974). If a secret keeper learns equally personal and potentially stigmatizing information about the partner, then the partner might fear retaliation enough that he or she would never reveal the secret even if the two were no longer in a relationship. Part of the trouble with the modern, mobile society with a very high rate of divorce is that husbands and wives tell each other very personal secrets, which still are protected in courts of law under "spousal privilege," and then often end up in new cities with new spouses. What they have divulged to their previous spouse is no longer as protected as they once had thought because there is less accountability now that they share different networks of friends. What this means is that people who have new networks do not necessarily feel the need to keep a former partner's secrets because they do not have to worry about losing that bond (i.e., it is already lost). At the same time, because of the "small-world problem" (see below) and increasing technology that is intensifying that problem, there is a greater risk than ever that one's reputation can be damaged by a former spouse's revelations. In a nutshell, revealing one's personal secrets to a relational partner puts the revealer in a vulnerable position. This vulnerability often is diminished because the revealer learns some equally stigmatizing information about the partner. A way of protecting oneself is to show the other that there is still some accountability and relational connection even after a breakup.

In sum, if a secret keeper believes that his partner is an appropriate confidant who will not tell others the secret, will not judge him negatively, and will not reject him, then he should reveal the secret to her. He needs to wait until the timing is right both to decide whether she has these qualities and to match her expectations of their intimacy level for the time that they have known each other. Also, he should tell her why the information should be kept secret, so that she can remember to do so. The fact that she usually will share secrets in return may enhance her level of continued discretion, even if the relationship ends. If he decides that she is not an appropriate confidant, however, then he next needs to consider how likely she is to discover the secret on her own before deciding whether to reveal the secret to her.

PROBABILITY OF BEING DISCOVERED

People typically expect to have to protect their social reputations, especially when they think that their actions will come to the attention of their family and friends from outside sources (Emler, 1990). Assuming that there are benefits associated with revealing hidden negative personal information oneself—so that one can put his or her own spin on the information and garner the support of intimates (Emler, 1990)—it would be helpful to be able to gauge the probability of a secret's being discovered when making the decision to reveal the secret. As yet, there is no objective way of knowing what these probabilities are. In the following paragraphs, I offer competing arguments concerning whether people are likely to underestimate or overestimate the likelihood of their secrets being discovered.

Emler (1990) proposed that because people rarely commit shameful or delinquent acts alone, these acts are not as concealable as they might think. Supporting this idea are the findings (described in Chapter 8) that confidants frequently reveal personal information about other people (e.g., Christophe & Rime, 1997). Moreover, researchers have demonstrated that when social reputations are measured, typically there is a consensus among knowledgeable informants (i.e., those who share community membership or having extensively overlapping personal networks with the target person) (Emler, 1990) about the attributes of the targets (e.g., Cheek, 1982; Moskowitz & Schwartz, 1982). Even though these reputational measures have been criticized for measuring more about the perceivers than the perceived (e.g., Cronbach, 1955), they do suggest that people's social networks may be more interconnected than they think. Emler (1990) noted that this is especially the case for people with high levels of social participation, such as actors, teachers, and politicians. Likewise, Milgram (1967) showed that people's social networks are surprisingly interconnected, calling this phenomenon the "small-world problem." Specifically, he observed in 1967 that starting with any two people, the probability that they will know each other is 1 chance in 200,000 for the American population. However, there is a 50/50 chance of linking any two people up with only two intermediate acquaintances! He demonstrated that the median interconnection between any two Americans chosen randomly is 5, with a range from 2 to 10. In addition, Emler and Fisher (1981) found that in informal conversations of students and teachers, the most common topic of conversation after self-disclosure was named acquaintances and the doings of these acquaintances. Thus, it seems both that people are more likely to be linked to others than they think and that these others are likely to be gossiping about common acquaintances.

I myself witnessed the "small-world" phenomenon firsthand at a recent hair-cutting appointment. My hairdresser told me that while his good-looking male friend was on vacation, the friend had sex with a beautiful and very famous young actress. My hairdresser did not tell me the name of his friend but certainly did tell me the name of the actress. This example fits Emler's point that a person's level of social participation affects how much people are aware of that person's social reputation. In this case, the actress has a much higher rate of social participation as compared with my hairdresser's friend, and thus needs to be much more aware of what people know about her if she is to manage her reputation. At the same time, however, because the actress is so famous, the listener is probably more likely to assume that the story was made up as a form of bragging.

In contrast to Emler's (1990) position that people tend to overestimate how concealable their stigmatizing actions are, I suggest that it also is possible that people might be too paranoid about how much people are likely to discover about them. Tversky and Kahneman (1973) demonstrated that people tend to overestimate the probability of the occurrence of events that are salient or vivid to them (i.e., those that come to mind more easily). These researchers referred to this phenomenon as the "availability bias." Moreover, as described in the previous chapter, Ross et al. (1977) demonstrated that people tend to see others as more similar to themselves than they actually are. Applying these well-documented principles to the model, I suggest that because people's own secrets are likely to be more vivid or salient to them than they are to other people, and because people tend to assume that others are more similar to themselves than they actually are, people may overestimate the probability that others are discussing or thinking about their secrets. They may draw this conclusion simply because they themselves are thinking about their secrets.

I suggest that a general guide for how likely it is that one's relational partner will discover a secret is whether there have been witnesses to this secret event; if there are witnesses and those witnesses have either direct or indirect contact with the partner, then one may assume that there is a reasonable chance that the partner will discover the secret. (Unless the witness is particularly discreet or is legally and ethically bound to confidentiality, such as one's doctor, therapist, or lawyer.) In cases where there are witnesses, the secret keeper and all the witnesses must keep track of what is secret information, and this is not an easy task. Wegner et al. (1994) observed that under conditions of high cognitive load, people are not very good at suppressing secret information. High cognitive load refers to diminished cognitive capacity, which can result from drinking alcohol, being very tired, or being nervous or distracted. This difficulty is illustrated by what happened to a couple (whom I will call Jim and Cindy) who dated for 2 years, broke up, and then each had a brief sexual relationship with another person. Their different sets of friends knew about their respective brief relationships. Then, when the couple got back together and their friends were sitting around having a drink, one of Cindy's friends mentioned her dislike of the man whom Cindy had dated briefly. Cindy had not yet told her boyfriend that she had another relationship when they broke up, so Jim became very embarrassed. His friends could see that he was not aware of the information and that he was stunned to be told under those circumstances.

If others know the secret and they have any contact with the partner, then the secret keeper should consider revealing the secret to the partner. This recommendation especially holds in clear cases in which the discovery of the secret is imminent, say, for example, a former lover threatens to tell one's husband about an affair. The secret keeper should explain her perspective on the once-hidden event. Even then, though, trying to put a spin on the revelation might not be that helpful if the husband believes that she was forced to reveal the secret. Thus, it is important to reveal the secret, focusing on the theme and not the details (if possible) at a time when the partner can believe that the decision to reveal it was initiated by the secret keeper herself.

If only the secret keeper knows the secret, however, then it is possible that he or she will be able to keep the secret quite well after a period of getting used to the secret. Moreover, the secret keeper should be better at keeping it than other people because he or she is more motivated to keep track of what should be kept secret. In the example of Nancy who had an abortion, it seems as though since no one knew about it except for her (and her doctor) from the beginning, she perhaps eventually could get used to the idea that it is private information that no one but her needs to know about. If it is not likely that the partner will discover the secret because only the secret keeper knows about the hidden information, then the secret keeper will need to move to the next step of the model in deciding whether to reveal the secret to the partner.

TROUBLING SECRETS

If the secret keeper determines that she does not think that the partner will discover the secret, she still needs to ask herself whether the secret is troubling in the context of the relationship. It may seem obvious that one only should reveal a secret if the secret is troubling. However, as described in the previous chapters, this idea contradicts the long-held supposition by psychoanalysts dating back to Freud (see Freud, 1958) that secret keepers ultimately will develop symptoms if they continue to squelch their secrets. Although there is a fair amount of recent correlational evidence that self-reports of secret keeping and symptoms are linked (e.g., Ichiyama et al., 1993; Larson & Chastain, 1990), there is no direct experimental evidence that people who choose to keep secrets actually develop symptoms as a result (see Chapter 3). It is possible that with practice, people can learn to suppress their unwanted thoughts with very little effort (Kelly & Kahn, 1994). In cases in which keeping secrets from the partner is relatively effortless for the secret keeper, I argue that the secret keeper should avoid sharing secrets to sidestep the rejecting feedback and other negative consequences that can be associated with sharing (e.g., see Lehman et al., 1986). It is the people who are suffering from carrying personal secrets whom I encourage to reveal their secrets.

How does one know if a secret is troubling in the context of a relationship? Sometimes the link between a secret and problems is apparent to the secret keeper because he or she is ruminating over the secret and is upset by such repetitious and intrusive thoughts. But at other times the connection between secrets and symptoms is less clear. I suggest that if a person is keeping a secret and is experiencing symptoms, such as depression, ulcers, and headaches, that have been found to be associated with secret keeping (e.g., Larson & Chastain, 1990), then the person should consider the possibility that the symptoms are the result of keeping the secret or that the secret is troubling. Also, if the person is worried that the partner would feel betrayed by the secrecy or that the partner will find out about the secret, then the person should view the secret as troubling.

I suggest that people who are troubled by their secrets in the context of particular relationships should talk about them with their relational partners. This decision to reveal is risky, however, because in reaching this last step in the model, the secret keeper already has assessed that the partner may not be an appropriate confidant (i.e., is not discreet, or is judgmental, or will reject the secret keeper). In the following paragraphs, I offer options to revealing troubling secrets to a relational partner who may not be an appropriate confidant. My emphasis is on avoiding the dangers associated with revealing to such a person who could not only end the relationship but also damage the secret keeper's reputation afterward by telling others about the secret.

OPTIONS TO REVEALING THE COMPLETE TRUTH

Revealing Themes as Opposed to Details

As noted in the previous paragraphs, there are two points in the model where the secret keepers are encouraged to focus on revealing the themes to their secrets rather than the details of them. These are when the partner is not perceived as an appropriate confidant and either (1) the partner is likely to discover the secret on his or her own or (2) the secret is troubling in the context of the relationship. For example, imagine that a young, conservative man asks his new girlfriend how many sexual partners she has had. Imagine, too, that she estimates that she has had 60 partners and fears that when they visit her hometown at Christmastime, he will discover that she had a reputation in high school for promiscuity. Because she is worried that he will reject her if he knows how many partners she has had, she can focus (truthfully) on the theme by saying, "I think it's crude to discuss numbers, but I can tell you that I used to be pretty sexually active when I was younger." Another example that is much more disturbing involves a psychotherapy client who has burned his children with lit cigarettes as a punishment for their misbehavior. The client may imagine or accurately perceive that his therapist will judge him negatively for this behavior, and the therapist is legally required to report such a revelation to the authorities. Yet he is very troubled by the secret, so he says, "I have trouble managing my anger with my children and want to learn what I need to do when my anger gets out of control." This way he can receive help for his abuse of the children and avoid losing his custody of them and being put in prison.

Even though I am offering this as a potential solution to the dilemma of wanting to be open and yet avoid negative judgments or rejection, Arkin and Hermann (2000) argued that themes, as compared with specific behaviors, have greater implications for one's identity (Vallacher & Wegner, 1987). In particular, they asserted that a focus on themes in the context of psychotherapy could encourage clients to experience a generalized sense of shame as opposed to a feeling of guilt, and that guilt can be adaptive in inducing clients to change their behaviors, whereas shame can prompt a maladaptive effort to change the self. As a solution to the dilemma surrounding negative disclosures, Arkin and Hermann (2000) indicated that

> it may be better to describe the event fully, but in a neutral, factual manner. This would allow the opportunity for client and therapist, when necessary, to reframe the client's understanding of specific events and help negate the tendency to move to broader, self-oriented levels of thinking and characterizing of the self. (p. 503)

Their suggestion certainly is reasonable for clients who can imagine that their therapists would view them favorably after a description of negative events. Moreover, it captures what many therapists, including psychoanalysts and cognitive–behavioral therapists, already do.

However, my recommendation targets those times when clients and secret keepers in general cannot imagine that their confidants would view them favorably after a revelation. I agree with Arkin and Hermann (2000) that it can be beneficial for a client to reveal behaviors like, "I sometimes slam the door, or stomp out" (p. 503). But these behaviors almost certainly would not be in the category of acts that most clients would fear revealing to their therapists. In Kelly (2000a), I used the example of the man who hit his wife with a bat one time because when people do such terrible things, those few acts often come to define them. The same is likely to be true for very humiliating details, such as those in the infamous Starr Report (1998), which was criticized for its gratuitous provision of sexual details: "According to Ms. Lewinsky, she performed oral sex on the President on nine occasions ... on one occasion, the President inserted a cigar into her vagina" (p. 5). I speculate that a client who feels burdened by similarly humiliating details could indicate something like "we had sexual contact" and could discuss her feelings about the events to let the therapist know what impact those events had on her. This option might be preferable to revealing the details and then imaging the undesirable themes that the therapist is developing about her. Of course, one must keep in mind that it is possible for a person to want others to hear such sexual details, because she anticipates that she will be seen in a desirable way (e.g., as a playful or adventurous woman). Also, what is considered to be undesirable by most people in one culture at one period of time may not be undesirable in another culture or at another time. My recommendation to focus on themes as opposed to details applies only to cases where the revealer expects to be viewed in an undesirable way if the details are revealed.

Support for my argument that a few noteworthy acts can be linked directly to their broader undesirable themes comes from evidence (see Mischel & Peake, 1982) that people judge others to have consistent traits, such as self-centeredness or conscientiousness, by stringing together their highly prototypical behaviors (i.e., behaviors that are representative of their broader categories). If a therapist hears that a client has beaten his wife on the back with a bat, the client might imagine that the therapist will weigh that detail heavily in evaluating that client's overall personality. This perception is likely to be accurate, too, given that Regan and Hill (1992) found that therapists formed very negative clinical conjectures about their clients, which they then hid from the clients. In addition, research has shown that therapists' perceptions of a target person are consistently less favorable than laypersons' perceptions, whether that target person is a client or nonclient (see Wills, 1978). It should not be surprising that clinicians form such negative opinions, because they are trained to use the *Diagnostic and Statistical Manual of Mental Disorders* (DSM) (see American Psychiatric Association, 1994), which lists behaviors that qualify their patients to have various disorders.

My suggestion about revealers' generating their own themes involves their creating relatively desirable themes, as opposed to the undesirable themes (e.g., having feelings of being self-centered) described by Arkin and Hermann (2000). For example, the man who hit his wife might say, "I am a person who is committed to dealing with my issues of rage" as opposed to, "I am a despicable wife-beater who has no place in society." If the client reveals the detail of hitting his wife, he might imagine getting feedback from the therapist that supports the more undesirable wife-beater label. Moreover, therapists probably are more apt to empathize with and like their clients if the clients can focus on their feelings of rage, frustration, hurt, and helplessness, rather than if the clients describe the heinous acts in a detached way. Empathy has been found to play an important role in clients' improvement (see Beutler et al., 1994), and clients who are more well liked by their therapists tend to show more progress in therapy (e.g., Stoler, 1963).

In the case of revealing to relational partners who are not ethically or legally bound to keep the secret information confidential the way therapists are, an important added benefit of revealing themes (which are phrased in ways that are desirable to the revealer) is that even if the partners turn out to be indiscreet, they still will be less able to use that information to damage the revealer's reputation. Themes, as compared with specific details, are less vivid and less interesting, and therefore are less likely to be fodder for gossip. For example, saying "I used to be more sexually active" is less noteworthy than "I had 60 sexual partners."

In sum, an alternative to complete revelation is to focus on the themes (which are phrased in desirable ways) as opposed to the details of the secrets. The problem with revealing details is that they may be readily linked to broader negative judgments, and relational partners may tell others these details and damage the revealer's reputation. Even in therapy, clients might consider revealing the themes to their problems when the details are particularly heinous and they would not be able to imagine that the therapist would view them favorably after hearing the details.

Establishing What Is Private Information

As mentioned earlier, the first steps in the model are to determine whether the relational partner expects access to the information and whether the partner is an appropriate confidant. I suggested that if the answer to both of those questions is yes, then the secret keeper should reveal the secret. However, it is still up to the secret keeper to decide whether he or she really wants to reveal that information. For example, even if the partner is an appropriate confidant who expects to be told certain information, such as whether the secret keeper has ever been pregnant, the secret keeper still may choose to keep this information to herself because she views it as something that he should not expect access to or because she would like to keep her personal boundaries firmly established in the relationship. Relationships are dynamic, and part of developing intimacy involves learning what level of revelation the two partners can expect from each other. If the partners have different expectations, they need to identify this difference early on in the relationship to avoid overstepping their boundaries and offending each other. They can set up rules such as "Don't ask questions when you can only accept one answer" or "Let me offer information about my sexual past if I wish—do not ask me specific questions."

An interesting paradox emerges when people respond to personal or embarrassing questions: They may view a completely factual and truthful set of responses as less representative of themselves than a more distorted, favorable set of disclosures (see Kelly et al., 1996; Schlenker, 1986). This distortion seems to be a normal part of everyday living and has even been construed as a sign a positive mental health (see Taylor & Brown, 1988). Imagine that someone who sees herself as a very moral and good person is cornered into a factual revelation about her past and in particular is asked whether she has ever had an affair with a married man. To herself, she acknowledges that she has had such an affair but is committed to never doing that again. As such, she does not see the whole, blunt truth as being representative of herself as she is now. So paradoxically she may be representing more honestly how she sees herself by omitting this previous bad act, especially if she feels that the listener will draw the wrong conclusions about her if she reveals this information. Even if she is factually truthful in her disclosures and then tries to explain the circumstances in which she had this affair, the chances are that the listener will not weigh that disqualifying information very heavily in judging her character. After all, researchers have demonstrated in a number of studies over the years that although people weigh situational causes for their own bad behaviors very heavily, they tend to attribute bad acts to other people's character (see, for example, Silvia & Duvak, 2001).

My suggestion for addressing this dilemma of wanting to be truthful but also to avoid presenting oneself in an undesirable way is to say something like, "As a matter of principle, I consider my previous sexual experiences—or lack thereof—to be private matters. If I answer this question, there may be more to follow like it, and I want to be clear that I would rather volunteer any such information than to be asked about it." If instead the question was how many sexual partners has a person had, the partner might have a legitimate concern for his safety as her new lover. In that case, she can use condoms and get tested for sexually transmitted diseases to address any potential risks that getting involved with her poses to his health. A revelation of the details of her sexual past is not required to address his concerns. This recommendation to declare what she finds to be private early in the relationship is consistent with the empirical findings that partners in successful relationships negotiate what they will talk about with each other (e.g., Coupland, Coupland, Giles, & Wieman, 1988).

Such negotiations can avoid some of the complications involving the dynamics between people. For example, there are times when a person perceives that the partner expects access to the hidden information when the partner really does not expect access. There also are times when the partner already knows about the hidden information and considers it private yet still gets upset because the partner believes that the person is keeping it secret. Because the process of keeping a secret from one's partner can be disconcerting, it may be especially useful to identify what is private information early in the relationship.

REVEALING TO SOMEONE ELSE

Imagine that a secret keeper has gotten through each of the steps of the model and has decided that a secret is troubling in the context of the relationship and that the partner is not an appropriate confidant and is unlikely to discover the secret on his own. In such a case, the secret keeper is in a bit of a dilemma. If the secret keeper could conquer her feelings of being troubled about the secret, then her relationship could remain undamaged by the secret. The example of Nancy, who had the abortion, comes to mind. She talked to her therapist about the abortion, and he encouraged her to reveal it to her fiancé. However, it might have been enough for her to work through her feelings about the abortion with the therapist, who could have helped her see the abortion as a private matter that could rest within her with no negative consequences. As described in Chapter 5, a possible route to feeling better about one's secrets is to gain new insights into them. Therapists are trained to offer interpretations to clients' problems, and secret keepers might benefit from sorting out their troubling secrets with the therapists instead of with relational partners in their immediate social context.

WRITING IT DOWN

A drawback to this last suggestion stems from the finding in my (Kelly, 1998) study, which showed that even with trained therapists who presumably fit all the positive qualities of confidants described in the previous chapter, clients who were keeping a relevant secret experienced greater symptom reduction than those who were not keeping one. The seeming contradiction between this finding and the model can be resolved by the fact that the model stresses that the secret keeper's perception of the relational partner as nonjudgmental is critical in his or her decision to reveal a personal secret. It is likely that at times secret keepers may imagine, or accurately perceive, that their relational partners are judgmental, particularly when the secret keepers have committed unusually heinous acts. Moreover, in some cases, even if a relational partner is completely trustworthy, the secret keeper may not perceive the partner's trustworthiness or may simply never feel comfortable telling anyone about an appalling or extremely embarrassing secret. In these cases, the secret keeper may benefit from privately writing down the secret and not sharing it with the partner (see Pennebaker, 1990). It is possible that he or she may benefit from writing about the secrets in an effort to gain new insights into them (see Kelly et al., 2001). However, this option is only reasonable in cases in which the partner who is an inappropriate confidant is unlikely to discover the information. If the partner is likely to discover the secret, then a more drastic step may be required, as described next.

Ending the Relationship

Sometimes it is better to end the relationship with a partner who is not perceived as an appropriate confidant and who nonetheless demands access to a particular secret, such as one's having herpes, than to reveal the secret. If the partner learns of the herpes secret, he or she might end the relationship anyway and then tell others about this potentially embarrassing and reputation-damaging secret. Since self-disclosure is such a crucial element of forging relationships (see Derlega et al., 1993), perceiving one's partner as an inappropriate confidant may be sufficient grounds for ending a relationship anyway.

LIMITATIONS

Encouraging Thought Suppression?

Elsewhere, social psychologists Arkin and Hermann (2000) criticized my recommendation for psychotherapy clients to reveal themes as opposed to details of really heinous acts to the therapists (see Kelly, 2000a,b) and argued that efforts to withhold information may have the ironic effect of enhancing the impact of that information on one's self-concept. They cited research on the negative effects of thought suppression (see Wegner, 1994) and suggested that encouraging clients to withhold details might make those thoughts even more vivid, salient, and central. Hill et al. (2000), too, suggested that clients' withholding information could cause them to miss out on the benefits of therapy, and they cited research on the negative effects of inhibiting information to support their claim (see Pennebaker, 1997a).

I have two sets of responses to this point. First, I am advocating an overhauling of current expectations of very high levels of revelation in therapy. If clients can come to believe that it is not a requirement of therapy for them to reveal unseemly details about themselves, then there would be no need for them to suppress such details. As described in Chapter 1, I make the following distinction between secrecy and privacy: Whereas privacy connotes the expectation of being free from unsanctioned intrusion, secrecy does not. Secrecy involves active attempts to prevent such intrusion or leaks, and the secret keeper exerts this energy, in part, because he or she perceives that other people may have some claim to the hidden information. It follows that if clients do not feel pressed for disclosure, then they could view these details as private, rather than as secrets that need to be suppressed.

Second, even if clients did choose to suppress some details, the evidence that those details would ironically become more significant is far from clear. Wegner and his colleagues have demonstrated that when people are given thoughts to suppress, they become more preoccupied with those thoughts than if they had not suppressed them (e.g., Wegner et al., 1987). However, one pair of experiments (Kelly & Kahn, 1994) showed that when participants were asked to suppress their own unwanted intrusive thoughts, they actually either became less preoccupied with the thoughts (Exp. 1) or did not experience any change in the frequency of the thoughts (Exp. 2). Also, the results from Pennebaker's (1997b) studies may not be relevant to the present discussion, because those studies focused on revelations in confidential, anonymous settings (i.e., they were not designed to look at the effects of revealing to an important audience). The crux of my argument for why it is acceptable for clients to censor some particularly heinous details is that the perceived feedback from an important audience (i.e., their therapists) could have negative implications for their self-concepts.

TYPE OF SECRET

As mentioned in Chapter 1, to date, the research comparing types of secrets has focused primarily on traumatic, negative secret keeping. This research has yet to support the idea that the type of negative or traumatic secret one is keeping (e.g., about having experienced incest vs. having been divorced several times) plays a role in whether one would benefit from revealing that secret to others. For example, when Pennebaker and O'Heeron (1984) surveyed spouses of people who had committed suicide or died in a car crash, they expected that the spouses of suicide victims would talk less about the trauma with others than would the spouses of the car crash victims due to the stigma associated with suicide. They also expected that the spouses of suicide victims would have poorer psychological functioning as a result of not discussing the trauma with others. However, whether the victims committed suicide or died in a car crash was not predictive of spouses' talking about the trauma or of their psychological functioning.

One reason for the lack of support for the idea that the type of traumatic secret is predictive of benefits from revealing is that there is a tremendous amount of variation in response to life stressors (e.g., Pennebaker, 1990; Silver et al., 1983; Silver & Wortman, 1980; Wortman & Silver, 1987, 1989). For instance, when my students and I (Kelly, Coenen, & Johnston, 1995) asked undergraduates to identify and evaluate their most traumatic life events, some individuals reported the breakup of a romantic relationship as their most traumatic life experience and rated it as "extremely disturbing," whereas others listed having been sexually molested by a close relative or having been violently raped as their most traumatic life event and rated it as somewhat less disturbing. Moreover, Silver et al. (1983) found that among a group of survivors of incest, although the majority reported a strong desire to make meaning of the incest experience, a small subset of them reported that they felt no need to make meaning out of the experience. Tait and Silver (1989) have argued that the type of major negative life event a person experiences is not what causes adjustment difficulties. What seems to be critical in determining how one responds to traumatic life events is how one interprets the experience (e.g., Epstein, 1985; Kelly, 1955).

Further research is necessary to compare the consequences of revealing various types of secrets: ones that are perceived to be negative or traumatic compared with ones that are perceived to be pleasant, such as having a high opinion of oneself. Researchers could explore how the controllability of the secret (from the potential listener's perspective), responsibility that the secret keeper has for the secret, number of people who are affected by the secret, and type of emotion associated with the secret may influence the outcome of revealing. In this section, I detail how the type of secret adds to the complexity of the model for when to reveal secrets in a particular relationship.

Controllability

Researchers studying social support have depicted controllability of stressful life events as the central organizing dimension for understanding what types of social support (e.g., instrumental vs. emotional support) victims need from their confidants (Cutrona, 1990; Cutrona & Russell, 1990;

Lazarus & Folkman, 1984). In a similar vein, I content that the controllability of a secret may be a central dimension in predicting whether a secret keeper will benefit from sharing a secret. As described in the previous chapter, there is evidence that depressed people tend to get rejected when they appear to be suffering or coping poorly with their problems (e.g., Silver & Wortman, 1980). However, if the secret seems controllable to the relational partner, then the partner most likely will not be burdened or overly distressed by the revelation and will be unlikely to reject the secret keeper. The secret keeper may wish to present her secret to a relational partner in such a way that the partner perceives that he can help with the secret disclosed. For instance, a rape victim may manage to tell her partner that what she really needs is for him to listen to her story and to accept and support her.

Responsibility

Whether a secret keeper is perceived as personally responsible for a problematic secret complicates the timing of the revelation. For example, if a student has cheated on a test and the teacher is likely to discover this cheating before the end of the semester, the student would probably get a more sympathetic response by admitting to the cheating sooner rather than later in the semester. Evidence for this claim comes from a study by Jones and Gordon (1972). They asked undergraduates to listen to an ostensible interview between a student and his academic advisor. There were two manipulations: The student on the tape had missed a semester of high school either because the student had engaged in cheating and plagiarism (personal responsibility condition) or because of the litigation surrounding his parents' divorce (no responsibility condition). The other manipulation was that the student revealed the negative information very early in the conversation or during a later segment when he was asked directly why he had transferred high schools. As it turned out, the participants liked the student who was responsible for the negative event (i.e., cheating) more when he disclosed that information early in the conversation rather than later when he was forced to "give it up." At the same time, the participants liked the student who was not responsible for the negative event more when he revealed it later rather than sooner. These findings were interpreted to mean that in the former condition, the student was seen as demonstrating trustworthiness by admitting to the act early on, whereas the student in the latter condition was seen as trying to obtain pity by revealing an event for which he was not responsible early in the dialogue. Thus, the findings provide support for the notion that revealing a secret for which one has personal responsibility could backfire if it is revealed too late.

Communality

Secrets often have adverse implications for other people besides the secret keeper. In deciding whether to reveal such secrets, secret keepers must take into account the collective consequences of such a decision. For example, if a woman is having an affair with her husband's best friend and business partner and she reveals this information to her husband, then her lover is likely to lose both his best friend and his job as a result. Many cases of physical and sexual abuse, criminal activity, cheating, lying, sexual indiscretion, and drug abuse either tacitly or explicitly involve other individuals who would be affected by the keeper's decision to reveal the secret. There also are times when the relational partners are likely to be hurt by a revelation, either because of their emotional ties to the secret keeper or because the secret involves them personally. For instance, if a man tells his wife that he is secretly lusting after another woman, his wife is likely to become jealous and depressed, and he may suffer as a result of seeing her this way. As such, the decision to reveal secrets that involve others is substantially more complex than the decision to reveal those that do not.

Emotion

There seem to be contradictions in the literature concerning whether disclosing secrets is associated with immediate or delayed relief for the secret keeper (e.g., see Pennebaker, 1985, 1990; Pennebaker & Beall, 1986). I speculate that if the secret involves guilt, typically around something the secret keeper has done (see Baumeister, Stillwell, & Heatherton, 1994), then the secret keeper may experience immediate benefits from disclosing. However, if the secret involves humiliation or anguish, typically around something that was done to the secret keeper, then the secret keeper may experience a delay before benefiting from revealing, assuming that the confidant is an appropriate one.

Clinical researchers have suggested that if clients are to benefit from therapy, they must first work through painful experiences (e.g., Courtois, 1992; Horowitz, 1986; Rando, 1993; Reichert, 1994). For example, studies of the treatment of anxiety disorders have shown that confronting or exposing oneself to feared stimuli as curative (Foa & Kozak, 1986; Foa et al., 1991; Kozak et al., 1988; Rachman, 1980). Similarly, research has shown that people feel worse after writing about traumas before they feel better (Pennebaker, 1990; Pennebaker & Beall, 1986). This pattern may be the result of their rehashing feelings of pain, humiliation, and anguish that prior to their writing were not directly influencing them. To be reminded of pain is painful initially, but the writing may then lead to the lasting relief associated with gaining new insights into the secret (see Chapter 5). In the case of the suspected criminals (see Pennebaker, 1985, 1990), an explanation for why they felt better immediately upon confessing is that they could relieve their guilt and could stop expending their cognitive resources to protect their lies. However, it remains to be seen whether this kind of relief lasts, especially once the negative implications (e.g., prison time) of their revelations materialize.

SUMMARY

The proposed model for when people should reveal hidden information in a particular relationship hinges on whether their relational partners (1) expect access to the information, (2) are appropriate confidants, and (3) would discover the information anyway. The model is intended to make people more aware of their ability to control how much access to themselves they allow others to have. Based on the fact that the majority of the previous work that has linked secret keeping with problems is only correlational, I encourage people to consider the likelihood that there will be times when keeping a secret is not harmful and may even be beneficial. In particular, I hope that they will make revelations with discretion and will evaluate closely whether their relational partners are discreet, nonjudgmental, and not rejecting of them. In cases where the relational partners do not have these fine qualities, I have offered alternatives to complete revelation, such as telling the partner that certain hidden information is private, revealing the theme as opposed to the details of the secret, and revealing the secret to another, more appropriate confidant. The decision to reveal a secret is complicated further by a consideration of the types of secrets people keep. For example, someone might decide that even if she personally will benefit from revealing, she may not want to reveal because revealing might hurt someone else too much. I have described several factors that add to the complexity of the model, which are how controllable the secret is (from the perspective of the relational partner), how responsible the secret keeper is for the secret, how many people the secret involves, and the kind of emotion that is associated with the secret.

TESTING THE MODEL WITH SAMPLE SECRETS

The model may sound reasonable to the reader so far, but how well does it hold up when applied to some of the most common, vexing secrets that people are likely to have in their close relationships? I am going to use sexual examples to "test" the model, because these have been the most frequently reported kinds of secrets (see Chapter 1).

HERPES

An example of a common stigmatizing sexual secret that comes to mind immediately is having genital herpes, which affects roughly 22% of adult Americans. Imagine that a man with genital herpes is entering a new sexual relationship with a woman who knows many of his friends and colleagues. Should he tell her about the herpes? The first step of the model is to ask himself whether she expects access to this information. The chances are that she does, especially since sexual contact with him puts her at risk for contracting the disease. Many people today even ask their new partners if they have any sexually transmitted diseases. Assuming that she does expect access to this knowledge, he next needs to ask himself if she is an appropriate confidant. Because she has previously expressed great fear of contracting a sexually transmitted disease, he fears that she might reject him for the disclosure. Also, she is closer to one of his female colleagues than she is to him, so he wonders if she would tell that colleague, especially if the relationship breaks up. To be safe, he concludes that she may not be an appropriate confidant. Next, he must ask himself whether she is likely to find out about the herpes, and the chances are good that she will, either because she might see his herpes suppression medication or sees the sores on his genitals, or worse yet develops sores for the first time herself. Normally, the model is helpful in offering the suggestion to reveal the secret by focusing on themes in such cases when the partner is likely to discover the secret on her own. However, in this case, the secret is quite specific. It is difficult to come up with any theme that represents herpes without saying what it is. My suggestion is either to abstain from sex or to wear condoms and avoid having sex when the sores are present while getting to know the partner well enough to decide whether she is an appropriate confidant and then either telling the secret if she is appropriate or ending the relationship.

NUMBER OF SEXUAL PARTNERS

The female protagonist in the movie, "Four Weddings and a Funeral," had 33 sexual partners. She simply tells the Hugh Grant character about the 33 relationships, because he asked her how many partners she had and does not reject her for the revelation. However, in many relationships, such a revelation might lead to rejection. If a young man asks his new girlfriend (who has had 33 partners) how many sexual partners she has had, he is making it obvious that he expects access to this information—the first step of the model. If he has expressed disdain for women he calls "sluts" in the past, then she might assume that he is not an appropriate confidant because he could reject her for the revelation—the second step of the model. Also, because she had a number of sexual partners in high school, he might discover this information when they visit her hometown during the holidays—the third step of the model. My suggestion is that because he may discover this information on his own, she should tell him the secret by focusing on the theme and not offering the specifics. She could say, "Even though I think it is dehumanizing to disclose specific numbers, I can tell you that I have been sexually active since high school. I have always used condoms and have been faithful when my boyfriends and I have agreed to be, as you and I have." This expresses that idea that there has been more than one lover and addresses the fears that may underlie the questions.

CONCLUSION

Secrets are a part of virtually every adult's life. Psychologists long have believed that keeping secrets is stressful and that it undermines mental and physical health. Even though they have not been able to show that keeping secrets causes problems, they recently have offered convincing experimental evidence that there are health benefits to revealing secrets in confidential and anonymous settings. Revealing in a private diary or journal, especially with an emphasis on gaining new meanings or new perspectives on the secrets, is likely ultimately to make secret keepers feel much better on the average.

However, once personal secrets are understood in their relational context, a number of potential drawbacks to revealing them become evident, including being rejected by the relational partner and receiving damage to one's reputation if the partner tells others the secret. It seems that making the decision to reveal personal secrets to others involves a trade-off. On the one hand, a secret keeper can feel better by revealing the secrets and no longer having to feel deceptive toward the partner. On the other hand, the secret keeper can avoid looking bad and risking rejection from the partner by not revealing to him or her. The key to making a wise decision to reveal one's personal secrets is to determine whether the relational partner is an appropriate confidant: someone who is discreet, who is perceived by the secret keeper to be nonjudgmental, and who will not reject the secret keeper. One also must take into account the probability of whether the secret will be discovered anyway when deciding to reveal to a partner, because there are potential benefits associated with putting one's own spin on undesirable events rather than letting the partner discover them on his or her own (see Emler, 1990).

In bringing this volume to a close, I wish to highlight several other points made earlier. One is that high self-concealers are sicker than low self-concealers. I have tried to explain this observation by offering a pre-dispositional model of concealment, wherein high self-concealers might be born with the predisposition to be vulnerable to physical and psychological problems. This idea is offered very cautiously and will need to be tested in future research. An important area of inquiry will be to see whether high self-concealers are especially vulnerable to specific illnesses the way repressors seem to be vulnerable to cancer. Also interesting will be to see how one's level of concealment interacts with a decision to reveal or conceal a secret in influencing the outcomes of that decision. In addition, independent of a person's self-concealment level, it will be important to find an ethical way of experimentally testing whether keeping a particular secret from a relational partner does make a person sick. Scientists need to determine once and for all whether persons' fears about the dangers of secrecy are warranted. It may seem odd that I am expecting that self-concealment (the dispositional quality) and secret keeping (the process variable) will predict illness in different directions, with keeping a particular secret possibly serving as a buffer against illness. However, this is where the discussion of the role of the confidant becomes so crucial. Telling others something really horrible about oneself offers so much more potential for damage than keeping that same horrible information a secret, especially since so many personal secrets actually may more appropriately be labeled private information anyway (i.e., their relational partners do not expect access to them). One of the solutions I have offered for times when some degree of revealing surrounding a heinous and stigmatizing personal problem is needed, such as in psychotherapy, is to reveal the themes instead of the really bad details. Even in therapy, people rightfully are concerned with presenting desirable impressions of themselves to their therapists, given that there is an interpersonal element to the self-concept, which can become more negative in the face of real or imagined undesirable feedback. It would be nice if people could not care what others think, the way some autonomy-oriented humanists advocated in the 1960s. However, given that what others think does seem to play a crucial role in the way people see themselves, I suggest that it is time for people to acknowledge that process and reveal personal secrets judiciously.

REFERENCES

Abbey, A., Abramis, D. J., & Caplan, R. D. (1985). Effects of different sources of social support and social conflict on emotional well-being. *Basic and Applied Social Psychology, 6,* 111–129.

Abraham, N., Torok, M., & Rand, N. (1994). *The shell and the kernel: Renewals of psychoanalysis, Vol. 1.* Chicago: University of Chicago Press.

Adams, J. F. (1993). The utilization of family secrets as constructive resources in strategic therapy. *Journal of Family Psychotherapy, 4,* 19–33.

Ajzen, I. (1977). Information processing approaches to interpersonal attraction. In S. W. Duck (Ed.), *Theory and practice in interpersonal attraction* (pp. 51–77). San Diego, CA: Academic Press.

Alloy, L. (1988). *Cognitive processes in depression.* New York: Guilford Press.

Altman, I., & Taylor, D. (1973). *Social penetration: The development of interpersonal relationships.* New York: Hold, Rinehart, & Winston.

American Psychiatric Association. (1994). *Diagnostic and statistical manual of mental disorders* (4th ed.). Washington, DC: Author.

Amini, F., Burke, E. L., & Edgerton, R. (1978). Social structure of a psychiatric ward for adolescents and the therapeutic implications of patient staff and intra staff conflicts. *Adolescence, 13,* 411–418.

Anderson, C. D. (1981). Expression of affect and physiological response in psychosomatic patients. *Journal of Psychosomatic Research, 25,* 143–149.

Andreasen, N. J. C., & Norris, A. S. (1972). Long-term adjustment and adaptation mechanisms in severely burned adults. *Journal of Nervous and Mental Disease, 154,* 352–362.

Antonovsky, A. (1990). Pathways leading to successful coping and health. In M. Rosenbaum (Ed.), *Learned resourcefulness: On coping skills, self-control, and adaptive behavior* (Vol. 24, pp. 31–63). New York: Springer.

Archer, R. L., & Berg, J. H. (1978). Disclosure reciprocity and its limits: A reactance analysis. *Journal of Experimental Social Psychology, 14,* 527–540.

Arkin, R. M., & Hermann, A. D. (2000). Constructing desirable identities—Self-

219

presentation in psychotherapy and daily life: Comment on Kelly (2000). *Psychological Bulletin, 126,* 501–504.

Arnow, B. (1996). Cognitive–behavioral therapy for bulimia nervosa. In J. Werne & I. Yalom (Eds.), *Treating eating disorders* (pp. 101–142). San Francisco: Jossey-Bass.

Asner, J. (1990). Reworking the myth of personal incompetence: Group psychotherapy for bulimia nervosa. *Psychiatric Annals, 20,* 395–397.

Avery, N. (1982). Family secrets. *Psychoanalytic Review, 69,* 471–486.

Baer, R., Hinkle, S., Smith, K., & Fenton, M. (1980). Reactance as a function of actual versus projected autonomy. *Journal of Personality and Social Psychology, 38,* 416–422.

Baldwin, M. W. (1992). Relational schemas and the processing of information. *Psychological Bulletin, 112,* 461–484.

Bandura, A., Lipsher, D. H., & Miller, P. E. (1960). Psychotherapists' approach–avoidance reactions to patients' expressions of hostility. *Journal of Consulting Psychology, 24,* 1–8.

Barak, A., & LaCross, M. B. (1975). Multidimensional perception of counselor behavior. *Journal of Counseling Psychology, 22,* 471–476.

Barger, S. D., Kircher, J. C., & Croyle, R. T. (1997). The effects of social context and defensiveness on the physiological responses of repressive copers. *Journal of Personality and Social Psychology, 73,* 1118–1128.

Barron, J. W., Beaumont, R., Goldsmith, G., & Good, M. I. (1991). Sigmund Freud: The secrets of nature and the nature of secrets. *International Review of Psycho-Analysis, 18,* 143–163.

Baumeister, R. F. (1982). A self-presentational view of social phenomena. *Psychological Bulletin, 91,* 3–26.

Baumeister, R. F. (1990). Suicide as escape from self. *Psychological Review, 97,* 90–113.

Baumeister, R. F. (1991). *Escaping the self.* New York: Basic Books.

Baumeister, R. F. (1998). The self. In D. T. Gilbert, S. T. Fiske, & G. Lindzay (Eds.), *The handbook of social psychology* (Vol. 2, 4th ed., pp. 680–740). Boston: McGraw-Hill.

Baumeister, R. F., & Leary, M. R. (1995). The need to belong: Desire for interpersonal attachments as a fundamental human motivation. *Psychological Bulletin, 117,* 497–529.

Baumeister, R. F., & Tice, D. M. (1984). Role of self-presentation and choice in cognitive dissonance under forced compliance: Necessary or sufficient causes? *Journal of Personality and Social Psychology, 46,* 5–13.

Baumeister, R. F., Stillwell, A. M., & Heatherton, T. F. (1994). Guilt: An interpersonal approach. *Psychological Bulletin, 115,* 243–267.

Baxter, L. A., & Wilmot, W. W. (1985). Taboo topics in close relationships. *Journal of Social and Personal Relationships, 2,* 253–269.

Bellman, B. L. (1981). The paradox of secrecy. *Human Studies, 4,* 1–24.

Bem, D. J. (1967). Self-perception: An alternative interpretation of cognitive dissonance phenomena. *Psychological Review, 74,* 183–200.

Bem, D. J. (1972). Self-perception theory. In L. Berkowitz (Ed.), *Advances in experimental social psychology* (Vol. 6, pp. 1–62). San Diego, CA: Academic Press.

Berg, J. H. (1987). Responsiveness and self-disclosure. In V. J. Derlega & J. H. Berg (Eds.), *Self-disclosure: Theory, research, and therapy* (pp. 101–130). New York: Plenum.

Berg, J. H., & Archer, R. L. (1980). Disclosure or concern: A second look at liking for the norm-breaker. *Journal of Personality, 48*, 245–257.

Bergmann, M. V. (1992). An infantile trauma, a trauma during analysis, and their psychic connexion. *International Journal of Psycho-Analysis, 73*, 447–454.

Bernfeld, S. (1941). The facts of observation in psychoanalysis. *The Journal of Psychology, 12*, 289–305.

Berry, D. S., & Pennebaker, J. W. (1993). Nonverbal and verbal emotional expression and health. *Psychotherapy and Psychosomatics, 59*, 11–19.

Beutler, L. E., Machado, P. P. P., & Neufeldt, S. A. (1994). Therapist variables. In A. E. Bergin & S. L. Garfield (Eds.), *Handbook of psychotherapy and behavior change* (4th ed., pp. 229–269). New York: John Wiley & Sons.

Biederman, J., Rosenbaum, J. F., Hirshfeld, D. R., Faraone, S. V. (1990). Psychiatric correlates of behavioral inhibition in young children of parents with and without psychiatric disorders. *Archives of General Psychiatry, 47*, 21–26.

Binder, R. (1981). Why women don't report sexual assault. *Journal of Clinical Psychiatry, 42*, 437–438.

Bingham, A., & Bargar, J. (1985). Children of alcoholic families: A group treatment approach for latency age children. *Journal of Psychosocial Nursing and Mental Health Services, 23*, 13–15.

Black, C. (1981). Innocent bystanders at risk: The children of alcoholics. *Alcoholism*, 22–26.

Bloch, S., & Reibstein, J. (1980). Perceptions by patients and therapists of therapeutic factors in group psychotherapy. *British Journal of Psychiatry, 137*, 274–278.

Bohart, A. C. (1980). Toward a cognitive theory of catharsis. *Psychotherapy: Theory, Research & Practice, 17*, 192–201.

Bohart, A., Allen, E., Jackson, M., & Freyer, R. (1976). *Understanding–sharing versus discharge in interpersonal counseling.* Paper presented at the 56th annual convention of the Western Psychological Association, Los Angeles, 1976. Accepted for inclusion in the ERIC/CAPS system.

Bok, S. (1982). *Secrets: On the ethics of concealment and revelation.* New York: Pantheon Books.

Bolger, N., Foster, M., Vinokur, A. D., & Ng, R. (1996). Close relationships and adjustments to a life crisis: The case of breast cancer. *Journal of Personality and Social Psychology, 70*, 283–294.

Booth, R. J., Petrie, K. J., & Pennebaker, J. W. (1997). Changes in circulating lymphocyte numbers following emotional disclosure: Evidence of buffering? *Stress Medicine, 13*, 23–29.

Bootzin, R. R. (1997). Examining the theory and clinical utility of writing about emotional experiences. *Psychological Science, 8*, 167–169.

Bor, R., Miller, R., Scher, I., & Salt, H. (1991). The practice of counseling HIV/AIDS clients. *British Journal of Guidance and Counseling, 19*, 129–138.

Braginsky, B. M., & Braginsky, D. D. (1967). Schizophrenic patients in the psychiatric interview: An experimental study of the manipulative tactics of mental patients. *Journal of Consulting Psychology, 31*, 543–547.

Braginsky, B. M., Grosse, M., & Ring, K. (1966). Controlling outcomes through impression management: An experimental study of the manipulative tactics of mental patients. *Journal of Consulting Psychology, 30*, 295–300.

Brehm, S. S., & Brehm, J. W. (1981). *Psychological reactance: A theory of freedom and control.* New York: Academic Press.

Breuer, J., & Freud, S. (1975). *Studies in hysteria.* New York: Basic Books. (Original work published 1893–1895)

Brewer, M. D., & Mittelman, J. (1980). Effects of normative control of self-disclosure on reciprocity. *Journal of Personality, 48*, 89–102.

Brickman, P., Rabinowitz, V., Karuza, J., Coates, D., Cohn, E., & Kidder, L. (1982). Models of helping and coping. *American Psychologist, 37*, 368–384.

Broadhead, W. E., Kaplan, B. H., James, S. A., Wagner, E. H., Schoenbach, V. J., Grimson, R., Heyden, S., Tibblin, G., & Gehlbach, S. H. (1983). The epidemiologic evidence for a relationship between social support and health. *American Journal of Epidemiology, 117*, 521–537.

Brown, E. (1991). Dealing with secret affairs in psychotherapy. In E. Brown (Ed.), *From patterns of infidelity and their treatment* (pp. 53–73). New York: Brunner-Mazel.

Buchele, B. J. (1993). Group psychotherapy for persons with multiple personality and dissociative disorders. *Bulletin of the Menninger Clinic, 57*, 362–370.

Buck, R. W. (1984). *The communication of emotion.* New York: Guilford.

Burger, J. M. (1997). *Personality* (4th ed.). Pacific Grove, CA: Brooks/Cole.

Burgess, A. W., & Holmstrom, L. L. (1974). Rape trauma syndrome. *American Journal of Psychiatry, 131*, 981–986.

Bush, L. K., Barr, C. L., McHugo, G. J., & Lanzetta, J. T. (1989). The effects of facial control and facial mimicry on subjective reactions to comedy routines. *Motivation and Emotion, 13*, 31–52.

Bushman, B. J., Baumeister, R. F., & Stack, A. D. (1999). Catharsis, aggression, and persuasive influence: Self-fulfilling or self-defeating prophecies? *Journal of Personality and Social Psychology, 76*, 367–376.

Buss, A. H., & Briggs, S. R. (1984). Drama and the self in social interaction. *Journal of Personality and Social Psychology, 47*, 1310–1324.

Butler, S. (1978). *Conspiracy of silence: The trauma of incest.* San Francisco: New Glide.

Caracena, P. F., & Victory, J. R. (1969). Correlates of the phenomological and judged empathy. *Journal of Counseling Psychology, 16*, 510–515.

Carlsmith, J. M., Ellsworth, P., & Whiteside, J. L. (1968). Guilt confession and compliance. Unpublished manuscript, as cited in Freedman, J. L., Carlsmith, J. M., & Sears, D. O. (1970). *Social psychology.* Englewood Cliffs, NJ: Prentice Hall.

Carver, C. S., & Scheier, M. F. (1985). Aspects of self and the control of behavior. In B. R. Schlenker (Ed.), *The self and social life* (pp. 146–174). New York: McGraw-Hill.

Casriel, D. (1972). *A scream away from happiness.* New York: Grosset & Dunlap.

Cass, V. (1979). Homosexual identity formation: A theoretical model. *Journal of Homosexuality, 4*, 219–235.

Castets, B. (1988). The place of secrecy in analysis. *Psychiatric Francaise, 19*, 15–18.

Cepeda-Benito, A., & Short, P. (1998). Self-concealment, avoidance of psychological services, and perceived likelihood of seeking professional help. *Journal of Counseling Psychology, 45*, 58–64.

Chafetez, J., Sampson, P., Beck, P., & West, J. (1974). A study of homosexual women. *Social Work, 19,* 714–723.

Chaikin, A. L., & Derlega, V. J. (1974). Liking for the norm-breaker in self-disclosure. *Journal of Personality, 42,* 117–129.

Champion, C. D. (2001). *Effects of deception on the perceptions of those deceived.* Unpublished manuscript. South Bend, IN: University of Notre Dame.

Cheek, J. M. (1982). Aggregation, moderator variables, and the validity of personality tests: A peer-rating study. *Journal of Personality and Social Psychology, 43,* 1254–1269.

Chevalier, A. J. (1995). *On the client's path: A manual for the practice of solution-focused therapy.* Oakland, CA: New Harbinger Publications.

Chodoff, P., Friedman, S. B., & Hamburg, D. A. (1964). Stress, defenses, and coping behavior: Observations in parents of children with malignant disease. *American Journal of Psychiatry, 120,* 743–749.

Christophe, B., & Rime, B. (1997). Exposure to the social sharing of emotion: Emotional impact, listener responses and secondary social sharing. *European Journal of Social Psychology, 27,* 37–54.

Christophe, V., & Di Giacomo, J. P. (1995). *Contenu du partage social secondaire suite a un episode emotionnel negatif ou positif.* Unpublished manuscript.

Cialdini, R. B., Schaller, M., Houlihan, D., Arps, K., Fultz, J., & Beaman, A. L. (1987). Empathy-based helping: Is it selflessly or selfishly based? *Journal of Personality and Social Psychology, 52,* 749–758.

Cioffi, D. (1996). Making public the private: Possible effects of expressing somatic experience. *Psychology and Health, 11,* 203–222.

Cioffi, D., & Holloway, J. (1993). Delayed costs of suppressed pain. *Journal of Personality and Social Psychology, 64,* 274–282.

Cline, R. J. W., & McKenzie, N. J. (2000). Dilemmas of disclosure in the age of HIV/AIDS: Balancing privacy and protection in the health care context. In S. Petronio (Ed.), *Balancing the secrets of private disclosure* (pp. 71–82). Mahwah, NJ: Lawrence Erlbaum.

Coates, D., Wortman, C. B., & Abbey, A. (1979). Reactions to victims. In I. H. Frieze, D. Bar-Tal, & J. S. Carroll (Eds.), *New approaches to social problems* (pp. 21–52). San Francisco: Jossey-Bass.

Cochrane, N., & Neilson, M. (1977). Depressive illness: The role of aggression further considered. *Psychological Medicine, 7,* 283–288.

Colby, C. Z., Lanzetta, J. T., & Kleck, R. E. (1977). Effects of the expression of pain on autonomic and pain tolerance responses to subject-controlled pain. *Psychophysiology, 14,* 537–540.

Cole, S. W., Kemeny, M. E., Taylor, S. E., & Visscher, B. R. (1996a). Elevated physical health risk among gay men who conceal their homosexual identity. *Health Psychology, 15,* 243–251.

Cole, S. W., Kemeny, M. E., Taylor, S. E., Visscher, B. R., & Fahey, J. L. (1996b). Accelerated course of human immunodeficiency virus infection in gay men who conceal their homosexual identity. *Psychosomatic Medicine, 58,* 219–231.

Cole, S. W., Kemeny, M. E., & Taylor, S. E. (1997). Social identity and physical health: Accelerated HIV progression in rejection-sensitive gay men. *Journal of Personality and Social Psychology, 72,* 320–335.

Cole, T. (2001). Lying to the one you love: The use of deception in romantic relationships. *Journal of Social and Personal Relationships, 18,* 107–129.

Collins, N. L., & Miller, L. C. (1994). Self-disclosure and liking: A meta-analytic review. *Psychological Bulletin, 116,* 457–475.

Consumer Reports. (1995). Mental health: Does therapy help? November, pp. 734–739.

Cooley, C. H. (1902). *Human nature and the social order.* New York: Charles Scribner's Sons.

Coons, P. M. (1986). Treatment progress in 20 patients with multiple personality disorder. *The Journal of Nervous and Mental Disease, 174,* 715–721.

Corcoran, K. J. (1988). *The Journal of Psychology, 122,* 193–195.

Cornwell, J., Nurcombe, B., & Stevens, L. (1977). Family response to loss of a child by sudden infant death syndrome. *The Medical Journal of Australia, 1,* 656–658.

Coupland, J., Coupland, H., Giles, H., & Wieman, J. (1988). My life in your hands: Processes of self-disclosure intergenerational talk. In N. Coupland (Ed.), *Styles of discourse* (pp. 201–253). London: Croon Helm.

Courtois, C. (1992). The memory retrieval process in incest survivor therapy. *Journal of Child Sexual Abuse, 1,* 15–31.

Cox, T., & McCay, C. (1982). Psychosocial factors and psychophysiological mechanisms in the aetiology and development of cancers. *Social Science and Medicine, 16,* 381–396.

Coyne, J. C., Kessler, R. C., Tal, M., Turnbull, J., Wortman, C. B., & Greden, J. F. (1987). Living with a depressed person. *Journal of Consulting and Clinical Psychology, 55,* 347–352.

Cozby, P. C. (1972) Self-disclosure, reciprocity, and liking. *Sociometry, 35,* 151–160.

Cramer, K. M., & Barry, J. E. (1999). Psychometric properties and confirmatory factor analysis of the Self-Concealment Scale. *Personality and Individual Differences, 27,* 629–637.

Cramer, K. M., & Lake, R. P. (1998). The Preference for Solitude Scale: Psychometric properties and factor structure. *Personality and Individual Differences, 24,* 193–199.

Cronbach, L. (1955). Processes affecting scores on "understanding of others" and "assumed similarity." *Psychological Bulletin, 52,* 177–193.

Cutrona, C. E. (1986). Behavioral manifestations of social support: A microanalytic investigation. *Journal of Personality and Social Psychology, 51,* 201–208.

Cutrona, C. E. (1990). Stress and social support—in search of optimal matching. *Journal of Social and Clinical Psychology, 59,* 3–14.

Cutrona, C. E., & Russell, D. (1990). Type of social support and specific stress: Toward a theory of optimal matching. In I. G. Sarason, B. R. Sarason, & G. R. Pierce (Eds.), *Social support: An interactional view* (pp. 319–336). New York: Wiley.

Dalto, C. A., Ajzen, I., & Kaplan, K. J. (1979). Self-disclosure and attraction: Effects of intimacy and desirability on beliefs and attitudes. *Journal of Research in Personality, 13,* 127–138.

Dattore, P. J., Shontz, F. C., & Coyne, L. (1980). Premorbid personality differentiation of cancer and noncancer groups: A test of the hypothesis of cancer proneness. *Journal of Consulting and Clinical Psychology, 48,* 388–394.

Davanloo, H. (1980). A method of short-term dynamic psychotherapy. In H. Davanloo (Ed.), *Short-term dynamic psychotherapy* (pp. 32–64). New York: Jason Aronson.

Davidowitz, M., & Myriak, R. D. (1984). Responding to the bereaved: An analysis of "helping" statements. *Research Record, 1,* 35–42.

Davis, C. G., Nolen-Hoeksema, S., & Larson, J. (1998). Making sense of loss and benefiting from the experience: Two construals of meaning. *Journal of Personality and Social Psychology, 75,* 561–574.

Davis, J. D., & Sloan, M. L. (1974). The basis of interviewee matching and interviewer self-disclosure. *British Journal of Social and Clinical Psychology, 13,* 359–367.

Davis, K. L., & Meara, N. M. (1982). So you think it is a secret. *Journal for Specialists in Group Work, 7,* 149–153.

Davis, P. J., & Schwartz, G. E. (1987). Repression and the inaccessibility of emotional memories. *Journal of Personality and Social Psychology, 52,* 155–162.

Denollet, J. (1991). Negative affectivity and repressive coping: Pervasive influence on self-reported mood, health, and coronary-prone behavior. *Psychosomatic Medicine, 53,* 538–556.

Denollet, J. (1993). Biobehavioral research on coronary heart disease: Where is the person? *Journal of Behavioural Medicine, 16,* 115–141.

DePaulo, B. M., Kashy, D. A., Kirkendol, S. E., Wyer, M. M., & Epstein, J. A. (1996). Lying in everyday life. *Journal of Personality and Social Psychology, 70,* 979–995.

Derlega, V. J. (1988). Self-disclosure: Inside or outside the mainstream of social psychological research? In M. R. Leary (Ed.), The state of social psychology. *Journal of Social Behavior and Personality, 3,* 27–34.

Derlega, V. J., & Grzelak, J. (1979). Appropriateness of self-disclosure. In G. J. Chelune (Ed.), *Self-disclosure: Origins, patterns, and implications of openness in interpersonal relationships* (pp. 151–176). San Francisco: Jossey-Bass.

Derlega, V. J., Metts, S., Petronio, S., & Margulis, S. T. (1993). *Self-disclosure.* Newbury Park, CA: Sage.

Derogatis, L. R. (1993). *Brief Symptom Inventory (BSI): Administration, scoring, and procedures manual* (3rd ed.). Minneapolis, MN: National Computer Systems.

Derogatis, L. R., Abeloff, M. D., & Melisaratos, N. (1979). Psychological coping mechanisms and survival time in metastatic breast cancer. *Journal of the American Medical Association, 242,* 1504–1508.

DiMatteo, M., & Hays, R. (1981). Social support and serious illness. In B. Gottlieb (Ed.), *Social networks and social support* (pp. 117–148). Beverly Hills, CA: Sage.

Doka, K. J., & Schwartz, E. (1978). Assigning blame: The restoration of the "sentimental order" following an accidental death. *Omega, 9,* 279–285.

Donnelly, D. A., & Murray, E. J. (1991). Cognitive and emotional changes in written essays and therapy interviews. *Journal of Social and Clinical Psychology, 10,* 334–350.

Dowd, E. T., & Milne, C. R. (1986). Paradoxical interventions in counseling psychology. *Counseling Psychologist, 14,* 237–282.

Dowd, E. T., Milne, C. R., & Wise, S. L. (1991). The Therapeutic Reactance Scale: A measure of psychological reactance. *Journal of Counseling and Development, 69,* 541–545.

Duck, S. W. (1988). *Relating to others.* Pacific Grove, CA: Brooks/Cole.

Dushman, R. D., & Bressler, M. J. (1991). Psychodrama in an adolescent chemical dependency treatment program. *Individual Psychology, 47,* 515–520.

Eaker, B. (1986). Unlocking the family secret in family play therapy. *Child and Adolescent Social Work, 3,* 235–253.

Ebbesen, E. B., Duncan, B., & Konecni, V. J. (1975). Effects of content of verbal aggression on future verbal aggression: A field experiment. *Journal of Experimental Social Psychology, 11,* 192–204.

Ehrlich, H. J., & Bauer, M. L. (1967). Therapists' feelings toward patients and patient treatment outcome. *Social Science and Medicine, 1,* 283–292.

Ekman, P. (1991). *Telling lies: Clues to deceit in the marketplace, politics, and marriage.* New York: W. W. Norton.

Ekman, P., & O'Sullivan, M. (1991). Who can catch a liar? *American Psychologist, 46,* 913–920.

Elliott, R. (1985). Helpful and nonhelpful events in brief counseling interviews: An empirical taxonomy. *Journal of Counseling Psychology, 32,* 307–322.

Emler, N. (1990). A social psychology of reputation. *European Review of Social Psychology, 1,* 171–193.

Engebretson, T. O., Matthews, K. A., & Scheier, M. F. (1989). Relations between anger expression and cardiovascular reactivity: Reconciling inconsistent findings through a matching hypothesis. *Journal of Personality and Social Psychology, 57,* 513–521.

Epstein, S. (1985). The implications of cognitive–experiential self-theory for research in social psychology and personality (special issue). *Journal for the Theory of Social Behavior, 15,* 283–310.

Esterling, B. A., Antoni, M. H., Kumar, M., & Schneiderman, N. (1990). Emotional repression, stress disclosure responses, and Epstein-Barr viral capsid antigen titers. *Psychosomatic Medicine, 52,* 397–410.

Esterling, B. A., Antoni, M. H., Kumar, M., & Schneiderman, N. (1993). Defensiveness, trait anxiety, and Epstein–Barr viral capsid antigen antibody titers in healthy college students. *Health Psychology, 12,* 132–139.

Esterling, B. A., Antoni, M. H., Fletcher, M. A., Marguiles, S., & Schneiderman, N. (1994). Emotional disclosure through writing or speaking modulates latent Epstein–Barr virus antibody titers. *Journal of Consulting and Clinical Psychology, 62,* 130–140.

Esterling, B. A., L'Abate, L., Murray, E. J., & Pennebaker, J. W. (1999). Empirical foundations for writing in prevention and psychotherapy: Mental and physical health outcomes. *Clinical Psychology Review, 19,* 79–96.

Eugster, S. L., & Wampold, B. E. (1996). Systematic effects of participant role on evaluation of the psychotherapy session. *Journal of Consulting and Clinical Psychology, 64,* 1020–1028.

Evans, N. (1976). Mourning as a family secret. *Journal of the American Academy of Child Psychiatry, 15,* 502– 509.

Fawzy, F. I., Fawzy, N. W., Hyun, C. S., Elashoff, R., Guthrie, D., Fahey, J. L., & Morton, D. L. (1993). Malignant melanoma: Effects of an early structured psychiatric intervention, coping, and affective state on recurrence and survival 6 years later. *Archives of General Psychiatry, 50,* 681–689.

Fazio, R. H., Effrein, E. A., & Falender, V. J. (1981). Self-perceptions following social interaction. *Journal of Personality and Social Psychology, 41,* 232–242.

Feldman, D. A., Strong, S. R., & Danser, D. B. (1982). A comparison of paradoxical and nonparadoxical interpretations and directives. *Journal of Counseling Psychology, 29,* 572–579.

Finkenauer, C., & Hazam, H. (2000). Disclosure and secrecy in marriage: Do both contribute to marital satisfaction? *Journal of Social and Personal Relationships, 17,* 245–263.

Finkenauer, C., & Rime, B. (1998a). Socially shared emotional experiences vs. emotional experiences kept secret: Differential characteristics and consequences. *Journal of Social and Clinical Psychology, 17,* 295–318.

Finkenauer, C., & Rime, B. (1998b). Keeping emotional memories secret: Health and subjective well-being when emotions are not shard. *Journal of Health Psychology, 3,* 47–58.

Fish, J. M. (1970). Empathy and the reported emotional experiences of beginning psychotherapists. *Journal of Consulting and Clinical Psychology, 35,* 64–69.

Fish, J. M. (1996). Prevention, solution-focused therapy, and the illusion of mental disorders. *Applied and Preventive Psychology, 5,* 37–40.

Fish, V., & Scott, C. G. (1999). Childhood abuse recollections in a nonclinical population: Forgetting and secrecy. *Child Abuse and Neglect, 23,* 791–802.

Fishbein, M. J., & Laird, J. D. (1979). Concealment and disclosure: Some effects of information control on the person who controls. *Journal of Experimental Social Psychology, 15,* 114–121.

Flowers, J. V., Armentrout, S. A., Booraem, C. D., Kraft, M. E., Maddi, S. R., & Wadhwa, P. D. (1995). The association between psychosocial factors and the incidence of breast cancer. *Annals of Behavioral Medicine, 17,* S081.

Foa, E. B., & Kozak, M. J. (1986). Emotional processing of fear: Exposure to corrective information. *Psychological Bulletin, 99,* 20–35.

Foa, E. B., & Rothbaum, B. O. (1989). Behavioural psychotherapy for posttraumatic stress disorder. *International Review of Psychiatry, 1,* 219–226.

Foa, E. B., Rothbaum, B. O., Riggs, D. S., & Murdock, T. B. (1991). Treatment of posttraumatic stress disorder in rape victims: A comparison between cognitive–behavioral procedures and counseling. *Journal of Consulting and Clinical Psychology, 59,* 715–723.

Foa, E. B., Molnar, C., & Cashman, L. (1995). Changes in rape narratives during exposure therapy for posttraumatic stress disorder. *Journal of Traumatic Stress, 8,* 675–690.

Fong, M. L., & Cox, B. G. (1983). Trust as an underlying dynamic in the counseling process: How clients test trust. *The Personnel and Guidance Journal, 63,* 163–166.

Frable, D. E. S., Wortman, C., & Joseph, J. (1997). Predicting self-esteem, well-being, and distress in a cohort of gay men: The importance of cultural stigma, personal visibility, community networks, and positive identity. *Journal of Personality, 65,* 599–624.

Frable, D. E. S., Platt L., & Hoey, S. (1998). Concealable stigmas and positive self-perceptions: Feeling better around similar others. *Journal of Personality and Social Psychology, 74*, 909–922.

Frank, J. D. (1974). Therapeutic components of psychotherapy. A 25-year progress report of research. *The Journal of Nervous and Mental Disease, 159*, 325–342.

Frankl, V. E. (1976/1959). *Man's search for meaning.* New York: Pocket.

Frederikson, M., & Engel, B. T. (1985). Cardiovascular and electrodermal adjustments during a vigilance task in patients with borderline and established hypertension. *Journal of Psychosomatic Research, 29*, 235–246.

Freud, S. (1958). *On the beginning of treatment: Further recommendations on the techniques of psychoanalysis.* London: Hogarth Press. (Original work published 1913)

Friedlander, M. L., & Schwartz, G. S. (1985). Toward a theory of strategic self-presentation in counseling and psychotherapy. *Journal of Counseling Psychology, 32*, 483–501.

Friedman, H. S., Hall, J. A., & Harris, M. J. (1985). Type A behavior, nonverbal expressive style and health. *Journal of Personality and Social Psychology, 48*, 1299–1315.

Fromm-Reichmann, F. (1950). *Principles of intensive psychotherapy.* Chicago: University of Chicago Press.

Fuller, F., & Hill, C. E. (1985). Counselor and helpee perceptions of counselor intentions in relation to outcome in a single counseling session. *Journal of Counseling Psychology, 32*, 329–338.

Garfield, S. L. (1980). *Psychotherapy: An eclectic approach.* New York: Wiley.

Garfield, S. L. (1991). Common and specific factors in psychotherapy. *Journal of Integrative and Eclectic Psychotherapy, 10*, 5–13.

Garfield, S. L. (1994). Research on client variables in psychotherapy. In A. E. Bergin & S. L. Garfield (Eds.), *Handbook of psychotherapy and behavior change* (4th ed., pp. 190–228). New York: Wiley.

Garron, D. C., & Leavitt, F. (1979). Demographic and affective covariates of pain. *Psychosomatic Medicine, 41*, 525–534.

Geiser, R. (1979). *Hidden victims: The sexual abuse of children.* Boston: Beacon.

Gelso, C. J., & Carter, J. A. (1994). Components of the psychotherapy relationship: Their interaction and unfolding during treatment. *Journal of Counseling Psychology, 41*, 296–306.

Gergen, K. J. (1965). Effects of interaction goals and personality feedback on the presentation of self. *Journal of Personality and Social Psychology, 1*, 413–424.

Gesell, S. B. (1999). The roles of personality and cognitive processing in secret keeping (anxiety). *Dissertation Abstracts International: Section B: The Sciences and Engineering, 60*(6-B): 2971.

Gillman, R. D. (1992). Rescue fantasies and the secret benefactor. *Psychoanalytic Study of the Child, 47*, 279–298.

Goffman, E. (1959). *The presentation of self in everyday life.* Garden City, NY: Doubleday Anchor.

Goldstein, D. A., & Antoni, M. H. (1989). The distribution of repressive coping styles among non-metastatic and metastatic breast cancer patients as compared to non-cancer patients. *Psychology and Health, 3*, 245–258.

Good, G. E., Dell, D. M., & Mintz, L. B. (1989). Male role and gender role conflict: Relations to help-seeking in men. *Journal of Counseling Psychology, 36*, 295–300.

Goodwin, S. (1982). *Sexual abuse: Incest victims and their families.* Boston: John Wright.

Greenberg, M. A., & Stone, A. A. (1992). Emotional disclosure about traumas and its relation to health: Effects of previous disclosure and trauma severity. *Journal of Personality and Social Psychology, 63*, 75–84.

Greenberg, M. A., Wortman, C. B., & Stone, A. A. (1996). Emotional expression and physical health: Revising traumatic memories or fostering self-regulation? *Journal of Personality and Social Psychology, 71*, 588–602.

Greer, S. (1983). Cancer and the mind. *British Journal of Psychiatry, 143*, 535–543.

Greif, G., & Porembski, E. (1988). Implications for therapy with significant others of persons with AIDS. *Journal of Gay and Lesbian Psychotherapy, 1*, 79–86.

Grencavage, L. M., & Norcross, J. C. (1990). Where are the commonalities among the therapeutic common factors? *Professional Psychology: Research and Practice, 21*, 372–378.

Grolnick, L. (1983). Ibsen's truth, family secrets, and family therapy. *Family Process, 22*, 275–288.

Gross, J. J., & Levenson, R. W. (1993). Emotional suppression: Physiology, self-report, and expressive behavior. *Journal of Personality and Social Psychology, 64*, 970–986.

Gross, J. J., & Levenson, R. W. (1997). Hiding feelings: The acute effects of inhibiting negative and positive emotion. *Journal of Abnormal Psychology, 106*, 95–103.

Gurtman, M. B. (1986). Depression and the response of others: Re-evaluating the re-evaluation. *Journal of Abnormal Psychology, 95*, 99–101.

Gutheil, T., & Avery, N. (1977). Multiple overt incest as family defense against loss. *Family Process, 16*, 106–116.

Haley, J. (1963). *Strategies of psychotherapy.* New York: Grune & Stratton.

Halpern, T. P. (1977). Degree of client disclosure as a function of past disclosure, counselor disclosure, and counselor facilitativeness. *Journal of Counseling Psychology, 24*, 41–47.

Handelman, S. (1981). Interpretation as devotion: Freud's relation to Rabbinic hermeneutics. *The Psychoanalytic Review, 68*, 201–218.

Hansen, J. C., Moore, G. D., & Carkhuff, R. R. (1968). The differential relationships of objective and client perceptions of counseling. *Journal of Clinical Psychology, 24*, 244–246.

Harber, K. D., & Pennebaker, J. W. (1992). Overcoming traumatic memories. In S. A. Christianson (Ed.), *The handbook of emotion and memory* (pp. 359–387). Hillsdale, NJ: Erlbaum.

Hartley, D., Roback, H. B., & Abramowitz, S. I. (1976). Deterioration effects in encounter groups. *American Psychologist*, 247–255.

Hays, K. F. (1987). The conspiracy of silence revisited: Group therapy with adult survivors of incest. *Journal of Group Psychotherapy, Psychodrama, and Sociometry, 39*, 143–156.

Heilman, M. E., & Garner, K. A. (1975). Counteracting the boomerang: The effects of choice on compliance to threats and promises. *Journal of Personality and Social Psychology, 31*, 911–917.

Heilman, M. E., & Toffler, B. L. (1976). Reacting to reactance: An interpersonal interpretation of the need for freedom. *Journal of Experimental Social Psychology, 12,* 519–529.

Helmrath, T. A., & Steinitz, E. M. (1978). Death of an infant: Parental grieving and the failure of social support. *The Journal of Family Practice, 6,* 785–790.

Hencken, J., & O'Dowd, W. T. (1977). Coming out as an aspect of identity formation. *Gay Academic Union Journal: Gai Saber, 1,* 18–22.

Henley, N. M. (1973). Power, sex, and nonverbal communication. *Berkeley Journal of Sociology, 18,* 1–26.

Herman, J. (1981). *Father–daughter incest.* Cambridge: Harvard University.

Herman, J., & Schatzow, E. (1984). Time-limited group therapy for women with a history of incest. *International Journal of Group Psychotherapy, 34,* 605–616.

Hesselman, S. (1983). Elective mutism in children 1877–1981: A literary review. *Acta Paedopsychiatrica, 49,* 297–310.

Heyn, D. (1992). *The erotic silence of the American wife.* New York: Turtle Bay (Random House).

Hill, C. E. (1974). A comparison of the perceptions of a therapy session by clients, therapists, and objective judges. *Journal Supplements Abstract Service, 4*(564).

Hill, C. E. (1982). Counseling process research: Philosophical and methodological dilemmas. *Counseling Psychologist, 10,* 7–19.

Hill, C. E. (1992). Research on therapist techniques in brief individual therapy: Implications for practitioners. *Counseling Psychologist, 20,* 689–711.

Hill, C. E., & Corbett, M. M. (1993). A perspective on the history of process and outcome research in counseling psychology. *Journal of Counseling Psychology, 40,* 3–24.

intentions illustrated in a case study and with therapists of varying theoretical orientations. *Journal of Counseling Psychology, 32,* 3–22.

Hill, C. E., Helms, J. E., Spiegel, S. B., & Tichenor, V. (1988a). Development of a system for categorizing client reactions to therapist interventions. *Journal of Counseling Psychology, 35,* 27–36.

Hill, C. E., Helms, J. E., Tichenor, V., Spiegel, S. B., O'Grady, K. E., & Perry, E. S. (1988b). The effects of therapist response modes in brief psychotherapy. *Journal of Counseling Psychology, 35,* 222–233.

Hill, C. E., Thompson, B. J., & Corbett, M. M. (1992). The impact of therapist ability to perceive displayed and hidden client reactions on immediate outcome in first sessions of brief therapy. *Psychotherapy Research, 2,* 148–160.

Hill, C. E., Thompson, B. J., Cogar, M. C., & Denman, D. W. (1993). Beneath the surface of long-term therapy: Therapist and client report of their own and each other's covert processes. *Journal of Counseling Psychology, 40,* 278–287.

Hill, C. E., Gelso, C. J., & Mohr, J. J. (2000). Client concealment and self-presentation in therapy: Comment on Kelly (2000). *Psychological Bulletin, 127,* 495–500.

Hoffman, I. Z. (1983). The patient as interpreter of the analyst's experience. *Contemporary Psychoanalysis, 19,* 389–422.

Hokanson, J. E., & Burgess, M. (1962). The effects of three types of aggression on vascular processes. *Journal of Abnormal and Social Psychology, 64,* 446–449.

Hokanson, J. E., & Shetler, S. (1961). The effect of overt aggression on physiological arousal level. *Journal of Abnormal and Social Psychology, 63*, 446–448.

Holahan, C. J., Moos, R. H., Holahan, C. K., & Brennan, P. L. (1997). Social context, coping strategies, and depressive symptoms: An expanded model with cardiac patients. *Journal of Personality and Social Psychology, 72*, 918–928.

Hoorwitz, A. (1983, November). Guidelines for treating father–daughter incest. *Social Casework: The Journal of Contemporary Social Work*, 515–524.

Horowitz, M. J. (1975). Intrusive and repetitive thoughts after experimental stress: A summary. *Archives of General Psychiatry, 32*, 1457–1463.

Horowitz, M. J. (1986). *Stress response syndromes* (2nd ed.). Northvale, NJ: Jason-Aronson.

Horowitz, M. J., & Wilner, N. (1976). Stress films, emotion, and cognitive response. *Archives of General Psychiatry, 33*, 1339–1344.

Horvath, A. O., & Symonds, B. D. (1991). Relation between working alliance and outcome in psychotherapy: A meta-analysis. *Journal of Counseling Psychology, 38*, 139–149.

Hough, G. (1992). When confidentiality mandates a secret be kept: A case report. *International Journal of Group Psychotherapy, 42*, 105–115.

House, J. S. (1981). *Work, stress, and social support*. Reading, MA: Addison-Wesley.

Howard, K. I., Orlinsky, D. E., & Hill, J. A. (1970). Patients' satisfactions in psychotherapy as a function of patient–therapist pairing. *Psychotherapy: Theory, Research, and Practice, 7*, 130–134.

Hoyt, M. F. (1978). Secrets in psychotherapy: Theoretical and practical considerations. *International Review of Psycho-Analysis, 5*, 231–241.

Hymer, S. (1982). The therapeutic nature of confessions. *Journal of Contemporary Psychotherapy, 13*, 129–143.

Ichiyama, M. A., Colbert, D., Laramore, H., Heim, M., Carone, K., & Schmidt, J. (1993). Self-concealment and correlates of adjustment in college students. *Journal of College Student Psychotherapy, 7*, 55–68.

Imber-Black, E. (1993). Secrets in families and family therapy: An overview. In E. Imber-Black (Ed.), *Secrets in families and family therapy* (pp. 3–28). New York: W. W. Norton.

Jackins, H. (1962). *Elementary counselor's manual*. Seattle, WA: Rational Island.

James, W. (1890). *The principles of psychology*. New York: Henry Holt.

Jammer, L. D., & Leigh, H. (1999). Repressive/defensive coping, endogenous opioids and health: How a life so perfect can make you sick. *Psychiatry Research, 85*, 17–31.

Jang, K. L., McCrae, R. R., Angleitner, A., Riemann, R., & Livesley, W. J. (1998). Heritability of facet-level traits in a cross-cultural twin sample: Support for a hierarchical model of personality. *Journal of Personality and Social Psychology, 74*, 1556–1565.

Janoff-Bulman, R. (1972). *Shattered assumptions: Towards a new psychology of trauma*. New York: The Free Press.

Janov, A. (1970). *The primal scream*. New York: Dell.

Jay, K., & Young, A. (1979). *The gay report*. New York: Summit Books.

Jensen, M. R. (1987). Psychobiological factors predicting the course of breast cancer. *Journal of Personality, 58*, 317–342.

Jones, E. E. (1990). *Interpersonal perception*. New York: W. H. Freeman.

Jones, E. E., & Archer, R. L. (1976). Are there special effects of personalistic self-disclosure? *Journal of Experimental Social Psychology, 12*, 180–193.

Jones, E. E., & Gordon, E. M. (1972). Timing of self-disclosure and its effects on personal attraction. *Journal of Personality and Social Psychology, 24*, 358–365.

Jones, E. E., & Pittman, T. S. (1982). Toward a general theory of strategic self-presentation. In J. Suls (Ed.), *Psychological perspectives on the self* (Vol. 1, pp. 231–262). Hillsdale, NJ: Erlbaum.

Jones, E. E., Rhodewalt, F., Berglas, S., & Skelton, J. A. (1981). Effects of strategic self presentation on subsequent self-esteem. *Journal of Personality and Social Psychology, 41*, 407–421.

Jourard, S. M. (1963). *Personal adjustment: An approach through the study of healthy personality* (2nd ed.). New York: Macmillan.

Jourard, S. M. (1971a). *Self-disclosure: An experimental analysis of the transparent self*. New York: Wiley.

Jourard, S. M. (1971b). *The transparent self*. New York: Van Nostrand Reinhold.

Jung, C. G. (1933). *Modern man in search of a soul*. New York: Harvest Books.

Justice, B., & Justice, R. (1979). *The broken taboo: Sex in the family*. New York: Human Sciences Press.

Kagan, J. (1994). *Galen's prophecy: Temperament in human nature*. New York: Basic Books.

Kagan, J., Reznick, J. S., & Snidman, N. (1988, April 8). Biological bases of childhood shyness. *Science, 240*, 167–171.

Kagan, J., Reznick, J. S., & Gibbons, J. (1989). Inhibited and uninhibited types of children. *Child Development, 60*, 838–845.

Kahn, J. H., & Kelly, A. E. (1998). *Dimensions of self-concealment*. Unpublished manuscript. Illinois State University.

Kahn, J. H., & Hessling, R. M. (2001). Measuring the tendency to conceal versus disclose psychological distress. *Journal of Social and Clinical Psychology, 20*, 41–65.

Kahn, J. H., Achter, J. A., & Shambaugh, E. J. (2001). Client distress disclosure, characteristics at intake, and outcome in brief counseling. *Journal of Counseling Psychology, 48*, 203–211.

Karpel, M. A. (1980). Family secrets. *Family Process, 19*, 295–306.

Kaslow, F. (1993). Attractions and affairs: Fabulous and fatal. *Journal of Family Psychotherapy, 4*, 1–34.

Kaufman, I., Peck, A., & Tagiuri, C. (1954). The family constellation and overt incestuous relations between father and daughter. *American Journal of Ortho-psychiatry, 24*, 266–279.

Kaufman, Y. (1989). Analytical psychotherapy. In R. J. Corsini & D. Wedding (Eds.), *Current psychotherapies* (pp. 119–154). Itasca, IL: F. E. Peacock.

Kazdin, A. E. (1986). Comparative outcome studies of psychotherapy: Methodological issues and strategies. *Journal of Consulting and Clinical Psychology, 54*, 95–105.

Kelly, A. E. (1997). Views of gaining catharsis versus new insights for coping with secrets. Unpublished raw data. South Bend, IN: University of Notre Dame.

Kelly, A E. (1998). Clients' secret keeping in outpatient therapy. *Journal of Counseling Psychology, 45,* 50–57.

Kelly, A. E. (1999). Revealing personal secrets. *Current Directions in Psychological Science, 8,* 105–109.

Kelly, A. E. (2000a). Helping construct desirable identities: A self-presentational view of psychotherapy. *Psychological Bulletin, 126,* 475–494.

Kelly, A. E. (2000b). A self-presentational view of psychotherapy: Reply to Hill, Gelso, and Mohr (2000) and to Arkin and Hermann (2000). *Psychological Bulletin, 126,* 505–511.

Kelly, A. E., & Achter, J. A. (1995). Self-concealment and attitudes toward counseling in university students. *Journal of Counseling Psychology, 42,* 40–46.

Kelly, A. E., & Kahn, J. H. (1994). Effects of suppression of personal intrusive thoughts. *Journal of Personality and Social Psychology, 66,* 998–1006.

Kelly, A. E., & McKillop, K. J. (1996). Consequences of revealing personal secrets. *Psychological Bulletin, 120,* 450–465.

Kelly, A. E., McKillop, K. J., & Neimeyer, G. J. (1991). Effects of counselor as audience on internalization of depressed and nondepressed self-presentations. *Journal of Counseling Psychology, 38,* 126–132.

Kelly, A E., Coenen, M. E., & Johnston, B. L. (1995). Confidants' feedback and traumatic life events. *Journal of Traumatic Stress, 8,* 161–169.

Kelly, A. E., Kahn, J. H., & Coulter, R. G. (1996). Client self-presentations at intake. *Journal of Counseling Psychology, 43,* 300–309.

Kelly, A. E., Klusas, J. A., von Weiss, R. T., & Kenny, C. (2001). What is it about revealing secrets that is beneficial? *Personality and Social Psychology Bulletin, 27,* 651–665.

Kelly, G. A. (1955). *The psychology of personal constructs* (Vols. 1 and 2). New York: Norton.

Kennedy, S., Kiecolt-Glaser, J. K., & Glaser, R. (1990). Social support, stress, and the immune system. In I. G. Sarason, B. R. Sarason, & G. R. Pierce (Eds.), *Social support: An interactional view* (pp. 253–266). New York: Wiley.

Kessler, R. C., & McLeod, J. D. (1985). Social support and mental health in community samples. In S. Cohen & S. L. Syme (Eds.), *Social support and health* (pp. 219–240). Orlando, FL: Academic Press.

Kessler, R. C., Price, R. H., & Wortman, C. B. (1985). Social factors in psychopathology: Stress, social support, and coping processes. *Annual Review of Psychology, 36,* 531–572.

Kiesler, D. J. (1981). Interpersonal theory for personality and psychotherapy. In J. C. Anchin & D. J. Kiesler (Eds.), *Handbook of interpersonal psychotherapy* (pp. 3–24). New York: Pergamon.

King, L. A., & Emmons, R. A. (1990). Conflict over emotional expression: Psychological and physical correlates. *Journal of Personality and Social Psychology, 58,* 864–877.

King, L. A., & Emmons, R. A. (1991). Psychological, physical, and interpersonal correlates of emotional expressiveness, conflict, and control. *European Journal of Personality, 5,* 131–150.

King, L. A., Emmons, R. A., & Woodley, S. (1992). The structure of inhibition. *Journal of Research in Personality, 26,* 85–102.

Kirman, W. J. (1991). Short-term modern analytic group therapy. *Modern Psychoanalysis, 16,* 151–159.

Kissen, D. M. (1966). The significance of personality in lung cancer among men. *Annals of the New York Academy of Science, 125,* 820–826.

Klein, J. W. (1976). Ethnotherapy with Jews. *International Journal of Mental Health, 5,* 26–38.

Klein, M. H., Mathieu, P. L., Gendlin, E. T., & Kiesler, D. J. (1969). *The experiencing scale: Vol. 1. A research and training manual.* Madison: Wisconsin Psychiatric Institute.

Klein, M. H., Mathieu-Coughlan, P., & Kiesler, D. J. (1986). The experiencing scales. In L. S. Greenberg & W. M. Pinsof (Eds.), *The psychotherapeutic process: A research handbook* (pp. 21–71). New York: Guilford Press.

Kleinke, C. L., & Kahn, M. L. (1980). Perceptions of self disclosers: Effects of sex and physical attractiveness. *Journal of Personality, 48,* 190–205.

Kliewer, W. L., Lepore, S. J., Oskin, D., & Johnson, P. D. (1998). The role of social and cognitive processes in children's adjustment to community violence. *Journal of Consulting and Clinical Psychology, 66,* 199–209.

Kneier, A. W., & Temoshok, L. (1984). Repressive coping reactions in patients with malignant melanoma as compared to cardiovascular disease patients. *Journal of Psychosomatic Research, 28,* 145–155.

Kobocow, B., McGuire, J. M., & Blau, B. J. (1983). The influence of confidentiality conditions on self-disclosure of early adolescence. *Professional Psychology, 4,* 435–443.

Koutstaal, W., Schacter, D. L., Johnson, M. K., Angell, K. E., & Gross, M. S. (1998). Post-event review in older and younger adults: Improving memory accessibility of complex everyday events. *Psychology and Aging, 13,* 277–296.

Kozak, M. J., Foa, E. B., & Steketee, G. (1988). Process and outcome of exposure treatment with obsessive–compulsives: Psychophysiological indicators of emotional processing. *Behavior Therapy, 19,* 157–169.

Kremer, T. G., & Gesten, E. L. (1998). Confidentiality limits of managed care and clients' willingness to self-disclose. *Professional Psychology: Research and Practice, 29,* 553–558.

Krestan, J., & Bepko, C. (1993). On lies, secrets, and silence: The multiple levels of denial in addictive families. In E. Imber-Black (Ed.), *Secrets in families and family therapy* (pp. 141–159). New York: W. W. Norton.

Kulik, J. A., Sledge, P., & Mahler, H. I. (1986). Self-confirmatory attribution, egocentrism, and the perpetuation of self-beliefs. *Journal of Personality and Social Psychology, 50,* 587–594.

Kurtz, R. R., & Grummon, D. L. (1972). Different approaches to the measurement of therapist empathy and their relations to therapy outcome. *Journal of Consulting and Clinical Psychology, 39,* 106–115.

Kyrios, M. (1998). A cognitive–behavioral approach to the understanding and management of obsessive–compulsive personality disorder. In C. Perris & P. D. McGorry (Eds.), *Cognitive psychotherapy of psychotic and personality disorders: Handbook of theory and practice* (pp. 351–378). Chichester, England: American Ethnological Press.

Labott, S. M., Ahleman, S., Wolever, M. E., & Martin, R. B. (1990). The physiological and psychological effects of the expression and inhibition of emotion. *Behavioral Medicine, 16,* 182–189.

Lamb, S. (1991). Acts without agents: An analysis of linguistic avoidance in journal articles on men who batter women. *American Journal of Orthopsychiatry, 61,* 250–257.

Lambert, M. J., & Bergin, A. E. (1994). The effectiveness of psychotherapy. In A. E. Bergin & S. L. Garfield (Eds.), *Handbook of psychotherapy and behavior change* (4th ed., pp. 143–189). New York: Wiley.

Lambert, M. J., & Hill, C. E. (1994). Assessing psychotherapy outcomes and processes. In A. E. Bergin & S. L. Garfield (Eds.), *Handbook of psychotherapy and behavior change* (4th ed., pp. 72–113). New York: Wiley.

Lambert, M. J., DeJulio, S. S., & Stein, D. M. (1978). Therapist interpersonal skills: Process, outcome, methodological considerations, and recommendations for future reference. *Psychological Bulletin, 85,* 467–489.

Lambert, M. J., Shapiro, D. A., & Bergin, A. E. (1986). The effectiveness of psychotherapy. In S. L. Garfield & A. E. Bergin (Eds.), *Handbook of psychotherapy and behavior change* (3rd ed., pp. 157–211). New York: Wiley.

Landman, J. T., & Dawes, R. M. (1982). Smith and Glass' conclusions stand up under scrutiny. *American Psychologist, 37,* 504–516.

Lane, J. D., & Wegner, D. M. (1995). The cognitive consequences of secrecy. *Journal of Personality and Social Psychology, 69,* 237–253.

Lanzetta, J. T., Cartwright-Smith, J., & Kleck, R. E. (1976). Effects of nonverbal dissimulation on emotional experience and autonomic arousal. *Journal of Personality and Social Psychology, 33,* 354–370.

Larson, D. G. (1993a). *The helper's journey: Working with people facing grief, loss, and life-threatening illness.* Champaign, IL: Research Press.

Larson, D. G. (1993b). Self-concealment: Implications for stress and empathy in oncology care. *Journal of Psychosocial Oncology, 11,* 1–16.

Larson, D. G., & Chastain, R. L. (1990). Self-concealment: Conceptualization, measurement, and health implications. *Journal of Social and Clinical Psychology, 9,* 439–455.

Lazarus, R. S. (1985). The trivialization of distress. In J. C. Rose & L. J. Solomon (Eds.), *Primary prevention of psychopathology: Vol. 8. Prevention in Health Psychology* (pp. 279–298). Hanover, NH: University Press of New England.

Lazarus, R. S., & Folkman, S. (1984). *Stress, appraisal, and coping.* New York: Springer.

Lazarus, R. S., Speisman, J. C., Mordkof, A. M., & Davison, L. A. (1962). A laboratory study of psychological stress produced by a motion picture film. *Psychological Monographs, 76*(34, entire No. 553).

Leary, M. R., & Kowalski, R. M. (1990). Impression management: A literature review and two-component model. *Psychological Bulletin, 107,* 34–47.

Lehman, D. R., & Hemphill, K. J. (1990). Recipients' perceptions of support attempts and attributions for support attempts that fail. *Journal of Social and Personal Relationships, 7,* 563–574.

Lehman, D. R., Ellard, J. H., & Wortman, C. B. (1986). Social support for the bereaved: Recipients' and providers' perspectives on what is helpful. *Journal of Consulting and Clinical Psychology, 54,* 438–446.

Lehman, D. R., Wortman, C. B., & Williams, A. F. (1987). Long-term effects of losing a spouse or child in a motor vehicle crash. *Journal of Personality and Social Psychology, 52,* 218–231.

Lepore, S. J. (1992). Social conflict, social support, and psychological distress: Evidence of cross-domain buffering effects. *Journal of Personality and Social Psychology, 63,* 857–867.

Lepore, S. J. (1997a, April). *Social constraints, intrusive thoughts, and negative affect in women with cancer.* Paper presented at the annual meeting of the Society of Behavioral Medicine, San Francisco, CA.

Lepore, S J. (1997b). Expressive writing moderates the relation between intrusive thoughts and depressive symptoms. *Journal of Personality and Social Psychology, 73,* 1030–1037.

Lepore, S. J., & Helgeson, V. S. (1998). Social constraints, intrusive thoughts, and mental health after prostate cancer. *Journal of Social and Clinical Psychology, 17,* 89–106.

Lepore, S. J., Silver, R. C., Wortman, C. B., & Wayment, H. A. (1996). Social constraints, intrusive thoughts, and depressive symptoms among bereaved mothers. *Journal of Personality and Social Psychology, 70,* 271–282.

Lepore, S. J., Ragan, J. D., & Jones, S. (2000). Talking facilitates cognitive–emotional processes of adaptation to an acute stressor. *Journal of Personality and Social Psychology, 78,* 499–508.

Lerner, M. J. (1980). *The belief in a just world: A fundamental delusion.* New York: Plenum Press.

Levy, R. L. (1983). Social support and compliance: A selective review and critique of treatment integrity and outcome measurement. *Social Science and Medicine, 17,* 1329–1338.

Lieberman, M., Yalom, I., & Miles, M. (1973). *Encounter groups: First facts.* New York: Basic Books.

Lifton, R. J. (1986). *The Nazi doctors: Medical killing and the psychology of genocide.* New York: Basic Books.

Lindberg, F. H., & Distad, L. J. (1985). Survival responses to incest: Adolescents in crisis. *Child Abuse and Neglect, 9,* 521–526.

Liotti, G. (1987). Structural cognitive therapy. In W. Dryden & W. L. Golden (Eds.), *Cognitive–behavioral approaches to psychotherapy* (pp. 92–128). Cambridge, UK: Hemisphere.

Lodge, D. (1995). *Therapy: A novel.* New York: Viking.

Loehlin, J. C. (1992). *Genes and environment in personality development.* Thousand Oaks, CA: Sage.

Lubell, D., & Soong, W. (1982). Group therapy with sexually abused adolescents. *Canadian Journal of Psychiatry, 27,* 311–315.

Luck, H. E., & Timaeus, E. (1969). Scales for the measurement of manifest anxiety (MAS) and social desirability (SDS-E and SDS-CM). *Diagnostica, 15,* 134–141.

Luminet, O., Bouts, P., Delie, F., Manstead, A. S. R., & Rime, B. (2000). Social sharing of emotion following exposure to a negatively valenced situation. *Cognition and Emotion, 14,* 661–688.

Lutgendorf, S. K., Antoni, M. H., Kumar, M., & Schneiderman, N. (1994). Changes in cognitive coping strategies predict EBV-antibody titre change following a stressor disclosure induction. *Journal of Psychosomatic Research, 38,* 63–78.

Lyubomirsky, S., & Nolen-Hoeksema, S. (1993). Self-perpetuating properties of dysphoric rumination. *Journal of Personality and Social Psychology, 65,* 339–349.

Lyubomirsky, S., & Nolen-Hoeksema, S. (1995). Effects of self-focused rumination on negative thinking and interpersonal problem solving. *Journal of Personality and Social Psychology, 69,* 176–190.

Macdonald, J., & Morley, I. (2001). Shame and non-disclosure: A study of the emotional isolation of people referred for psychotherapy. *British Journal of Medical Psychology, 74,* 1–21.

Maddison, D. C., & Walker, W. L. (1967). Factors affecting the outcome of conjugal bereavement. *British Journal of Psychiatry, 113,* 1057–1067.

Mahony, P. J. (1996). *Freud's Dora: A psychoanalytic, historical, and textual study.* New Haven, CT: Yale University Press.

Major, B., & Gramzow, R. H. (1999). Abortion as stigma: Cognitive and emotional implications of concealment. *Journal of Personality and Social Psychology, 77,* 735–745.

Major, B., Cozzarelli, C., Sciacchittano, A. M., Cooper, M. L., Testa, M., & Mueller, P. M. (1990). Perceived social support, self-efficacy, and adjustment to abortion. *Journal of Personality and Social Psychology, 59,* 452–463.

Major, B., Zubek, J. M., Cooper, M. L., Cozzarelli, C., & Richards, C. (1997). Mixed messages: Implications of social conflict and social support within close relationships for adjustment to a stressful life event. *Journal of Personality and Social Psychology, 72,* 1349–1363.

Manne, S. L., Taylor, K. L., Dougherty, J., & Kemeny, N. (1997). Supportive and negative responses in the partner relationship: Their association with psychological adjustment among individuals with cancer. *Journal of Behavioral Medicine, 20,* 101–125.

Maracek, J., & Mettee, D. R. (1972). Avoidance of continued success as a function of self-esteem, level of esteem certainty, and responsibility for success. *Journal of Personality and Social Psychology, 22,* 90–107.

Margolis, G. J. (1966). Secrecy and identity. *International Journal of Psycho-Analysis, 47,* 517–522.

Margolis, G. J. (1974). The psychology of keeping secrets. *International Review of Psycho-Analysis, 1,* 291–296.

Markus, H., & Nurius, P. (1986). Possible selves. *American Psychologist, 41,* 954–969.

Martin, J. (1984). The cognitive mediational paradigm for research on counseling. *Journal of Counseling Psychology, 31,* 558–571.

Martin, J., Martin, W., Meyer, M., & Slemon, A. (1986). Empirical investigation of the cognitive mediational paradigm for research on counseling. *Journal of Counseling Psychology, 33,* 115–123.

Martin, J., Martin, W., & Slemon, A. G. (1987). Cognitive mediation in person-centered and rational–emotive therapy. *Journal of Counseling Psychology, 34,* 251–260.

Martin, L. L., Tesser, A., & McIntosh, W. D. (1993). Wanting but not having: The effects of unattained goals on thoughts and feelings. In D. M. Wegner & J. W. Pennebaker (Eds.), *Handbook of mental control* (pp. 552–572). Englewood Cliffs, NJ: Prentice-Hall.

McArdle, J. (1974). Impression management by alcoholics. *Quarterly Journal of the Study of Alcoholism, 35,* 911–916.

McCanne, T. R., & Anderson, J. A. (1987). Emotional responding following experimental manipulation of facial electromyographic activity. *Journal of Personality and Social Psychology, 52,* 759–768.

McCarthy, B. W. (1995). Learning from unsuccessful sex therapy patients. *Journal of Sex and Marital Therapy, 21,* 31–38.

McCrae, R. R., & Costa, P. T., Jr. (1995). Trait explanations in personality psychology. *European Journal of Personality, 9,* 231–252.

McDaniel, S. H., Stiles, W. B., & McGaughey, K. J. (1981). Correlations of male college students' verbal response mode use in psychotherapy with measures of psychological disturbance and psychotherapy outcome. *Journal of Consulting and Clinical Psychology, 49,* 571–582.

McFarlin, D. B., & Blascovich, J. (1981). Effects of self-esteem and performance feedback on future affective preferences and cognitive expectations. *Journal of Personality and Social Psychology, 22,* 90–107.

McGaughey, K. J., & Stiles, W. B. (1983). Courtroom interrogation of rape victims: Verbal response mode use by attorneys and witnesses during direct examination vs. cross-examination. *Journal of Applied Social Psychology, 13,* 78–87.

McKillop, K. J. (1991). Multiple self-presentations and the resiliency of the self. *Dissertation Abstracts International, 52*(5-B), 2822.

McKillop, K. J., & Schlenker, B. R. (1988). *Audience effects on the internalization of depressed vs. nondepressed self-presentations.* Paper presented at the Annual Meeting of the American Psychological Association, Atlanta, Georgia.

McKillop, K. J., Berzonsky, M. D., & Schlenker, B. R. (1992). The impact of self-presentations on self-beliefs: Effects of social identity and self-presentational context. *Journal of Personality, 60,* 789–808.

Mead, G. H. (1934). *Mind, self, and society.* Chicago: University of Chicago Press.

Meichenbaum, D. (1977). *Cognitive–behavior modification: An integrative approach.* New York: Plenum Press.

Meiselman, K. C. (1978). *Incest.* San Francisco: Jossey-Bass.

Mendola, M. (1980). *The Mendola Report: A new look at gay couples.* New York: Crown.

Mendola, M., & Kleck, R. E. (1993). Effects of talking about a stressful event on arousal: Does what we talk about make a difference? *Journal of Personality and Social Psychology, 64,* 283–292.

Merton, R. K. (1948). The self fulfilling prophecy. *Antioch Review, 8,* 193–210.

Miell, D. E., & Duck, S. W. (1986). Strategies in developing friendship. In V. J.

Derlega & B. A. Winstead (Eds.), *Friendship and social interaction* (pp. 129–144). New York: Springer-Verlag.

Milgram, S. (1967). The small world problem. *Psychology Today, 1,* 60–67.

Miller, R., Goldman, E., & Bor, R. (1994). Application of a family systems approach to working with people affected by HIV disease—Two case studies. *Journal of Family Therapy, 16,* 295–312.

Minoff, L. A. (1992). A case of rape: Real and imagined. *Psychoanalytic Review, 79,* 537–553.

Mischel, W., & Peake, P. K. (1982). Beyond dejá vu in the search for cross-situational consistency. *Psychological Review, 89,* 730–755.

Mitchell, R. G. (1993). *Secrecy and fieldwork.* Thousand Oaks, CA: Sage.

Mook, D. G. (1983). In defense of external invalidity. *American Psychologist, 38,* 379–387.

Moos, R. H., & Solomon, G. F. (1965). Psychologic comparisons between women with rheumatoid arthritis and their non-arthritic sisters: II. Content analysis of interviews. *Psychosomatic Medicine, 27,* 150–164.

Moreno, J. (1958). *Psychodrama* (Vol. II). New York: Beacon House.

Moultrop, D. (1992). *Husbands, wives, and lovers.* New York: Guilford.

Mueller, D. P. (1980). Social networks: A promising direction for research on the relationship of the social environment to psychiatric disorder. *Social Science Medicine, 14,* 147–161.

Murphy, B. (1989). Lesbian couples and their parents: The effects of perceived parental attitudes on the couples. *Journal of Counseling and Development, 68,* 46–51.

Murray, E. J., & Segal, D. L. (1994). Emotional processing in vocal and written expression of feelings about traumatic experiences. *Journal of Traumatic Stress, 7,* 391–405.

Murray, E. J., Lamnin, A. D., & Carver, C. S. (1989). Emotional expression in written essays and psychotherapy. *Journal of Social and Clinical Psychology, 8,* 414–429.

Myers, L. B., & Brewin, C. R. (1994). Recall of early experience and the repressive coping style. *Journal of Abnormal Psychology, 103,* 288–292.

Nash, E. H., Hoehn-Saric, R., Battle, C. C., Stone, A. R., Imber, S. D., & Frank, J. D. (1965). Systematic preparation of patients for short-term psychotherapy. II. Relations to characteristics of patient, therapist, and the psychotherapeutic process. *Journal of Nervous and Mental Disease, 140,* 374–383.

Nichols, M. (1974). Outcome of brief cathartic psychotherapy. *Journal of Consulting and Clinical Psychology, 42,* 403–410.

Nichols, M., & Efran, J. (1985). Catharsis in psychotherapy: A new perspective. *Psychotherapy, 22,* 46–58.

Nisbett, R. E., & Wilson, T. D. (1977). Telling more than we can know: Verbal reports and mental processes. *Psychological Review, 84,* 231–259.

Nolen-Hoeksema, S., & Morrow, J. (1993). Effects of rumination and distraction on naturally occurring depressed mood. *Cognition and Emotion, 7,* 561–570.

Nolen-Hoeksema, S., McBride, A., & Larson, J. (1997). Rumination and psychological distress among bereaved partners. *Journal of Personality and Social Psychology, 72,* 855–862.

Norton, R., Feldman, C., & Tafoya, D. (1974). Risk parameters across types of secrets. *Journal of Counseling Psychology, 21*, 450–454.

Nowak, A., Szamrej, J., & Latane, B. (1990). From private attitude to public opinion: A dynamic theory of social impact. *Psychological Review, 97*, 362–376.

O'Brien, R. A., & Pilar, B. R. (1997). Application of solution-focused interventions to nurse home visitation for pregnant women and parents of young children. *Journal of Community Psychology, 25*, 47–57.

Okun, B. F. (1997). *Effective helping: Interviewing and counseling techniques* (5th ed.). Pacific Grove, CA: Brooks/Cole.

Olson, J. M., Barefoot, J. C., & Strickland, L. H. (1976). What the shadow knows: Person perception in a surveillance situation. *Journal of Personality and Social Psychology, 34*, 583–589.

Orlinsky, D. E., & Howard, K. I. (1966). *Therapy Session Report, Form P.* Chicago: Institute for Juvenile Research.

Palazzoli, M. S., & Prata, G. (1982, October). Snares in family therapy. *Journal of Marital and Family Therapy*, 443–450.

Paul, N. L., & Bloom, J. D. (1970). Multiple-family therapy: Secrets and scapegoating in family crisis. *International Journal of Group Psychotherapy, 20*(1), 37–47.

Pennebaker, J. W. (1985). Traumatic experience and psychosomatic disease: Exploring the roles of behavioral inhibition, obsession, and confiding. *Canadian Psychology, 26*, 82–95.

Pennebaker, J. W. (1989). Confession, inhibition, and disease. *Advances in Experimental Social Psychology, 22*, 211–244.

Pennebaker, J. W. (1990). *Opening up: The healing powers of confiding in others.* New York: Morrow.

Pennebaker, J. W. (1993). Mechanisms of social constraint. In D. Wegner & J. W. Pennebaker (Eds.), *Handbook of mental control* (pp. 200–212). Englewood Cliffs, NJ: Prentice-Hall.

Pennebaker, J. W. (1997a). Writing about emotional experiences as a therapeutic process. *Psychological Science, 8*, 162–166.

Pennebaker, J. W. (1997b). *Opening up: The healing power of expressing emotion.* New York: Guilford.

Pennebaker, J. W., & Beall, S. K. (1986). Confronting a traumatic event: Toward an understanding of inhibition and disease. *Journal of Abnormal Psychology, 95*, 274–281.

Pennebaker, J. W., & Chew, C. H. (1985). Behavioral inhibition and electrodermal activity during deception. *Journal of Personality and Social Psychology, 49*, 1427–1433.

Pennebaker, J. W., & Hoover, C. W. (1985). Inhibition and cognition: Toward an understanding of trauma and disease. In R. J. Davidson, G. E. Schwartz, & D. Shapiro (Eds.), *Consciousness and self-regulation* (Vol. 4, pp. 107–136). New York: Plenum Press.

Pennebaker, J. W., & O'Heeron, R. C. (1984). Confiding in others and illness rates among spouses of suicide and accidental-death victims. *Journal of Abnormal Psychology, 93*, 473–476.

Pennebaker, J. W., & Harber, K. D. (1993). A social stage model of collective coping:

The Loma Prieta earthquake and the Persian Gulf War. *Journal of Social Issues,* 49, 125–145.

Pennebaker, J. W., & Susman, J. R. (1988). Disclosure of traumas and psychosomatic processes. *Social Science and Medicine,* 26, 327–332.

Pennebaker, J. W., Hughes, C. F., & O'Heeron, R. C. (1987). The psychopathology of confession: Linking inhibitory and psychosomatic processes. *Journal of Personality and Social Psychology,* 52, 781–793.

Pennebaker, J. W., Kiecolt-Glaser, J. K., & Glaser, R. (1988). Disclosure of traumas and immune function: Health implications for psychotherapy. *Journal of Consulting and Clinical Psychology,* 56, 239–245.

Pennebaker, J. W., Barger, S. D., & Tiebout, J. (1989). Disclosure of traumas and health among holocaust survivors. *Psychosomatic Medicine,* 51, 577–589.

Pennebaker, J. W., Colder, M., & Sharp, L. K. (1990). Accelerating the coping process. *Journal of Personality and Social Psychology,* 58, 528–537.

Pennebaker, J. W., Mayne, T. J., & Francis, M. E. (1997). Linguistic predictors of adaptive bereavement. *Journal of Personality and Social Psychology,* 72, 863–871.

Peskin, J. (1992). Ruse and representations: On children's ability to conceal information. *Developmental Psychology,* 28, 84–89.

Peters-Golden, H. (1982). Breast cancer: Varied perceptions of social support in the illness experience. *Social Science and Medicine,* 16, 483–491.

Petrie, K. J., Booth, R. J., Pennebaker, J. W., Davison, K. P., & Thomas, M. G. (1995). Disclosure of trauma and immune response to a hepatitis B vaccination program. *Journal of Consulting and Clinical Psychology,* 63, 787–792.

Petronio, S. (2000). *Balancing the secrets of private disclosures.* Mahwah, NJ: Erlbaum.

Petronio, S., & Bantz, C. (1991). Controlling the ramifications of disclosure: "Don't tell anybody but …" *Journal of Language and Social Psychology,* 10, 263–269.

Pincus, L., & Dare, C. (1978). *Secrets in the family.* New York: Pantheon Books.

Pittman, F. (1989). *Private lies.* New York: Norton.

Polivy, J. (1998). The effects of behavioral inhibition: Integrating internal cues, cognition, behavior, and affect. *Psychological Inquiry,* 9, 181–204.

Ponse, B. (1978). *Identities in the lesbian world.* Westport, CT: Greenwood.

Premo, B. E., & Stiles, W. B. (1983). Familiarity in verbal interactions of married couples versus strangers. *Journal of Social and Clinical Psychology,* 1, 209–230.

Quintana, S. M., & Meara, N. M. (1990). Internalization of therapeutic relationships in short-term psychotherapy. *Journal of Counseling Psychology,* 37, 123–130.

Rachman, S. (1980). Emotional processing. *Behaviour Research and Therapy,* 18, 51–60.

Rando, T. (1993). *Treatment of complicated mourning.* Champaign, IL: Research Press.

Regan, A. M., & Hill, C. E. (1992). Investigation of what clients and counselors do not say in brief therapy. *Journal of Counseling Psychology,* 39, 240–246.

Regan, J. W. (1968). Guilt, inequity, and altruistic behavior. Unpublished doctoral dissertation, as cited in Freedman, J. L., Carlsmith, J. M., & Sears, D. O. (1970). *Social psychology.* Englewood Cliffs, NJ: Prentice Hall.

Reichert, E. (1994). Expressive group therapy with adult survivors of sexual abuse. *Family Therapy,* 21, 99–105.

Reik, T. (1945). *The compulsion to confess: On the psychoanalysis of crime and punishment.* New York: Grove Press.

Rennie, D. L. (1985, June). *Client deference in the psychotherapy relationship*. Paper presented at the annual meeting of the Society for Psychotherapy Research, Evanston, IL.

Rennie, D. L. (1992). Qualitative analysis of client's experience of psychotherapy: The unfolding of reflexivity. In S. G. Toukmanian & D. L. Rennie (Eds.), *Psychotherapy process research: Paradigmatic and narrative approaches. Sage focus editions* (Vol. 143, pp. 211–233). Newbury Park, CA: Sage.

Rhodes, R. H., Hill, C. E., Thompson, B. J., & Elliott, R. (1994). Client retrospective recall of resolved and unresolved misunderstanding events. Special section: Qualitative research in counseling process and outcome. *Journal of Counseling Psychology, 41,* 473–483.

Rhodewalt, F., & Agustsdottir, S. (1986). Effects of self-presentation on the phenomenal self. *Journal of Personality and Social Psychology, 50,* 47–55.

Richardson, L. (1988). Secrecy and status: The social construction of forbidden relationships. *American Sociological Review, 53,* 209–219.

Rimé, B. (1995a). Mental rumination, social sharing, and the recovery from emotional exposure. In J. W. Pennebaker (Ed.), *Emotion, disclosure, and health* (pp. 271–291). Washington, DC: American Psychological Association.

Rimé, B. (1995b). The social sharing of emotion as a source for the social knowledge of emotion. In J. A. Russell, D. Fernandez, & M. Jose (Eds.), *Everyday conceptions of emotion: An introduction to the psychology, anthropology and linguistics of emotion. NATO ASI series D: Behavioural and social sciences* (Vol. 81, pp. 475–489). Norwell, MA: Kluwer.

Rimé, B., & Schiaratura, L. (1991). Gesture and speech. In R. S. Feldman & B. Rimé (Eds.), *Fundamentals of nonverbal behavior. Studies in emotion and social interaction* (pp. 239–281). New York: Cambridge University Press.

Rimé, B., Mesquita, B., Philippot, P., & Boca, S. (1991a). Beyond the emotional event: Six studies on the social sharing of emotion. *Cognition and Emotion, 5,* 435–465.

Rimé, B., Noel, P., & Philippot, P. (1991b). Episode emotionnel, reminiscences mentales et reminiscences sociales. (Mental rumination, social sharing, and everyday life emotions.) *Cahiers Internationaux de Psychologie Sociale, 7(11),* 93–104.

Rimé, B., Philippot, P., Boca, S., & Mesquita, B. (1992). Long-lasting cognitive and social consequences of emotion: Social sharing and rumination. In W. Stroebe & M. Hewstone (Eds.), *European review of social psychology* (Vol. 3, pp. 225–258). New York: Wiley.

Rimé, B., Philippot, P., Finkenauer, C., Legast, S., Moorkens, P., & Tornqvist, J. (1995). *Mental rumination and social sharing in current life emotion*. Unpublished manuscript. Louvain-la-Neuver, Belgium: University of Louvain.

Rippa, B. (1994). Groups in Israel during the Gulf War. *Group Analysis, 27,* 87–94.

Roback, H. B., & Shelton, M. (1995). Effects of confidentiality limitations on the psychotherapeutic process. *Journal of Psychotherapy Practice and Research, 4,* 185–193.

Robertson, J. M., & Fitzgerald, L. F. (1992). Overcoming the masculine mystique: Preferences for alternative forms of assistance. *Journal of Counseling Psychology, 39,* 240–246.

Rodriguez, N., & Ryave, A. L. (1992). The structural organization and micropolitics of everyday secret telling interactions. *Qualitative Sociology, 15,* 297–318.

Roger, D., & Najarian, B. (1998). The relationship between emotional rumination and cortisol secretion under stress. *Personality and Individual Differences, 24,* 531–538.

Rogers, C. R. (1951). *Client-centered therapy: Its current practice, implications, and theory.* Boston: Houghton Mifflin.

Rogers, C. R. (1957). The necessary and sufficient conditions of therapeutic personality change. *Journal of Counseling Psychology, 21,* 95–103.

Rook, K. S. (1984). The negative side of social interaction: Impact on psychological well-being. *Journal of Personality and Social Psychology, 46,* 1097–1108.

Rosenberg, M. (1979). *Conceiving the self.* New York: Basic Books.

Rosenfeld, D. (1980). The handling of resistances in adult patients. *International Journal of Psychoanalysis, 61,* 71–83.

Ross, L., Greene, D., & House, P. (1977). The false consensus effect: An egocentric bias in social perception and attribution processes. *Journal of Experimental Social Psychology, 13,* 279–301.

Roth, S. (1985). Psychotherapy with lesbian couples: Individual issues, female socialization, and the social context. *Journal of Marital and Family Therapy, 11,* 273–286.

Russell, D. E. (1986). *The secret trauma: Incest in the lives of girls and women.* New York: Basic Books.

Russell, P. D., & Snyder, W. U. (1963). Counselor anxiety in relation to amount of clinical experience and quality of affect demonstrated by clients. *Journal of Consulting Psychology, 27,* 358–363.

Saffer, J. B., Sansone, P., & Gentry, J. (1979). The awesome burden upon the child who must keep a family secret. *Child Psychiatry and Human Development, 10,* 35–40.

Sagarin, B. J., Rhoads, K. V. L., & Cialdini, R. B. (1998). Deceiver's distrust: Denigration as a consequences of undiscovered deception. *Personality and Social Psychology Bulletin, 24,* 1167–1176.

Salkovskis, P. M., & Campbell, P. (1994). Thought suppression induces intrusion in naturally occurring negative intrusive thoughts. *Behaviour Research and Therapy, 32,* 1–8.

Scheff, T. J. (1979). *Catharsis in healing, ritual, and drama.* Berkeley: University of California Press.

Schlenker, B. R. (1980). *Impression management: The self-concept, social identity, and interpersonal relations.* Monterey, CA: Brooks/Cole.

Schlenker, B. R. (1985). Identity and self-identification. In B. R. Schlenker (Ed.), *The self and social life* (pp. 65–99). New York: McGraw-Hill.

Schlenker, B. R. (1986). Self-identification: Toward an integration of the private and public self. In R. Baumeister (Ed.), *Public self and private self* (pp. 21–62). New York: Springer-Verlag.

Schlenker, B. R. (1987). Threats to identity: Self-identification and social stress. In C. R. Snyder & C. E. Ford (Eds.), *Coping with negative life events: Clinical and social psychological perspectives* (pp. 273–321). New York: Plenum Press.

Schlenker, B. R., & Trudeau, J. V. (1990). Impact of self-presentations on private self-beliefs: Effects of prior self-beliefs and misattribution. *Journal of Personality and Social Psychology, 58*, 22–32.

Schlenker, B. R., & Weigold, M. F. (1989). Goals and the self-identification process: Constructing desired identities. In L. A. Pervin (Ed.), *Goal concepts in personality and social psychology* (pp. 243–290). Hillsdale, NJ: Erlbaum.

Schlenker, B. R., & Weigold, M. F. (1990). Self-consciousness and self-presentation: Being autonomous versus appearing autonomous. *Journal of Personality and Social Psychology, 59*, 820–828.

Schlenker, B. R., & Weigold, M. F. (1992). Interpersonal processes involving impression regulation and management. *Annual Review of Psychology, 43*, 133–168.

Schlenker, B. R., Dlugolecki, D. W., & Doherty, K. (1994). The impact of self-presentations on self-appraisals and behavior: The power of public commitment. *Personality and Social Psychology Bulletin, 20*, 20–33.

Schlenker, B. R., Britt, T. W., & Pennington, J. (1996). Impression regulation and management: Highlights of a theory of self-identification. In R. M. Sorrentino & E. T. Higgins (Eds.), *Handbook of motivation and cognition: The interpersonal context* (Vol. 3, pp. 118–147). New York: Guilford.

Schmidt, L. A., & Fox, N. A. (1995). Individual differences in young adults shyness and sociability: Personality and health correlates. *Personality and Individual Differences, 19*, 455–462.

Schoicket, S. (1980). Secrets. *American Journal of Psychoanalysis, 40*, 179–182.

Schwartz, G. E. (1990). Psychobiology of repression and health: A systems approach. In J. L. Singer (Ed.), *Repression and dissociation: Implications for personality theory, psychopathology, and health* (pp. 405–434). Chicago: University of Chicago Press.

Schwartz, G. S., Friedlander, M. L., & Tedeschi, J. T. (1986). Effects of clients' attributional explanations and reasons for seeking help on counselors' impressions. *Journal of Counseling Psychology, 33*, 90–93.

Schwartz, R. S. (1984). Confidentiality and secret-keeping on an inpatient unit. *Psychiatry, 47*, 279–284.

Segal, D. L., & Murray, E. J. (1994). Emotional processing in cognitive therapy and vocal expression of feeling. *Journal of Social and Clinical Psychology, 13*, 189–206.

Servaes, P., Vingerhoets, A. J. J. M., Vreugdenhil, G., Keuning, J. J., & Broekhuijsen, A. M. (1999). Inhibition of emotional expression in breast cancer patients. *Behavioral Medicine, 25*, 23–27.

Shapiro, D. A., & Firth, J. A. (1987). Prescriptive vs. exploratory psychotherapy: Outcomes of the Sheffield Psychotherapy Project. *British Journal of Psychiatry, 151*, 790–799.

Shapiro, D., Jamner, L. D., & Goldstein, I. B. (1993). Ambulatory stress psychophysiology: The study of "compensatory and defensive counterforces" and conflict in a natural setting. *Psychosomatic Medicine, 55*, 309–323.

Shlien, J. (1984). Secrets and the psychology of secrecy. In R. Levant & J. Shlien (Eds.), *Client centered therapy and the person centered approach* (pp. 390–399). New York: Praeger.

Shneidman, E. S., & Farberow, N. L. (1961). Statistical comparisons between attempted and committed suicides. In N. L. Farberow & E. S. Shneidman (Eds.), *The cry for help* (pp. 19–47). New York: McGraw-Hill.

Shneidman, E. S., & Farberow, N. L. (1970). Attempted and committed suicides. In E. S. Shneidman, N. L. Farberow, & R. E. Litman (Eds.), *The psychology of suicide* (pp. 199–225). New York: Science House.

Shoham-Salomon, V., & Rosenthal, R. (1987). Paradoxical interventions: A meta-analysis. *Journal of Consulting and Clinical Psychology, 55,* 22–28.

Shortt, J. W., & Pennebaker, J. W. (1992). Talking versus hearing about Holocaust experiences. *Basic and Applied Social Psychology, 13,* 165–179.

Shrauger, J. S., & Schoeneman, T. J. (1979). Symbolic interactionist view of self-concept: Through the looking glass darkly. *Psychological Bulletin, 86,* 549–573.

Siegman, A. W. (1993). Cardiovascular consequences of expressing, experiencing, and repressing anger. *Journal of Behavioral Medicine, 16,* 539–569.

Siegman, A. W. (1994a). From type A to hostility to anger: Reflections on the history of coronary-prone behavior. In A. W. Siegman & T. W. Smith (Eds.), *Anger, hostility, and the heart* (pp. 1–21). Hillsdale, NJ: Lawrence Erlbaum.

Siegman, A. W. (1994b). Cardiovascular consequences of expressing and repressing anger. In A. W. Siegman & T. W. Smith (Eds.), *Anger, hostility, and the heart* (pp. 173–197). Hillsdale, NJ: Lawrence Erlbaum.

Siegman, A. W., & Snow, S. C. (1997). The outward expression of anger, the inward experience of anger and CVR: The role of vocal expression. *Journal of Behavioral Medicine, 20,* 29–45.

Siegman, A. W., Anderson, R. W., & Boyle, S. (1991, March). *Repression, impression management, trait anxiety, and cardiovascular reactivity in men and women.* Paper presented at the annual meeting of the Society for Behavioral Medicine, Washington, DC.

Siegman, A. W., Anderson, R., Herbst, J., Boyle, S., & Wilkinson, J. (1992). Dimensions of anger–hostility and cardiovascular reactivity in provoked and angered men. *Journal of Behavioral Medicine, 15,* 257–272.

Sifneos, P. (1979). *Short-term dynamic psychotherapy.* New York: Plenum Press.

Silver, D. (1983). Psychotherapy and the characterologically difficult patient. *Canadian Journal of Psychiatry, 28,* 513–521.

Silver, R. L., & Wortman, C. B. (1980). Coping with undesirable life events. In J. Garber & M. E. P. Seligman (Eds.), *Human helplessness: Theory and applications* (pp. 279–375). New York: Academic Press.

Silver, R. L., Boon, C., & Stones, M. H. (1983). Searching for meaning in misfortune: Making sense of incest. *Journal of Social Issues, 39,* 81–102.

Silver, R. C., Wortman, C. B., & Crofton, C. V. (1990). The role of coping in support provision: The self-presentation dilemma of victims of life crises. In B. R. Sarason, I. G. Sarason, & G. R. Pierce (Eds.), *Social support: An interactional view* (pp. 397–426). New York: Wiley.

Silverstein, J. L. (1993). Secrets versus privacy in group psychotherapy. *Group, 17,* 107–114.

Silvia, P. J., & Duval, T. S. (2001). Predicting the interpersonal targets of self-serving attributions. *Journal of Experimental Social Psychology, 37,* 333–340.

Sloan, W. W., & Stiles, W. B. (1994). *Client self-disclosure and psychotherapy outcome.* Unpublished manuscript.

Smart, L., & Wegner, D. M. (1999). Covering up what can't be seen: Concealable stigma and mental control. *Journal of Personality and Social Psychology, 77,* 474–486.

Smith, M. L., Glass, G. V., & Miller, T. I. (1980). *The benefits of psychotherapy.* Baltimore: The Johns Hopkins University Press.

Smyth, J. M., (1998). Written emotional expression: Effect sizes, outcome types, and moderating variables. *Journal of Consulting and Clinical Psychology, 66,* 174–184.

Smyth, J. M., Stone, A. A., Hurewitz, A., & Kaell, A. (1999). Effects of writing about stressful experiences on symptom reduction in patients with asthma or rheumatoid arthritis: A randomized trial. *Journal of the American Medical Association, 281,* 1304–1309.

Sophie, J. (1988). Internalized homophobia and lesbian identity. In E. Coleman (Ed.), *Integrated identity for gay men and lesbians* (pp. 53–65). New York: Harrington Park.

Spera, S. P., Buhrfeind, E. D., & Pennebaker, J. W. (1994). Expressive writing and coping with job loss. *Academy of Management Journal, 37,* 722–733.

Spiegel, D. (1992). Effects of psychosocial support on patients with metastatic breast cancer. *Journal of Psychosocial Oncology, 10,* 113–120.

Spiegel, D., Bloom, J. H., Kraemer, H. C., & Gottheil, E. (1989). Effects of psychosocial treatment of patients with metastatic breast cancer. *Lancet, 2,* 888–891.

Spielberger, C. D., Crane, R. S., Kearns, W. D., Pellegrin, K. L., Rickman, R. L., & Johnson, E. H. (1991). Anger and anxiety in essential hypertension. In C. D. Spielberger, I. G. Sarason, Z. Kulcsar, & G. L. Van Heck (Eds.), *Stress and emotion: Anxiety, anger, and curiosity* (Vol. 14, pp. 265–283). Washington, DC: Hemisphere.

Starr, K. W. (1998, September 9). Narrative. In *The Starr report* (online). Available: http://www.all links.com/icreport/6narrit.htm#N_42_.

Steinbeck, J. (1961). *The winter of our discontent.* New York: Viking Press.

Stice, E. (1992). The similarities between cognitive dissonance and guilt: Confession as a relief of dissonance. *Current Psychology: Research and Reviews, 11,* 69–77.

Stiles, W. B. (1984). Client disclosure and psychotherapy session evaluations. *British Journal of Clinical Psychology, 23,* 311–314.

Stiles, W. B. (1987). "I have to talk to somebody." A fever model of disclosure. In V. J. Derlega & J. H. Berg (Eds.), *Self-disclosure: Theory, research, and therapy* (pp. 257–282). New York: Plenum Press.

Stiles, W. B. (1995). Disclosure as a speech act: Is it psychotherapeutic to disclose? In J. W. Pennebaker (Ed.), *Emotion, disclosure, and health* (pp. 71–91). Washington, DC: American Psychological Association.

Stiles, W. B., & Shapiro, D. A. (1994). Disabuse of the drug metaphor: Psychotherapy of process–outcome correlations. *Journal of Consulting and Clinical Psychology, 62,* 942–948.

Stiles, W. B., & Sultan, F. E. (1979). Verbal response mode use by clients in psychotherapy. *Journal of Consulting and Clinical Psychology, 47,* 611–613.

Stiles, W. B., McDaniel, S. H., & McGaughey, K. (1979). Verbal response mode correlates of experiencing. *Journal of Consulting and Clinical Psychology, 47,* 795–797.

Stiles, W. B., Putnam, S. M., & Jacob, M. C. (1982). Verbal exchange structure of initial medical interviews. *Health Psychology, 1,* 315–336.

Stokes, J. P. (1983). Predicting satisfaction with social support from social network structure. *American Journal of Community Psychology, 11,* 141–152.

Stoler, N. (1963). Client likability: A variable in the study of psychotherapy. *Journal of Consulting Psychology, 27,* 175–178.

Stone, A., Kennedy-Moore, E., & Neale, J. (1995). Association between daily coping and end-of-the-day mood. *Health Psychology, 14,* 341–349.

Strack, S., & Coyne, J. C. (1983). Social confirmation of dysphoria: Shared and private reactions to depression. *Journal of Personality and Social Psychology, 44,* 798–806.

Strassberg, D. S., & Anchor, K. N. (1977). Ratings of client self-disclosure and improvement as a function of sex of client and therapist. *Journal of Clinical Psychology, 33,* 239–241.

Strassberg, D. S., Roback, H. B., Anchor, K. N., & Abramowitz, S. I. (1975). Self-disclosure in group therapy with schizophrenics. *Archives of General Psychiatry, 32,* 1259–1261.

Strassberg, D. S., Anchor, K. N., Gabel, H., & Cohen, B. (1978). Client self-disclosure in short-term psychotherapy. *Psychotherapy: Theory, Research, and Practice, 15,* 153–157.

Strong, S. R. (1968). Counseling: An interpersonal influence process. *Journal of Counseling Psychology, 15,* 215–224.

Strong, S. R. (1987). Interpersonal influence theory as a common language for psychotherapy. *Journal of Integrative and Eclectic Psychotherapy, 6,* 173–184.

Strong, S. R. (1991). Theory-driven science and naive empiricism in counseling psychology. *Journal of Counseling Psychology, 38,* 204–210.

Strong, S. R. (1995). Interpersonal influence theory: The situational and individual determinants of interpersonal behavior. In D. J. Lubinski & R. Dawis (Eds.), *Assessing individual differences in human behavior: New concepts, methods, and findings* (pp. 263–295). Palo Alto, CA: Davies-Black Publishing.

Strong, S. R., & Claiborn, C. D. (1982). *Change through interaction: Social psychological processes of counseling and psychotherapy.* New York: Wiley-Interscience.

Stroop, J. R. (1935). Studies of interference in serial verbal reactions. *Journal of Experimental Psychology, 18,* 643–662.

Strupp, H. H., & Hadley, S. W. (1979). Specific vs. nonspecific factors in psychotherapy: A controlled study of outcome. *Archives of General Psychiatry, 36,* 1125–1136.

Sturkie, K. (1983). Structured group treatment for sexually abused children. *Health and Social Work, 8,* 299–308.

Suarez, E. C., & Williams, R. B. (1990). The relationships between dimensions of hostility and cardiovascular reactivity as a function of task characteristics. *Psychosomatic Medicine, 52,* 558–570.

248

Suedfeld, P., & Pennebaker, J. W. (1997). Health outcomes and cognitive aspects of recalled negative life events. *Psychosomatic Medicine, 59*, 172–177.

Sullivan, H. S. (1953). *The interpersonal theory of psychiatry.* New York: W. W. Norton.

Suls, J., & Fletcher, B. (1985). The relative efficacy of avoidant and nonavoidant coping strategies: A meta-analysis. *Health Psychology, 4*, 249–288.

Suomi, S. J. (1991). Uptight and laid-back monkeys: Individual differences in the response to social challenges. In S. Branch, W. Hall, & E. Dooling (Eds.), *Plasticity of development* (pp. 27–55). Cambridge, MA: MIT Press.

Swann, W. B. (1987). Identity negotiation: Where two roads meet. *Journal of Personality and Social Psychology, 53*, 1038–1051.

Swann, W. B. (1996). *Self-traps: The elusive quest for higher self-esteem.* New York: W. H. Freeman.

Swann, W. B., & Ely, R. J. (1984). A battle of wills: Self-verification versus behavioral confirmation. *Journal of Personality and Social Psychology, 46*, 1287–1302.

Swann, W. B., & Hill, C. A. (1982). When our identities are mistaken: Reaffirming self-conceptions through social interaction. *Journal of Personality and Social Psychology, 43*, 59–66.

Swann, W. B., & Predmore, S. C. (1985). Intimates as agents of social support: Sources of consolation or despair? *Journal of Personality and Social Psychology, 49*, 1609–1617.

Swann, W. B., & Read, S. J. (1981). Acquiring self-knowledge: The search for feedback that fits. *Journal of Personality and Social Psychology, 41*, 1119–1128.

Swanson, L., & Biaggio, M. K. (1985). Therapeutic perspectives on father–daughter incest. *American Journal of Psychiatry, 142*, 667–674.

Sweetser, E. E. (1987). The definition of "lie": An examination of the folk models underlying a semantic prototype. In D. Holland & N. Quinn (Eds.), *Cultural models in language and thought* (pp. 43–66). New York: Cambridge University Press.

Swink, K. K., & Leveille, A. E. (1986). From victim to survivor: A new look at the issues and recovery process for adult incest survivors. *Women and Therapy, 5*, 119–141.

Szajnberg, N. (1988). The developmental continuum from secrecy to privacy in a psychodynamic milieu. *Residential Treatment for Children and Youth, 6*, 9–28.

Tait, R., & Silver, R. C. (1989). Coming to terms with major negative life events. In J. S. Uleman & J. A. Bargh (Eds.), *Unintended thought* (pp. 351–381). New York: Guilford.

Tannenbaum, P. H., & Gaer, E. P. (1965). Mood changes as a function of stress of protagonist and degree of identification in a film viewing situation. *Journal of Personality and Social Psychology, 2*, 612–616.

Tausk, V. (1933). On the origin of the "influencing machine" in schizophrenia. *Psychoanalysis Quarterly, 2*, 519–556.

Taylor, S. E. (1990). Health psychology: The science and the field. *American Psychologist, 45*, 40–50.

Taylor, S. E., & Armor, D. A. (1996). Positive illusions and coping with adversity. *Journal of Personality, 64*, 873–898.

Taylor, S. E., & Brown, J. D. (1988). Illusion and well-being: A social psychological perspective on mental health. *Psychological Bulletin, 103*, 193–210.

Taylor, S. E., & Brown, J. D. (1994). Positive illusions and well-being revisited: Separating fact from fiction. *Psychological Bulletin, 116*, 21–27.

Taylor, S. E., & Gollwitzer, P. M. (1995). Effects of mindset on positive illusions. *Journal of Personality and Social Psychology, 69*, 213–226.

Temoshok, L. (1983). Emotion, adaptation, and disease: A multidimensional theory. In L. Temoshok, C. v. Dyke. & L. S. Zegans (Eds.), *Emotions in health and illness*. New York: Grune & Stratton.

Temoshok, L. (1987). Personality, coping style, emotion, and cancer: Towards an integrative model. *Cancer Surveys, 6*, 545–567.

Tesser, A. (1988). Toward a self-evaluation maintenance model of social behavior. In L. Berkowitz (Ed.), *Advances in experimental social psychology* (Vol. 21, pp. 181–227). San Diego, CA: Academic Press.

Tesser, A., Leone, C., & Clary, E. (1978). Affect control: Process constraints versus catharsis. *Cognitive Therapy and Research, 2*, 265–274.

Thompson, B. J., & Hill, C. E. (1991). Therapist perceptions of client reactions. *Journal of Counseling and Development, 69*, 261–265.

Thoits, P. (1982). Conceptual, methodological and theoretical problems in studying social support as a buffer against life stress. *Journal of Health and Social Behavior, 23*, 145–159.

Tice, D. M. (1992). Self-concept change and self-presentation: The looking glass self is also a magnifying glass. *Journal of Personality and Social Psychology, 63*, 435–451.

Tice, D. M., & Ciarocco, N. J. (1998). Inhibition and self-control. *Psychological Inquiry, 9*, 228–231.

Tichenor, V., & Hill, C. E. (1989). A comparison of six measures of working alliance. *Psychotherapy, 26*, 195–199.

Traue, H. C. (1995). Inhibition and muscle tension in myogenic pain. In J. W. Pennebaker (Ed.), *Emotion, disclosure, and health* (pp. 155–175). Washington, DC: American Psychological Association.

Traue, H. C., & Kraus, W. (1988). Ausdruckshemmung als Risikofaktor: Eine verhaltensmedizinische Analyses. *Praxis der angewandten Verhaltensmedizin und Rehabilitation, 2*, 85–95.

Traue, H. C., & Michael, A. (1993). Behavioral and emotional inhibition in head pain. In H. C. Traue & J. W. Pennebaker (Eds.), *Emotion, inhibition, and health* (pp. 226–246). Kirkland, WA: Hogrefe & Huber.

Trinder, H., & Salkovskis, P. N. (1994). Personally relevant intrusions outside the laboratory: Long-term suppression increases intrusion. *Behaviour Research and Therapy, 32*, 833–842.

Truax, C. B. (1966). Therapist empathy, warmth, and genuineness and patient personality change in group psychotherapy: A comparison between interaction unit measures, time sample measures, and patient perception measures. *Journal of Clinical Psychology, 22*, 225–229.

Truax, C. B., & Carkhuff, R. R. (1967). *Toward effective counseling and psychotherapy: Training and practice*. Chicago: Aldine.

Truax, C. B., & Mitchell, K. M. (1971). Research on certain therapist interpersonal skills in relation to process and outcome. In A. E. Bergin & S. L. Garfield (Eds.), *Handbook of psychotherapy and behavior change* (pp. 299–344). New York: Wiley.

Tsai, M., & Wagner, N. N. (1978). Therapy groups for women sexually molested as children. *Archives of Sexual Behavior, 7*, 417–427.

Turner, R. J. (1983). Direct, indirect, and moderating effects of social support on psychological distress and associated conditions. In H. B. Kaplan (Ed.), *Psychological stress: Trends in theory and research* (pp. 105–155). New York: Academic Press.

Tversky, A., & Kahneman, D. (1973). Availability: A heuristic for judging frequency and probability. *Cognitive Psychology, 5*, 207–232.

Vallacher, R. R., & Wegner, D. M. (1987). What do people think they're doing? Action identification and human behavior. *Psychological Review, 94*, 3–15.

Vangelisti, A. L. (1994). Family secrets: Forms, functions, and correlates. *Journal of Social and Personal Relationships, 11*, 113–135.

Vangelisti, A. L., & Caughlin, J. P. (1997). Revealing family secrets: The influence of topic, function, and relationships. *Journal of Social and Personal Relationships, 14*, 679–705.

Van Rood, Y. R., Bogaards, M., Goulmy, E., & Van Houwelingen, H. C. (1993). The effects of stress and relaxation on the *in vitro* immune response in man: A meta-analytic study. *Journal of Behavioral Medicine, 16*, 163–181.

Vinokur, A. D., & Van Ryn, M. (1993). Social support and undermining in close relationships: Their independent effects on the mental health of unemployed persons. *Journal of Personality and Social Psychology, 65*, 350–359.

Wallerstein, R. S. (1986). *Forty-two lives in treatment: A study of psychoanalysis and psychotherapy* (pp. 265–277). New York: Guilford.

Watson, D., Clark, L. A., & Tellegen, A. (1988). Development and validation of brief measures of positive and negative affect: The PANAS scales. *Journal of Personality and Social Psychology, 54*, 1063–1070.

Wegner, D. M. (1989). *White bears and other unwanted thoughts*. New York: Penguin Books.

Wegner, D. M. (1992). You can't always think what you want: Problems in the suppression of unwanted thoughts. In M. Zanna (Ed.), *Advances in experimental social psychology* (Vol. 25, pp. 193–225). San Diego, CA: Academic Press.

Wegner, D. M. (1994). Ironic processes of mental control. *Psychological Review, 101*, 34–52.

Wegner, D. M., & Erber, R. (1992). The hyperaccessibility of suppressed thoughts. *Journal of Personality and Social Psychology, 63*, 903–912.

Wegner, D. M., & Gold, D. B. (1995). Fanning old flames: Emotional and cognitive effects of suppressing thoughts of a past relationship. *Journal of Personality and Social Psychology, 68*, 782–792.

Wegner, D. M., & Wenzlaff, R. M. (1996). Mental control. In E. T. Higgins & A. W. Kruglanski (Eds.), *Social psychology: Handbook of basic principles*. New York: Guilford.

Wegner, D. M., Schneider, D. J., Carter, S. R., III, & White, T. (1987). Paradoxical effects of thought suppression. *Journal of Personality and Social Psychology, 53*, 5–13.

Wegner, D. M., Shortt, J. W., Blake, A. W., & Page, M. S. (1990). The suppression of exciting thoughts. *Journal of Personality and Social Psychology, 58,* 409–418.

Wegner, D. M., Lane, J. D., & Dimitri, S. (1994). The allure of secret relationships. *Journal of Personality and Social Psychology, 66,* 287–300.

Weigel, R. G., Dinges, N., Dyer, R., & Straumfjord, A. A. (1972). Perceived self-disclosure, mental health, and who is liked in group treatment. *Journal of Counseling Psychology, 19,* 47–52.

Weinberger, D. A. (1990). The construct validity of the repressive coping style. In J. L. Singer (Ed.), *Repression and dissociation: Implications for personality theory, psychopathology, and health* (pp. 337–386). Chicago: Chicago University Press.

Weinberger, D. A., Schwartz, G. E., & Davidson, R. J. (1979). Low-anxious, high-anxious, and repressive coping styles: Psychometric patterns and behavioral and physiological responses to stress. *Journal of Abnormal Psychology, 88,* 369–380.

Weinberger, J. (1995). Common factors aren't so common: The common factors dilemma. *Clinical Psychology: Science and Practice, 2,* 45–69.

Weinstein, H. M., & Richman, A. (1984). The group treatment of bulimia. *Journal of American College Health, 32,* 208–215.

Weiss, J. (1995). Bernfeld's "The facts of observation in psychoanalysis: A response from psychoanalytic research." *Psychoanalytic Quarterly, 64,* 699–716.

Welsh, A. (1994). *Freud's wishful dream book* (pp. 29–50). Princeton, NJ: Princeton University Press.

Wenzlaff, R. M., Wegner, D. M., & Klein, S. B. (1991). The role of thought suppression in the association of thought and mood. *Journal of Personality and Social Psychology, 60,* 500–508.

Wergeland, H. (1980). Elective mutism. *Annual Progress in Child Psychiatry and Child Development, 65,* 373–385.

Westfall, A. (1989). Extramarital sex: The treatment of the couple. In G. R. Weeks (Ed.), *Treating couples* (pp. 163–190). New York: Brunner/Mazel.

Wills, T. A. (1978). Perceptions of clients by professional helpers. *Psychological Bulletin, 85,* 968–1000.

Wilner, N., & Horowitz, M. J. (1975). Intrusive and repetitive thoughts after a depressing film: A pilot study. *Psychological Reports, 37,* 135–138.

Wilson, T. D., & Kraft, D. (1993). Why do I love thee? Effects of repeated introspections about a dating relationship on attitudes toward the relationship. *Personality and Social Psychology Bulletin, 19,* 409–418.

Wilson, T. D., Lisle, D. J., & Schooler, J. (1988). Some undesirable effects of self-reflection. Unpublished manuscript, Charlottesville: University of Virginia.

Wilson, T. D., Dunn, D. S., Kraft, D., & Lisle, D. J. (1989). Introspection, attitude change, and attitude–behavior consistency: The disruptive effects of explaining why we feel the way we do. In L. Berkowitz (Ed.), *Advances in experimental social psychology* (Vol. 19, pp. 123–205). Orlando, FL: Academic Press.

Windle, M. (1994). Temperamental inhibition and activation: Hormonal and psychosocial correlates and associated psychiatric disorders. *Personality and Individual Differences, 17,* 61–70.

Winnicott, D. W. (1980). *Playing and reality.* New York: Penguin Books.

Winter, D. A. (1985). Group psychotherapy with depressives: A personal construct theory perspective. *International Journal of Mental Health, 13*, 26–38.

Wolff, C. T., Friedman, S. B., Hofer, M. A., & Mason, J. W. (1964). Relationship between psychological defenses and mean urinary 17-hydroxycorticosteroid excretion rates: I. A predictive study of parents of fatally ill children. *Psychosomatic Medicine, 26*, 576–591.

Woods, K., & McNamara, J. R. (1980). Confidentiality: Its effect on interviewee behavior. *Professional Psychology, 11*, 714–721.

Wortman, C. B. (1984). Social support and the cancer patient: Conceptual and methodological issues. *Cancer, 53*, 2339–2360.

Wortman, C. B., & Conway, T. (1985). The role of social support in adaptation and recovery from physical illness. In S. Cohen (Ed.), *Social support and health* (pp. 281–308). New York: Academic.

Wortman, C. B., & Lehman, D. R. (1985). Reactions to victims of life crises: Support attempts that fail. In I. G. Sarason & B. R. Sarason (Eds.), *Social support: Theory, research, and applications* (pp. 463–489). Dordrecht, The Netherlands: Martinus Nijhoff.

Wortman, C. B., & Silver, R. C. (1987). Coping with irrevocable loss. In G. R. Vanden Bos & B. K. Bryant (Eds.), *Cataclysms, crises, and catastrophes: Psychology in action* (pp. 189–235). Washington, DC: American Psychological Association.

Wortman, C. B., & Silver, R. C. (1989). The myths of coping with loss. *Journal of Consulting and Clinical Psychology, 57*, 349–357.

Wortman, C. B., Adesman, P., Herman, E., & Greenberg, R. (1976). Self-disclosure: An attributional perspective. *Journal of Personality and Social Psychology, 33*, 184–191.

Wright, F. (1990). Discussion: Of "common dilemmas in combined individual and group treatment" by Anne Alsonso and J. Scott Rutan. *Group, 14*, 13–15.

Wright, T. L., Ingraham, L. J., Chemtob, H. J., & Perez-Arce, P. (1985). Satisfaction and things not said: Clinical tools for group therapists. *Small Group Behavior, 16*, 565–572.

Yalom, I. D. (1985). *The theory and practice of group psychotherapy* (4th ed.). New York: Basic Books.

Yep, G. A. (2000). Disclosure of HIV infection in interpersonal relationships: A communication boundary management approach. In S. Petronio (Ed.), *Balancing the secrets of private disclosures*. LEA's communication series (pp. 83–96). Mahwah, NJ: Erlbaum.

Yovetich, N. A., & Drigotas, S. M. (1999). Secret transmission: A relative intimacy hypothesis. *Personality and Social Psychology Bulletin, 25*, 1135–1146.

Zeigarnik, B. (1927). Uber das behalten von erledigten und underledigten handlungen. *Psychologische Forschung, 9*, 1–85.

Zuckerman, M., Klorman, R., Larrance, D. T., & Spiegel, N. H. (1981). Facial, autonomic, and subjective components of emotion: The facial feedback hypothesis versus the externalizer–internalizer distinction. *Journal of Personality and Social Psychology, 41*, 929–944.

Zung, W. W., & Gianturco, J. A. (1971). Personality dimension and the Self-Rating Depression Scale. *Journal of Clinical Psychology, 27*, 247–248.

INDEX

Abortion, concealment or disclosure of, 50, 54, 179, 192–193, 194, 202
Acquaintances, shared, 200
Advice, unhelpful, 170
Aggression, avoidance of, 24–25
AIDS (acquired immunodeficiency syndrome), as family secret, 112
Alcoholism
  revelation of, in group therapy, 114–116
  as trauma response, 82
Allen, Joan, 187
Amygdala, overresponsive, 58, 59
Anger
  as cardiovascular hyperactivity risk factor, 29
  as coronary heart disease risk factor, 29, 31
  expression of, 29, 87, 90–01
  suppression of, as low-back pain risk factor, 25
Anxiety
  genetic factors in, 59
  effect on immunologic functioning, 30–31
  positive correlation with secrecy, 23–24
  positive correlation with self-concealment, 32, 37
Anxiety disorders, exposure therapy for, 213
Arabs, in psychotherapy training groups, 114
Arousal
  catharsis-related decrease in, 86
  endogenous opioids-mediated, 31

Arousal (*cont.*)
  negative emotional, effect of revelation of secrets on, 174
  repression-related increase in, 27–28
  as response to others' distress, 168–169
Asthma patients, trauma writing experiment with, 77–78
Audience effects, in self-presentation, 138–140, 166, 167
Autonomic reactivity: *see also* Arousal
  repression-related increase in, 25, 27–28
Availability bias phenomenon, 201

Back pain
  repression as risk factor for, 25
  self-concealment as risk factor for, 32, 37
Behavioral control, negative correlation with self-concealment, 34, 35
Belonging, as basic human need, 16, 169–170
Bereaved persons
  depression in, 83
  mothers, of sudden infant death syndrome victims, 180
  negative advice given to, 170
  spouses, of suicide and automobile crash victims, 210–211
Blaming, of victims, 169
Borderline personality disorder, 107
Boundaries
  personal, effect of secrecy on, 172–173
  for revelation of secrets, 206–208